Called to Conquer

CALLED TO CONQUER

A DAILY DEVOTIONAL
TO ENERGIZE AND ENCOURAGE
YOU IN WORD AND SPIRIT

EDDIE LONG

THOMAS NELSON PUBLISHERS
Nashville

Published in Nashville, Tennessee, by Thomas Nelson, Inc., and distributed in Canada by Word Communications, Ltd., Richmond, British Columbia, and in the United Kingdom by Word (UK), Ltd., Milton Keynes, England.

Selected devotions have been adapted from themes found in the book by Eddie Long, *Taking Over,* published by Creation House.

ISBN 0-7852-6765-4

Printed in the United States of America
1 2 3 4 5 6 7 PHX 06 05 04 03 02 01 00

Contents

January

The Power of Dreaming

Start Your Day the Bright Way

Today's Scripture Reading: Psalm 118:17–24 *Key Verse:* Psalm 118:24

This is the day the Lord has made;
We will rejoice and be glad in it.

Millions of people will wake up this morning feeling like a truck ran over them because of the hangover from last night's "celebration." The prospects for the New Year somehow look dimmer through bloodshot eyes. There is a better way to greet each new day.

I will never forget the twenty-year-old man who told me how hard his life was while he wiped away the tears trickling down his cheeks. But then he looked at me and said, "You know, some days I have to wear sunglasses."

He aroused my curiosity, so I asked, "Why?"

"Because my future is so bright that I have to shade my eyes."

That ministered to me. We need more people who wake up every morning and say by faith, "You know, I probably need to put on some sunglasses. My future is so bright that I need to cover up my eyes. It is so bright that it is interfering with my view of my problems."

Tomorrow morning when you wake up, get out your sunglasses. Your future in Christ is too bright for the naked eye!

Pray this prayer with me today:

Heavenly Father, I thank You for giving me a bright future in Your Son. Now I can dare to dream the unthinkable and reach for the impossible. I owe it all to You, and I give it all back to You in Jesus' name. Amen.

JANUARY 2

SAY THE THINGS GOD SAYS ABOUT YOU

Today's Scripture Reading: Proverbs 18:20–21 *Key Verse:* Proverbs 18:21

Death and life are in the power of the tongue.

What were you thinking about when you woke up this morning? Were you thinking about God, or were you thinking about the awful taste in your mouth? Your body, soul, and spirit are simply components of a missile, a heavenly arrow waiting for direction. Things will go better if you learn how to wake up with a great expectation in God.

Ask yourself, *Do I really know God?* If you really know Him, then let His light and "unlimitedness" flood every part of your being. Wake up with expectations of such great light and magnitude that you cannot bear to look at them. You should be an artesian well springing up with a continual flow of bright ideas and new revelation.

I know that God is changing me from what I am to what I am destined to be. Because of Him, I am about to do accomplish great exploits. My future is incredibly bright because I am speaking it into the light. I am calling out everything that God says I am and everything that He said I will have forevermore. I am saying the same things about me that God is saying about me.

How about you? It really does not matter if you are fourteen, forty, or eighty-four years old. God has invested power in your words. Your future will be what you say it will be, and that is why words are so important. Speak the words of God and release His creative ability in your life. Speak up and speak out about the bright future God has shown you. Speak it in the light!

Make this prayer declaration with me:

God, I am speaking out about a bright future. Everything You have said about me is coming to pass! I will accomplish great exploits!

IT TAKES GOD TO BELIEVE GOD

Today's Scripture Reading: Galatians 2:20; Philippians 2:13 *Key Verse:* Philippians 2:13

It is God who works in you both to will and to do for His good pleasure.

It takes God to believe God. What does that mean? Perhaps you have not grasped the reality that God has been saying some big things to you. It is hard to take something great and run with it if you do not know about it. It may sound strange, but it takes something bigger than yourself to believe what God is saying. In other words, it takes God to believe God.

The "Christ in you" can grasp what God is telling you to do. That only happens, though, when you have been so crucified in yourself that it is no longer you who live, but Christ who lives in you. When the life you now live in the flesh is Christ living through you, the Christ in you answers God's challenge or assignment with a firm "Amen."

When there is nothing but Christ in you, there is nothing left in you to resist what God says. Then you can say, "I am going to do it because I believe God." At that point, nothing can stop you from living out your destiny.

Pray this prayer with me today:

Jesus, I want to believe what the Father is saying. Forgive me for not letting You in me answer God's call. With Paul, I say that I am crucified with You and it is You who lives through me! And I am going to do it because I believe God!

January 4

Too Small to Contain It All

Today's Scripture Reading: 1 Corinthians 2:9–16 *Key Verse:* 1 Corinthians 2:9

Eye has not seen, nor ear heard,
Nor have entered into the heart of man
The things which God has prepared for those who love Him.

When God speaks big things to you, He is speaking things that only He believes at that moment. When you hear something that your head just is not big enough to contain, you are listening to God. On the other hand, if you hear something that fits easily in your head—if you can explain it and accomplish it all on your own—then the devil has whispered something to you. God inspires only deeds, dreams, and declarations that push us beyond our natural abilities and into His arms of supernatural supply.

A single word from the lips of God can immediately overload your intellect. Do not be surprised if your vocabulary falls short when you try to explain what God says to you. No one has words enough to describe the eternal and the infinite. As usual, we can communicate the revelations of God only by *doing them* for all to see.

Do not be discouraged. It is normal to feel too small and inadequate to contain and communicate the revelations of God. He steps into our inadequacy with His Spirit and makes a way where there is no way.

Pray this prayer with me today:

Lord Jesus, I give up. The only way I can hold the things You have shown me, the only way I can do the things You have asked me to do, is through Your strength and ability. Reveal Your glory, power, and grace through my inadequacies and weakness. All I can do is yield to Your Spirit and say, "Yes, Lord. May Your will be done in my life."

Pregnant with Divine Purpose

Today's Scripture Reading: Isaiah 43:18–19 *Key Verse:* Isaiah 43:19

Behold, I will do a new thing,
Now it shall spring forth;
Shall you not know it?

The dreams and visions of God develop in us much as a baby grows from a tiny beginning in its mother's womb to a magnificent life at birth.

When my wife became pregnant, we did not know it at first. After a few weeks Vanessa told me she was "feeling funny." I said, "Honey, you need to go to the drugstore and get one of those home-pregnancy tests. We need to see what is going on."

Sure enough, our do-it-yourself pregnancy test was positive and the doctor later confirmed it. Vanessa did not get any better; she started "feeling funny" all of the time. Then she started stretching.

You need to understand this important kingdom principle: *revelation never comes in its mature state*. When you first get pregnant with a vision or message from God, you receive the seed of the revelation. It has to get *in you* before it can grow and begin to stretch you.

If God has been talking big things to you, then you had better get ready for some change.

Pray this prayer with me today:

Dear Father, I am "feeling funny" today, and I think You are behind it all. Like Mary before me, I say, "Be it unto me . . ." Help me to bring to pass the dream You put in me. Grant me grace to walk in obedience and faith as You stretch me and mold me. Help me to carry Your seed until it is fully revealed to the world. In Jesus' name, amen.

JANUARY 6

DARE TO TRUST GOD

Today's Scripture Reading: Matthew 14:22–33 *Key Verses:* Matthew 14:28–29

"Lord, if it is You, command me to come to You on the water."
So He said, "Come."

What has God been speaking to you? Wait, let me tell you. He has been talking about big things and great dreams. In fact, He may have directed you to go to some very uncomfortable arenas. Why?

God believes that you are qualified because you should have grown up enough to trust Him by now. He thinks that you know Him well enough to hear what He says and do something about it.

Are you debating with God? Do not argue, and do not sit around and talk about what you think He is saying. Please, do not say you have to "fast on it" for a while. You should be already "fasted up." Do not make God change His mind.

I challenge you to hear and obey God. If you dare to trust Him, your life will never be the same!

Make this prayer declaration with me:

Lord Jesus, I am going to unplug my ears and hear what the Father is saying. I trust You to help me every step I take in obedience, and I thank You for it. Today, I decide to hear and obey!

YOU START IT AND YOUR GRANDCHILDREN WILL FINISH IT

Today's Scripture Reading: Psalm 105:6–8 *Key Verse:* Psalm 105:8

He remembers His covenant forever,
The word which He commanded, for a thousand generations.

Sometimes (or should I say *every time*) God gives you such a great vision that you alone can never accomplish it.

In fact, when God gives you a vision, you should know that *whatever He speaks to you, you cannot accomplish it in one lifetime*. If you can, it is not a vision from God; it is simply a task or a short-term mission. True visions are transgenerational. This may explain why you thought you were crazy when you heard God's idea. You were trying to figure out how you were going to get it all done before you died; now you know that God never intended that you accomplish the vision in your lifetime alone. He intended that you start it and then pass along the vision of your heart to someone else at God's direction.

If this truth caught you off guard today, then you will need to make some serious changes in your thinking, planning, and preparing. It is all part of our adventure as we follow the God who knows the beginning from the end.

Pray this prayer with me today:

Father, forgive me for thinking too small and for my failure to perceive that Your vision for my life extends beyond my own lifetime into the lives of my children and grandchildren (both physical and spiritual). You are the God of generations, and You delight to bless the seed of the righteous from generation to generation. Those things I do well today in Your name become blessings for my great-great-grandchildren another day. In Jesus' name, amen.

January 8

Supernatural by Definition

Today's Scripture Reading: John 15:1–8 *Key Verse:* John 15:5

Without Me you can do nothing.

When God places a call or vision in your life, by definition it is *supernatural*. You cannot ever accomplish it with just your strength, resources, or abilities. You will need God to pull it off, so why even play the game of saying, "God, I cannot do it"? Of course you cannot! Why would God ask you to do something that you could do in your own strength? You would not need His provision, His wisdom, or His power. In other words, it then would be a work of the flesh. Trust me, God does not work that way.

God is looking for people who have mountain-moving faith. Do you qualify? Then let Him speak big things to you.

Pray this prayer with me today:

Father, by myself I know I cannot do what You want me to do. But in Christ, I can do all things because He strengthens me. I have faith that You can move mountains with a single word, and I trust You to move every mountain in my way today. In Jesus' name I pray, amen.

GOD WANTS WILLINGNESS, NOT PERFECTION

Today's Scripture Reading: Jeremiah 1:4–6 *Key Verse:* Jeremiah 1:6

Said I:
"Ah, Lord God!
Behold, I cannot speak, for I am a youth."

When God gave the prophet Jeremiah an awesome assignment, he sat up and said, "But I am a youth." Jeremiah was probably about twenty years old at the time, so he was actually saying, "This just overwhelms me. I am not equipped to handle this, Lord. Why are You calling me to do this?"

You will know when God speaks to you because you will feel like Jeremiah did. It happened to me. God has blessed me with a growing church of more than ten thousand people, and every time I step in front of the congregation, I do so with awe and a reverent fear before God. Week after week I ask Him, "Why do You permit me to come before these people? You know how often I miss it and how inadequate I feel."

In His sovereign grace, God always tells me, "I know how often you fail and miss it. Just keep your heart toward Me, keep reverencing Me, and continue to stand every time I say, 'Get up.' I am not looking for a perfect vessel; all I require is a willing vessel. I want someone who understands that he *needs Me* every step of the way. I am looking for someone who will get up every time he falls down. I am looking for someone who loves."

Trust me: God is not interested in your credentials. He is interested in your love and loyalty to Him.

Pray this prayer with me today:

Lord, You know how often I fail You and miss the mark. All I know is that I need You desperately. I reverence You, and I long to do Your will. Grant me the grace to stand and sit only as You direct. Thank You for saving my soul and calling me in spite of my weaknesses. Where You lead, I will follow, as long as You direct my every step. In Jesus' name, amen.

January 10

Everything God Says About You Will Come to Pass

Today's Scripture Reading: Joshua 21:43–45 *Key Verse:* Joshua 21:45

Not a word failed of any good thing which the Lord had spoken to the house of Israel. All came to pass.

How do you react to God's vision and destiny for your life? Do you feel amazement, excitement, or fear? All of these emotions are natural, but you cannot afford to base your experience on feelings.

Sarah, the wife of Abraham, actually laughed out loud when she heard the angel of God (who was probably Jesus Christ Himself) say that she would have a child in her old age. Sarah's next response was fear.

Sarah was a woman who basically had lost her faith because of her assessment in the physical world. One of the greatest problems in the church today is our "sight problem." We see everything in the natural, but we insist on calling ourselves spiritual beings. Once we conclude that God has missed His mark and failed to come through on a promise, we feel we should help Him along.

Perhaps you have been dealing with some serious problems in your marriage or on the job for years, yet God told you a long time ago, "I am going to fix this." Since several years have gone by with no noticeable change, you have settled in and accepted the situation. So when God says it is time to *change*, you will not accept it *because of what you see* and what you have been through over the last many months. Can you see what has happened? You have lowered your aim; you have lived with a low expectancy.

Trust God to keep His promises, and they will come to pass. Apply Joshua's statement about God's faithfulness to your own situation: "Not a word will fail of any good thing which the Lord has spoken to my house. All will come to pass."

Pray this prayer with me today:

Father, forgive me for doubting Your promises to me and my house. You are faithful in all things, and I trust You. You will keep every promise and honor every word You have spoken to me and over me, because You are faithful. Help me to be faithful too. I love You, and by Your grace I wait for the fulfillment of Your promises, in Jesus' name. Amen.

JANUARY 11

START WITH A DREAM

Today's Scripture Reading: Habakkuk 2:1–3 *Key Verse:* Habbakuk 2:2

Write the vision
And make it plain on tablets,
That he may run who reads it.

"God, I cannot do that; I do not have enough money. Lord, are You really serious about this?"

Have you ever said these things? Has God spoken to you about starting a business or launching some great enterprise? Why are you sitting there, looking at your finances? You *never* start with finances—you start with a *dream*.

Forget your doubts and questions; go back to your dream. Start talking about it to other people, and above all, *write it down*. Put it down in simple terms so it will get past your head and into your heart. The more you talk about it, declare it, and write it down, the sooner the money will come.

Money always follows vision. If God spoke it, then you start speaking it too. Share the dream with people who also can receive it and run with it. Then God will see that the money comes your way.

Pray this prayer with me right now:

Jesus, even though the dream does not seem possible, I believe that You will bring it to pass! Show me who will receive the dream, and I will make it plain to them. And Jesus, in advance, I thank You for the capital I need!

January 12

Perhaps You Need to Go Back . . .

Today's Scripture Reading: Exodus 3:1–5 *Key Verse:* Exodus 3:5

He said, "Do not draw near this place. Take your sandals off your feet, for the place where you stand is holy ground."

God gave Moses instructions and vision when they were face-to-face on holy ground. If God has spoken to you in an unmistakable way sometime in your life, then you have received holy words on holy ground. It was a holy message in the sense that there was nothing mixed with it.

When God speaks pure words to us, we add nothing to them. These revelations come to us in holy, pure, and direct encounters with God. So in case you are wondering, no, you are not crazy. You did not think up the vision on your own. Do not expect fireworks: God does not need driving music or heavy doses of adrenaline to spark His creativity in our hearts. All He needs is a willing heart and an open ear.

Holy words are not the products of a "spiritual idea" or someone's concept of a "good, spiritual thing to do." That is the stuff of religion, not revelation. When He speaks, you know beyond a shadow of a doubt that the voice is God's, and the message remains pure over the passage of time.

You need to go back to that pure word. Perhaps you allowed someone to mix manufactured ideas or personal agendas to that thing you received on holy ground. If you or someone else perverted or added to God's holy word to your heart, simply repent and return to the pure thing God gave you. All He asks is that you be faithful in what He told you—nothing more, nothing less.

Pray this prayer with me today:

Lord Jesus, I repent and ask Your forgiveness for allowing Your pure word to become unholy. Right now, I return to what You and You alone told me. Thank You for Your grace.

January 13

He Brought You out of Sin for a Supernatural Purpose

Today's Scripture Reading: Ephesians 2:4–10 *Key Verse:* Ephesians 2:10

We are His workmanship, created in Christ Jesus for good works, which God prepared beforehand that we should walk in them.

The Israelites just wanted to get out of Egypt, so they did not look ahead to the end of the journey. They did not bother to search for the purpose behind their deliverance from bondage. They were not interested in the destiny propelling them to the promised land.

We must take time to look ahead, to search for God's purpose, and to seek out our divine destiny. God saved us for a holy purpose, not just because we were lost.

My friend, God brought you out of sin to take you into something supernatural. He has a holy purpose for you; He has a divine dream and destiny for your life. Accomplishing it is just part of our adventure in Christ.

Pray this prayer with me today:

Lord Jesus, deliver me from spiritual nearsightedness. Forgive me for my short-term focus; I realize now that You deal in eternal destinies and infinite possibilities. That is why You gave me the mind of Christ. It is the only way I can see beyond the rim of my limitations and the forest of my temporary wants. Lead me as You choose, Good Shepherd, and I will follow.

JANUARY 14

WHO TOLD YOU THAT YOU COULDN'T?

Today's Scripture Reading: Genesis 3:11; Psalm 37 *Key Verse:* Genesis: 3:11a

"Who told you that you were naked?"

Too many of us make the mistake of living up to fleshly job descriptions created by other people: "You are stupid." "You cannot do that." "You are nobody."

Do not let somebody else tell you who you are! Adam sought knowledge outside of God's blessing, and God called him on it! When he told the Creator that he was naked, God immediately asked, "Who told you that you were naked?"

Now I ask you: who told you that you were a fool and that you were no good? Who told you that you were ugly or that you could not do this or that? Who told you that you are not "qualified" because you did not graduate from Morehouse or Princeton University? Who told you that you couldn't?

Tune out the ever-changing whims and opinions of man and listen to God's eternal decrees about who you are and why He made you. Go back to the original Manufacturer and ask Him why you were made.

He will tell you this: you have a *holy calling*. You are a *child of God* and an *heir of all the promises*. You are a *chosen vessel*, and a *priest* in His kingdom. You are *holy*.

Peel away the false name tags, pick yourself up off the ground, and dust yourself off. You are holy and you have a holy calling, so do not pay attention to the unholy comments of other people. They do not realize it, but when they talk about you they are meddling with the child of God (let Him deal with them). Your only job is to hear and obey the things you hear your Father in heaven say.

Pray this prayer with me today:

Dear Father, help me to start over today. I want to return to the things You say about me, and I cast away all the negative, limiting opinions and predictions of others. If the things I hear are not in Your Word, grant me the wisdom and grace to set them aside as mere noise and focus on Your decrees. Your Word is a lamp unto my feet. In Jesus' name, amen.

AVOID THOSE FALSE PURSUITS

Today's Scripture Reading: Genesis 12:1–3; Mark 10:17–31 *Key Verse:* Genesis 12:2

I will make you a great nation;
I will bless you
And make your name great;
And you shall be a blessing.

God promised Abram, "I will make your name great"—if he would leave his father's house and enter into a new house with a new name. Abram moved in such a dynamic realm of faith and personal sacrifice that most of the known world knew his name. He always pursued the vision God gave him, even though he made mistakes and sinned from time to time. The Lord blessed Abram in the same measure that Abram sacrificed his will for God's.

In the book of Mark, Jesus talked about giving up things for the sake of the gospel. Sacrifices are involved wherever you find the genuine vision of God. Too many of us have "wish-ions" (a wish with a God twist) instead of visions. Most "wish-ions" are based on something spiritual we see in another person's life, which helps explain all the jealousy and backbiting in the church. (People who do not know where they are supposed to be feel a need to protect what they think they have.)

Check your faith. If you have a "wish-ion" and not a vision, do not bother to make a sacrifice. God is not obligated to reward you a hundredfold for pursuing something He never told you to do.

Return to the genuine vision and make whatever sacrifices necessary to fulfill it. God will joyfully reward you beyond your every dream.

Pray this prayer with me today:

Lord Jesus, I lay aside every plan, desire, and project that You never told me to pursue. Please forgive me for my presumption and set my life back on the track of destiny. I set my eyes on the pure vision You gave me, the vision that is too great for me to accomplish alone. By Your grace and provision, I will see Your vision for my life come to pass to Your glory.

January 16

God Told Me to Do It Because No One Else Would!

Today's Scripture Reading: Genesis 37, 50:20 *Key Verse:* Genesis 37:20

"Come therefore, let us now kill him . . .
We shall see what will become of his dreams!"

Do you have the vacant look of someone who has lost his dream? Perhaps you have not lost it at all. The problem may be that you have shared it with the wrong people. Joseph shared his heavenly vision with his brothers and in their jealousy, they tried to kill him to keep it from coming to pass.

Some people just cannot stand to see you dream. They get jealous when you start talking about big things and climbing higher than they have. They almost always say, "You cannot do that. Nobody else has done it, so why are you so special?"

If someone says this to you, tell him, "That is exactly why God told me to do this—because nobody else has done it yet. Sorry, I cannot afford to talk to you anymore. Bye!" Then walk worthy of your calling and be faithful to step out on the water by yourself and walk.

Make this prayer declaration with me now:

Lord, I am stepping out on the water. I am forgetting the "Joseph's brothers" who tried to kill my dream and quench my faith. I am resurrecting it right now, and I am stepping out of the boat. Hallelujah!

FIND FAITHFUL FRIENDS WHO VALUE YOUR VISION

Today's Scripture Reading: 2 Timothy 1:3–7; Proverbs 18:24 *Key Verse:* 2 Timothy 1:6

I remind you to stir up the gift of God which is in you through the laying on of my hands.

When God gives you a divine dream and heavenly vision, you have to do more than avoid people who are jealous of your dream. You must find people who will encourage you and help you fulfill the vision. You need to find spiritual allies who will constantly remind you of your gifts and abilities (and the One who gave them to you).

It is easy to forget the gift God gave you when you are in the middle of the hunt or in the heat of battle. Everyday pressures can bog you down and cause you to forget your God-given abilities. You need true friends who know you so well that they can tell when you get depressed or discouraged. Before you know it, they will be at your side, reminding you of the vision and of all the times God has come through for you.

It is important to stir up the gifts inside you. Paul the apostle made it clear that it is your job; so stir them up! Let me speak to you as a friend and brother in Christ: *You are not what those jealous people say you are. Get up and keep going. Do not just lie there; God has invested great gifts in you for a great purpose. You have a special God-given ability to get through this!*

Declare this prayer by faith:

God, I am stirring up the gift. I remember the dream You gave me. Please show me the friends I need to encourage me on my journey.

DO NOT ADD TO OR SUBTRACT FROM YOUR CALL

Today's Scripture Reading: Luke 1:30–38 *Key Verse:* Luke 1:38

Let it be to me according to your word.

You know that God has spoken holy things to you. Perhaps He called you to be an intercessor and gave you a special ability to pray with supernatural results.

Then something happened. Somebody told you that since you pray so wonderfully, you also should be laying on hands. You added the laying on of hands and "moved on" to prophesying. Who told you to do that? (It was not God; He called you simply to pray.)

Who said praying is not "good enough"? Even if God gave you your gift so you could pray for one person's salvation, does that somehow make it less important?

Perhaps you are one of the millions of mothers who devote their lives to birthing and raising godly children. The most famous woman in human history is remembered precisely for that ministry. (I am speaking of Mary, the mother of Jesus, of course.)

If you are called to motherhood, do not be angry because God did not make you the CEO of a major corporation. Forget about being a career woman. Look at your child and remember that you knew he was not yours even before he arrived. You perceived the finger of God upon him from the beginning, and you can already see the spiritual warfare swirling around your special child. Remember your call and remember there is something in that child.

Never negate God's call or dilute it with man's "mixture," no matter what it looks like in the eyes of others. Your part in the kingdom is crucial, so do not add or subtract from it. God is looking for faithfulness. Will He find it in you?

Pray this prayer with me today:

Lord, forgive me for the times I have changed my prayer to say, "Let it be to me according to man's word and ideas." Help me to renew my mind and to redefine success to mean obedience to Your purpose and design for my life. Only Your plans are good enough for me. Anything less is second best. In Jesus' name, amen.

ENDURE THE PROCESS, ENJOY THE BIRTH

Today's Scripture Reading: James 1:2–4, 12 *Key Verse:* James 1:12

Blessed is the man who endures temptation;
for when he has been approved, he will receive the crown of life
which the Lord has promised to those who love Him.

God, what is happening? Why is everything around me falling apart?"

Do you really want to know why you go through so much? James the apostle said trials help us to develop godly character. Life's struggles test the reality of God's Word in our lives along with our ability and willingness to hook up with the skills and ability He has given us. They confirm that every word we operated on came to pass.

Trials are part of the preparation process to transform dreams and visions into realities. It is as if you are pregnant with God's revelatory word for your life, and now you are going through the labor and strain of delivery from the realm of faith to the realm of the physical.

You know that birth is inevitable, so you do not have to manipulate things to speed up the blessings. When God gets ready to bless you, He will bless you because your character and your word represent the kingdom.

The Christian life involves more than merely accumulating "stuff." When you operate on character and the word of God, He gives you creative ideas so you can start your own business and prosper where others have failed. You do not need earth's money; all you need is heaven's idea. If the idea came from God, then He will finance it. True wealth is not the mere accumulation of things; you *are* wealthy because of who you are.

Trials and tribulations do not mess you up and rob you of blessings; they develop your character—and that is where true wealth lies.

Pray this prayer with me right now:

Jesus, I do not always understand why I go through these trials, but I trust You and I will let them develop my character. I will go through the process and enjoy the birth of Your word in my life.

THEN GOD SAID, "YOU ARE GETTING WARMER . . ."

Today's Scripture Reading: Genesis 1:3; 2 Timothy 3:16–17 *Key Verse:* Genesis 1:3

God said, "Let there be light"; and there was light.

Does it seem like it takes forever for God's promises to come to pass? Do you wonder why you have not heard God speak, even though you have been praying about something for a long time? Perhaps it is not time yet.

God's words are so powerful that if He opens His mouth to simply suggest a thing, it will happen instantly. (That is how He created the universe.) That also explains why He can give you only clues. Do you remember playing a game where your only clue consisted of the words, "You are getting warmer" or "You are getting colder"?

God lets you know when you are getting warmer, but He will not give you the full story now because it would come to pass before its time and season. In His infinite wisdom, He gives you just enough to hold onto.

God will give you a preview in the theater of life, but it is not finished yet because it is still in the process of birth. Words are extremely important. God gave us His Word to build up our spirits, to renew our minds to His way of thinking and doing things, to help us through the birth process. When you speak His words, they affect you, body, soul, and spirit. Not only do you understand them, but your body and spirit also respond to them in unity and power.

Pray this prayer with me today:

Lord Jesus, thank You for the previews. Thank You for the vision of what will one day be, and thank You for allowing me to help bring it to pass on earth as it is in heaven.

DO NOT ASK GOD TO BLESS YOUR MESS

Today's Scripture Reading: Matthew 6:24–33 *Key Verse:* Matthew 6:33

Seek first the kingdom of God and His righteousness,
and all these things shall be added to you.

A lot of people work out their own dreams and plans while asking God to bless them. That is not how things work in God's kingdom. The only way to operate under the favor of God is to pursue His plan and alignment with His heavenly vision.

God's kingdom always flows in God's favor. If you operate under kingdom principles, then you will automatically walk in God's provision and blessing. You will not have to work at it at all.

Seek God for a vision of His kingdom and get His picture of what He wants you to do. Then walk forward, confident in His provision.

Pray this prayer with me today:

Heavenly Father, I have made up my mind to seek You first, and then act with Your blessing. Forgive me for the times I have made up my mind and acted first, and then asked You to bless my mess. Show me what You want me to do today and grant me the grace to do it Your way. In Jesus' name, amen.

January 22

Do Not Get Stuck in the Middle—Press On

Today's Scripture Reading: Philippians 3:12–14 *Key Verses:* Philippians 3:13–14

Forgetting those things which are behind and reaching forward to those things which are ahead, I press toward the goal for the prize of the upward call of God in Christ Jesus.

Have you noticed that God gives us a great and wonderful vision, plus the first and the last steps necessary to attain it? He gives us the first line and the last line of the story, but He never informs us of the fine print.

God does not discuss the "in-between" part, but He will tell us the ultimate goal or aim of the vision. He may even tell us about where we must go, but He never gives us enough to go on apart from faith and total dependence on Him.

One of the reasons so many saints get frustrated is that they settle for less than their destiny. They get stuck in the middle and never press through to the end.

Let me encourage you. Yes, you heard from God. Do not worry about unexpected situations—they are not "unexpected" to God. You and I both know that something inside is telling you that something bigger, better, and greater is waiting for you just on the other side of the middle. So just keep pressing forward until you make it to your dream!

Pray this prayer with me:

Lord, forgive me for getting stuck in the fine print in the middle. I know that You finish what You start. I determine today to press forward to fulfill my destiny!

Everything God Said About You Will Come to Pass

Today's Scripture Reading: Genesis 37:5–36, 45:1–15 *Key Verse:* Genesis 45:8

It was not you who sent me here, but God;
and He has made me a father to Pharaoh, and lord of all his house,
and a ruler throughout all the land of Egypt.

After Joseph's jealous brothers threw him into a pit and sold him into slavery because of his visions, he soon found himself in Potiphar's house where he again faced mistreatment. Although he was only seventeen years old at the time, Joseph held on because somehow he received and believed the vision of God despite his circumstances and the many people who tried to stop him.

Whatever God spoke about you in eternity will happen in your life, no matter what people try to do to you financially, politically, physically, or spiritually. If God said it, you will get it.

God said in Jeremiah 1:5 that before you were formed in your mother's womb, He knew you. Paul added in 2 Timothy 1:9 that not only did God call you, but He gave you a holy calling. No one can add to it or subtract from it. The devil cannot add or take anything away, no matter what he throws at you.

God said it, so it has to happen. Regardless of whatever happens in the "in-between" time, the things God said will come to pass. He will see to it that you make it through to the end.

Pray this prayer with me today:

Heavenly Father, thank You for divine purpose and the holy calling You have given me. Today I am reminded that it was You who sent me here and not other men or women. What You have said about me will come to pass as surely as the sun rises each day, and no one can add to or subtract from Your decrees. Thank You, in Jesus' name.

January 24

By the Way, Things May Get Worse—But I Will Be with You

Today's Scripture Reading: Hebrews 13:5–6; Matthew 28:20; Psalm 23:4

Key Verses: Hebrews 13:5b–6

He Himself has said, "I will never leave you nor forsake you."
So we may boldly say:
"The Lord is my helper; I will not fear. What can man do to me?"

The first thing God told Joseph about his destiny was that the sun, the moon, and the stars would bow down to him. God would raise him up as a ruler and even his parents and brothers would bow before him.

Joseph received the vision directly from God, so he wanted to share his vision with his brothers. That introduced him to the "in-between" part of his call. God did not tell him that his brothers would throw him in a pit or sell him to the Midianites. The Lord did not mention the part about the attempts of Potiphar's wife to seduce him or the prison sentence that would be extended an extra two years due to the forgetfulness of Pharaoh's butler. God never mentioned the mess "in between" the first line and the last line of the heavenly vision.

So you should understand why you are having problems with the "in-between" part of your call: it is normal. I know God did not tell you about the stuff you are dealing with now. He gave you a glorious picture of what will be, but He did not tell you about the fine print of what will come first. Perhaps He did not tell you that someone would die, or that you would lose a child or a spouse, or go through a divorce. Perhaps He did not mention the eviction, the drugs, or the pain.

He did not tell you all that. What now? He expects you to go through the "in-between" time with faith in His word. Best of all, He promises that He will never leave us and that He will walk through the valley of the shadow with us!

Pray this prayer with me today:

Lord, I know that You did not mention the "in-between" part of this calling to me because You knew I would have avoided it. I am in the middle of the middle right now, and I put all my trust in You. Only You can know the beginning from the end, and my future is rooted and grounded in Your faithfulness. Thank You for walking through this with me. I still remember the vision. In Jesus' name I thank You, Father.

STAY DILIGENT BETWEEN YESTERDAY'S BONDAGE AND TOMORROW'S PROMISE

Today's Scripture Reading: Hebrews 11:1–6 *Key Verse:* Hebrews 11:6

Without faith it is impossible to please Him, for he who comes to God must believe that He is, and that He is a rewarder of those who diligently seek Him.

Diligence is an awesome word, and it may be the key to winning your struggle with the "in-between" time of your life. God already gave you the first step and the goal of your vision, but now you have to go through the process (the part He did not mention earlier).

All kinds of things happen in the "in-between" times. If you are not careful, you can forget the reason for your journey and trip over your doubt and unbelief. That is why Moses and the older generation of Israelites died in the wilderness, the land "in between" the land of bondage and the land of promise.

Do not let that wilderness, the "in-between" journey from your bondage to your promise from God, cause you to forget why the Lord put you here.

Be diligent. Stay with your faith. The reward will surely come.

Pray this prayer with me today:

Lord Jesus, I ask Your forgiveness for falling in the wilderness. Forgive me for grumbling in this "in-between" time. Lord, I know that You are a rewarder of those who diligently seek You. With Your help, I decide today to diligently follow You and Your kingdom principles.

JANUARY 26

GOD IS WAITING FOR YOU IN THE MIDDLE OF YOUR FIRE

Today's Scripture Reading: Daniel 3 *Key Verses:* Daniel 3:24–25

"Did we not cast three men bound into the midst of the fire?"
They answered and said to the king, "True, O king."
"Look!" he answered, "I see four men loose, walking in the midst of the fire;
and they are not hurt, and the form of the fourth is like the Son of God."

God does not tell you what will happen in between His call and its fulfillment in your life, but He does show you the blessings.

By now, most of us realize that those blessings are hidden in the circumstances He did not tell us about. God uses circumstances to hide His reward from those who are less diligent. He knows they do not have what it takes to walk through the trials and tribulations of life.

The three Hebrew youths described in the book of Daniel did not know what would happen when they took their stand for God and defied the king of Babylon. They knew that their decision would probably land them in the fire, but they never thought God Himself would meet them in the middle of it.

When God tells you to do something in a situation, He is already there. He placed hidden treasure in that situation long before you ever arrived.

If God was in the midst of the problem before you ever arrived, do you not think He knows the way out? (He also knows what you will need to carry out the treasure you find there.)

Pray this prayer with me today:

Heavenly Father, by Your grace I will diligently seek You in the middle of my circumstances and problems. You always reward me with treasures from Your heart when I do it; please forgive me for forgetting just how faithful You are. I am glad You were already here waiting for me when I fell into this pit, and I am also reassured by the fact that You know the way out. Thank You, Lord, in Jesus' name.

THE BEST IS STILL AHEAD

Today's Scripture Reading: John 3:1–21 *Key Verse:* John 3:4

Nicodemus said to Him, "How can a man be born when he is old? Can he enter a second time into his mother's womb and be born?"

It amazes me that Nicodemus asked Jesus about eternal life in one breath, and then asked with the next, "How can a man go back into his mother's womb when he is old?"

I believe Nicodemus actually understood what Jesus was saying. He had been a ruler and knew the Law. The problem was that Nicodemus also knew that he was old. He wondered if his opportunity for eternal life was past.

When you are young, you believe that you own everything and can do everything. Something happens in the years between youth and old age. Anyone who has set timetables for himself knows what I am talking about. We usually think we are ready for something when we really are not, according to God's timetable.

God does not use us the moment He speaks destiny and purpose into our lives. He waits until we feel like we are *not* equipped, which usually happens in our older and wiser years. We end up asking, "God, why did not You ask me to do this when I was young?" We know the answer already: it is because His timetable is a lot different from ours.

I do not care how old you are: the best still lies in front of you. If you feel like it is over, though, then it is over. Pray this prayer of new beginnings with me right now:

Jesus, I admit to feeling impatient at times. I want to do great things for You right now, but I choose to submit to Your timetable. Thank You, Jesus, for doing all things well in my life.

YOU ARE ON SCHEDULE—IT IS JUST NOT *YOUR* SCHEDULE

Today's Scripture Reading: Isaiah 46:9–10 *Key Verses:* Isaiah 46:9b–10a

I am God, and there is none like Me,
Declaring the end from the beginning,
And from ancient times things that are not yet done.

Have you complained to God because He would not "hurry up" your destiny? I have.

I did not become the pastor of a church until I was in my thirties. Yet very early in my life, God informed me that I would be the pastor of a major church. At that time, my definition of a "major church" was a congregation of about fifteen hundred people. That was thinking on a big scale for me, because at my daddy's church, fifty people showed up for Easter (if you included the twenty family members).

I began to complain to God about the delay between His promise and its delivery. "Time is rolling by," I told Him. I thought I understood how long it took to grow a church—at least, according to my mind-set and timetable. I was about to discover the reality of Isaiah's statement that God's thoughts are not our thoughts and His ways are not our ways (Isa. 55:8–9).

Sometimes we step out of the divine move of God by trying to fit God into our plans instead of conforming ourselves to His plans. Do you realize how impossible that is? Some of us have very limited faith because we look for God only within the realm of what we can see. Stop trying to fit God's infinite plans into your puny blueprint of life. Instead, let Him do things according to His infinitely wise timetable. He will set you into His perfect place and plan, and things will be well with you.

Pray this prayer with me today:

Lord, I am throwing away my man-made blueprints and timetables. They resemble a child's grade-school scribbling more than an architect's building plans. Forgive me for my presumption and plant me in the center of Your eternal purposes and divine timetable. I trust You to move me where I must go in the fullness of time and to supply me with everything I need to succeed in the task You have given me. In Jesus' name, amen.

Let Your Faith Extend Beyond Your Lifetime

Today's Scripture Reading: Genesis 23 *Key Verses:* Genesis 23:8–9

Meet with Ephron the son of Zohar for me, that he may give me the cave of Machpelah which he has, which is at the end of his field. Let him give it to me at the full price, as property for a burial place among you.

Faith is not just for the here and now. Sometimes it stretches beyond a lifetime. Abraham was in the land that God promised, but he never physically possessed it. He possessed the land by faith, but not in reality in his lifetime. The land was in sight, but not in hand. In fact, Abraham never owned more than a small plot to bury his wife. He never saw God's promise fulfilled. He just waited.

When God promises us something, we want it *now* because our faith is for only this life. The Bible says Abraham "waited for the city which has foundations, whose builder and maker is God" (Heb. 11:10 NKJV). Abraham had an eternal viewpoint of God's promises, whereas most of us lock our views in time. Abraham understood that the vision God spoke to him was so big and so far-reaching that all he had to do was get it started. It motivated him to know that he would be in the presence of God when he completed his part.

Begin to change your vision too. Let God show you His plan beyond the artificial limitations of time; let Him give you an eternal view of His glorious plan for you. Let your faith expand to encompass multiple generations!

Pray this prayer with me today:

Lord, stretch my thinking and expand my vision to step outside the limitations of time and space. Help me to see things as You see them and to understand that time is merely a tool and not a limitation in Your eternal kingdom. You will bring all things to pass in their proper season. Help me to see Your eternal purpose for my life so that, like Abraham before me, I can look for a city with foundations.

JANUARY 30

SOMETIMES YOU GET STUCK ON THE HIGHWAY OF FAITH

Today's Scripture Reading: Matthew 17:14–21 *Key Verse:* Matthew 17:20

I say to you, if you have faith as a mustard seed, you will say to this mountain, "Move from here to there," and it will move; and nothing will be impossible for you.

God, is something wrong with me? Why is nothing happening?" Have you ever felt stuck, even though you knew you were operating in a degree of faith? Do not stop; you are experiencing only a temporary delay.

Always remember that when God speaks to you and gives you vision, He never gives you a bad idea. Because of His nature, the Creator can give you nothing but perfection. He is perfection itself.

This also means that God does not have nightmares and or get nervous about the future. He knows the end from the beginning. So although things do not look good now, just keep diligently seeking Him by faith. You need to be diligent in order to turn that corner and escape that temporary "sticking point."

The flip side of all this is simple: if you do not keep after faith—if you do not go after God—then your hope and inspiration will die. Remember: you do not diligently seek Him merely by showing up at church on Sunday!

Stick with it. Do not give up on your dream or on the all-wise God who gave it to you. Keep after it in faith!

Make this faith declaration with me:

Jesus, I refuse to give up! I will turn this corner. I look to You more and more. I believe that with Your help, this too will add to my destiny.

JANUARY 31

MAKE SURE YOU DEAL WITH THE ENEMY IN THE MIRROR

Today's Scripture Reading: Hebrews 12:5–17 *Key Verse:* Hebrews 12:13

Make straight paths for your feet, so that what is lame may not be dislocated, but rather be healed.

God has written a script for your life that the devil cannot alter. No matter what the adversary throws against you, he cannot change your destiny. Nor can he keep you from reaching the end of your story.

The devil cannot change what God has set into place. No one can change what God has established in your life—*except you!* You are the only one who can stop you from experiencing what God has planned for you. You literally determine your destiny.

How? You determine your destiny by your obedience. Check your obedience level right now. Do you want to accomplish God's kingdom purpose in your life? Then release every area of disobedience or "lameness" to which you cling. Do not be a worse enemy to yourself than the devil already is!

Pray this prayer with me today:

Lord, I receive Your loving correction and repent of every sin against You and against other people. Forgive me for loving things, appetites, comforts, and my own will more than I have loved You. I offer You my life anew. Thank You for giving me a new beginning today and for placing my feet back on the path of obedience to Your perfect will. In Jesus' name I pray, amen.

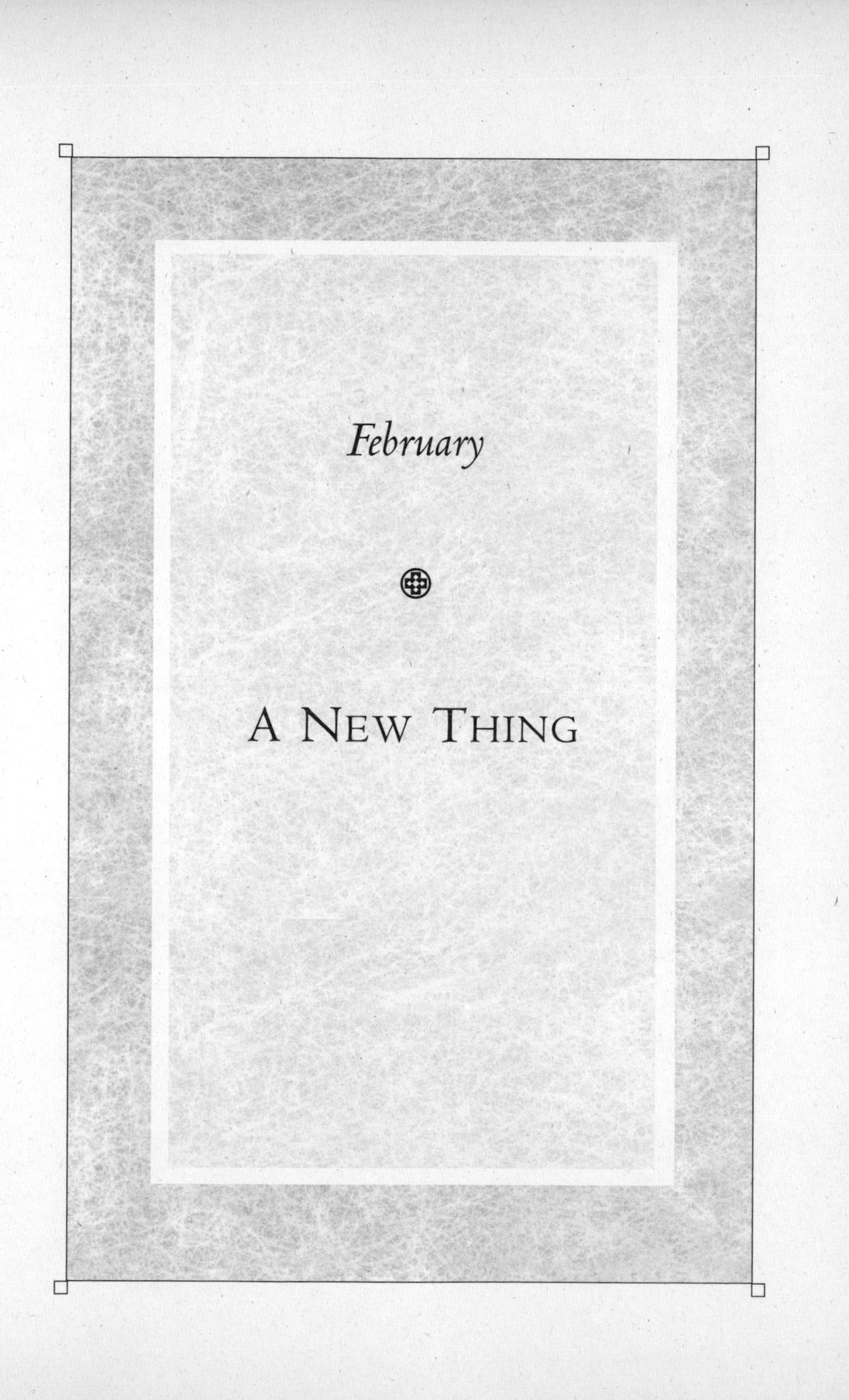

February

A New Thing

SOUL-WINNERS HAVE MORE FUN

Today's Scripture Reading: Luke 15:10; Jude 22–23; Proverbs 11:30

Key Verse: Luke 15:10

There is joy in the presence of the angels of God over one sinner who repents.

God has a new assignment for you, with a fresh anointing for a greater joy this year!

What is the greatest joy you could ever experience? It is not getting a sportier car, receiving a hefty raise, relocating to a new city, or moving into a bigger house. It is not even the day you get married. Your greatest joy comes when you step into the kingdom of darkness, snatch someone out of Satan's grip, and pull him into the marvelous light of God!

If that does not give you joy, then nothing will. The more people you rescue from darkness and draw into the light, the greater the joy that God gives you.

It is harvesttime. Go and fulfill your joy! But before you go, pray this prayer with me:

Jesus, nothing is more joyous than bringing someone to You. I want to snatch as many as I can from the kingdom of darkness! I expect You to give me opportunities, and I promise to take them.

IT IS YOUR SEASON TO BLOOM

Today's Scripture Reading: Numbers 13:1–20 *Key Verses:* Numbers 13:18, 20

[Moses said,] "See what the land is like: . . . whether the land is rich or poor; and whether there are forests there or not. Be of good courage. And bring some of the fruit of the land." Now the time was the season of the first ripe grapes.

When Moses wrote that it was the "season of the first ripe grapes," he was referring to the time of the harvest. The church also is entering a season of harvest today. It is time for the fulfillment of God's promise in your life. Now is the season.

There is something about seasons that you must remember: they change. That means if you do not move when and where God directs you to go, then the season will change and your opportunity will be lost.

This is no time to stall, ponder, consult, and delay. Now is the time to move forward in the vision of God—it is a new season!

Pray with me:

Lord, I hear You telling me to go forward whether the future looks rich or poor. I sense Your courage rising up in me, and I am ready to cross the river from the known to the unknown realm of faith. This is my season, and by Your Spirit, I will bear much fruit today and in the days to come. In Jesus' name, amen.

FEBRUARY 3

BE PREPARED: IT IS "OUT WITH THE OLD, IN WITH THE NEW"

Today's Scripture Reading: Isaiah 43:16–21 *Key Verse:* Isaiah 43:19

Behold, I will do a new thing,
Now it shall spring forth;
Shall you not know it?
I will even make a road in the wilderness
And rivers in the desert.

God is doing something new. He is ready to tear down the old system and build something new.

God is telling us today, "The old system, which I never ordained or blessed, is out, and I am raising up new folks of whom you have never heard."

When God starts to work on your life, be prepared. He will move out the old things that you considered to be anchors in your life. He will clean out your old ways of thinking. He is moving you into a new position, for it is a new season.

Pray this prayer with me today:

Lord Jesus, I am ready for a housecleaning; I want to embrace every new thing You send my way. Grant me the discernment to see what is old in my life and my thinking patterns, and give me the grace to embrace Your new assignments, correction, direction, and purpose for my life. I trust You to make a road where there is no road and to provide abundant streams of water in the middle of the worst deserts I encounter. I want to be a part of Your new move in the earth. Thank You for calling and anointing me for the new.

LORD, DELIVER US FROM THE SPECTATOR'S SEAT

Today's Scripture Reading: Galatians 6:7–10 *Key Verse:* Galatians 6:9

Let us not grow weary while doing good,
for in due season we shall reap if we do not lose heart.

The King James Version of this verse says, "And let us not be weary in well doing: for in due season we shall reap, if we faint not." No matter what Bible translation you read, you will come to the same conclusion: there are just too many "sissified" (uncommitted) converts in the church.

Jesus did not tell His disciples (and that includes us) in Matthew 28:19, "Go therefore and make *converts* of all the nations." He would never say that because converts just sit and look. Converts are candidates for career spectators, and we have entire churches filled with them.

No, Jesus commanded us to make *disciples*. Disciples say, "God said it, and I am going to stand here whether seeing His vision come to pass takes all my life or not. I will be here until God accomplishes it. It might take a year, it might take two years, but I am not moving. Why? Because I have to watch and pray until the Lord comes through, and I know He will!"

Are you a casual convert or a determined disciple? If you are a convert, leave your spectator's seat right now and become a participant in God's great kingdom plan.

Before you do anything else today, pray this prayer of declaration to the Lord:

Lord Jesus, the only way I can risk "losing heart" is if I put my heart into something in the first place. Please forgive me for being a watcher when You called me to be a doer. It is time for me to raise up disciples who will follow You faithfully for all eternity—help me to be a godly example before them. Thank You for delivering me from complacency and for planting Your vision in my heart.

Count the Cost Before You Wear His Colors

Today's Scripture Reading: Luke 14:25–33 *Key Verse:* Luke 14:28

Which of you, intending to build a tower, does not sit down first and count the cost, whether he has enough to finish it?

Do you have enough to finish what you have started? Have you counted the cost?

After the Lord rose again, He appeared to the disciples and said, "All authority has been given to Me in heaven and on earth. *Go therefore and make disciples of all the nations*" (Matt. 28:18–19 NKJV, emphasis mine). You have to be a disciple before you can make one. Jesus set a high standard for disciples when He said in Luke 14:33 that if we do not forsake all that we have, we cannot be His followers.

If you have not forsaken all, then you are just a "wanna-be." You have to count the cost first. What is the cost? Your life. This is the *gospel*.

It is easy to pick out people who have not counted the cost; they pick and choose what they will do for Christ. When something costs your life, your whole priority scheme changes the moment you decide you must possess that thing.

Converts just want to benefit from the blessings of Christ and the cross without enduring to the end. Disciples, however, have forsaken all for the sake of the gospel and the Lord of the gospel. The Lord is not someone they "add" to their lives—He is the life.

Pray this prayer with me:

Lord Jesus, You gave everything to purchase my freedom and restore me to Your kingdom. How can I give You less? Please forgive me for those times I have slipped into "country-club Christianity" and played the fashionable follower. The colors of Your kingdom are red for the blood You shed and white for the righteousness of God You have given us. My life is no longer my own, for I have been bought with a price. Thank You, Lord.

February 6

It Is Time to Move, Not to Delay or Disobey

Today's Scripture Reading: Genesis 11:31–12:4 *Key Verse:* Genesis 12:4

Abram departed as the Lord had spoken to him, and Lot went with him. And Abram was seventy-five years old when he departed from Haran.

This is the season to move, but count the cost before you do.

Do not say you will follow Jesus "no matter what" if your love for someone is holding you back. You have some rethinking to do. God ordained that we have many loving relationships in this life, but He will not tolerate taking second place behind a man, a woman, children, a career, or things of any kind. Do not hang on so long that you force God into rearranging things for you.

At first Abram's response to God was partial and slow. God called him to leave his father's house at once and take only his immediate family. He did not move until after his father died, then he took his nephew, Lot. Eventually Abraham learned to obey God's commands immediately and fully.

God has a place for you to be, and His plans for your life are big. This is not the time to be partial or slow in your obedience by faith. It is the season to move. Make this faith declaration with me today:

Jesus, I choose to follow You. I count the cost, and right now I let go of that relationship. Your plans are more important than anything else in this life. Thank You, Jesus, for including me in Your kingdom. I know that I can make a difference.

THERE IS NEW LIFE AFTER THE DIVINE INTERRUPTION

Today's Scripture Reading: Matthew 4:19–20; Genesis 12:1–7

Key Verses: Matthew 4:19–20

He said to them, "Follow Me, and I will make you fishers of men." They immediately left their nets and followed Him.

Has God interrupted your life? Abram was minding his own business when God intervened through a divine interruption and told him to leave his country, his extended family, and his father's house and go to a land He would show him.

Perhaps God interrupted you at a party. Maybe He interrupted you in a traffic jam on a freeway, or in the middle of a class or a meeting at work. God cannot be controlled or managed. He can invade any circumstance to blow up your plans and mess up your game. When He does, you can count on it being a lifelong interruption. He will suddenly show up and tell you to step out of your comfort zone and follow Him into the unknown.

One thing I have noticed about God is that when He tells us to get up, He usually does not tell us where He is taking us. All we know is that when He says, "Go," we have to go.

God has interrupted your life or you would not be investing this time with Him through this devotional book. You had some plans of your own, but God changed them.

God often places us in areas in which we feel conspicuously ill equipped. He interrupts our lives so we will lean on and draw closer to Him. Enjoy the journey.

Pray this prayer if you dare:

Lord Jesus, I know You interrupted my life for a purpose. Today, I choose to walk away from all those things and get up so I can follow You. I do not know where You are taking me, but I trust You every step of the way, and I know there is a blessing in store for those who obey.

IT IS TIME TO CHANGE YOUR MIND

Today's Scripture Reading: Romans 12 *Key Verse:* Romans 12:2

Do not be conformed to this world, but be transformed by the renewing of your mind, that you may prove what is that good and acceptable and perfect will of God.

This is a whole new season in your life and in God's kingdom. Walking in this new season requires a lot of changes on your part, one of which is an adjustment in your mind-set.

God wants you to start thinking "kingdom," and that requires you to completely change your old brain activity. The only way to make the change is to understand what God has ordained regarding the kingdom.

God's kingdom operates according to kingdom principles. So once you start thinking and acting in alignment with His kingdom—as you deepen your discipleship and forsake former patterns of behavior—you will receive an abundant flow of divine favor, blessings, and provision. It is the way the Lord set up His kingdom.

Pray this prayer with me:

Lord, I want to change my mind. I give You my old way of thinking, reasoning, and justifying my actions. Now I receive the mind of Christ by grace. Grant me the wisdom to faithfully follow the Holy Spirit into all truth and the grace to accept change no matter how much it hurts for the moment.

SPEAK, LORD—I AM LISTENING

Today's Scripture Reading: 1 Samuel 3:1–10 *Key Verse:* 1 Samuel 3:10

The LORD came and stood and called as at other times, "Samuel! Samuel!" And Samuel answered, "Speak, for Your servant hears."

I am thoroughly convinced that God is speaking to everyone who will listen to His creative word. Count on it: God is not going to do something that He did before. He is looking for someone who has enough faith to declare, "If nobody else is going to go with God on this thing, then I am just going to sit up and say, 'Speak, Lord, for Your servant hears.'"

God is creating something new in the world, and He is speaking fresh things into your heart and life. I urge you to obey. It is a new season.

Before you go, pray this prayer with me:

Lord, I tremble every time I sense You calling my name. Speak, Lord, I am listening. If someone is hurting and You want to heal his pain, send me. If one person, family, village, or nation is struggling in darkness and You are ready to send light, use me. Only know from the beginning that I know I am weak and that You are strong. Speak to me, lead me, send me; but send me in Your strength. In Jesus' name, amen.

FIRST THINGS FIRST (EVERYTHING ELSE COMES LAST)

Today's Scripture Reading: Matthew 22:37–40, 6:33 *Key Verse:* Matthew 6:33

Seek first the kingdom of God and His righteousness,
and all these things shall be added to you.

Kingdom is God's top priority in this new season. Nothing else matters except God's kingdom and His righteousness. Do not say, "I have heard it before." You have a part to play in it.

Every saint has an assignment and a seat of rulership in the kingdom of God, so do not belittle what He has called you to do. Do you exemplify God's kingdom at your job? How do you raise your children? Were you obedient to minister to that stranger on the street yesterday? Whatever you do in this life has a major impact on the kingdom because you no longer belong to yourself. You belong to and represent *Him*.

No part is too small because God wastes nothing. There are no accidents in His kingdom. This is the season, so do not miss your assignment.

Pray this prayer with me:

Heavenly Father, I want to make two clichés regain their original power in my life. I want to "put first things first," and I have decided to "major on majors and minor on minors." You said it better: "Seek first My kingdom." Please forgive me for all the times I have placed people, things, and fleshly appetites ahead of You. At last, I present my body as a living sacrifice.

YOU ARE QUALIFIED FOR THE JOB GOD ASSIGNS YOU

Today's Scripture Reading: Exodus 3; Philippians 4:13 *Key Verse:* Exodus 3:11

Moses said to God, "Who am I that I should go to Pharaoh, and that I should bring the children of Israel out of Egypt?"

God has a purpose for this generation. And you have a part to play in it. Do not let any man-made limitation in your life keep you from saying yes to God's plan and purpose for you! If you say yes, I guarantee you that your life—and the lives of those around you—will change.

A forgotten boy, the youngest in his family, said yes to God and became the most famous king in human history. All David knew was that he could not say no to the God who had never failed him.

An eighty-year-old runaway murderer said yes to God on a desert mountainside, and the Lord used him to alter history and deliver an entire nation from slavery. All Moses knew was that he was not qualified for the job—and that was the exact qualification God was looking for. You have the same job qualification.

She was still dreaming of the day she would marry, but the teenage girl said yes when God asked her to become an unwed mother for Him. Mary is still remembered two thousand years later as the mother of Jesus, the woman who birthed a miracle and changed man's destiny for all time.

Say yes to God now, and let Him deal with your limitations, fears, and lack of credentials. The rest, as we say, will be history. Just be prepared for the wildest ride of your life.

Pray this prayer with me:

Lord, I cannot, but You can. I would not, but You would. I do not know, but You know all things. I cannot see, but You see all. I do not have enough, but You are the God of More Than Enough. What else can I say? Yes, Lord. Yes, Lord. Yes, Lord. In Jesus' name, yes!

BEWARE OF BOGUS SAVIORS

Today's Scripture Reading: Galatians 1:6–24 *Key Verse:* Galatians 1:6

I marvel that you are turning away so soon from Him who called you in the grace of Christ, to a different gospel.

There is only one gospel, so we should be surprised that Paul marveled at the Galatians when they started following something different.

The kingdom gospel is tough. It does not allow us to remain comfortable in Sunday-only church. Kingdom gospel focuses on God and what He wants, not on the whims and wants of man. The God who birthed that gospel wants to see you move out in this new season!

How could the Galatians turn from God to a different gospel? They did it the same way you will *if* you get uncomfortable with the truth and go looking for the most appealing lie. After laboring on a crop for months, no farmer leaves his field of labor in harvest season to shop for comfortable new furniture.

This is no season to seek out comforts; this is the season to press forward in the kingdom! (The Comforter will take care of your needs if you take care of kingdom business.)

Do not become a marvel of foolishness for other saints. Stick to the one pure gospel and avoid every counterfeit. No matter how appealing counterfeit money may be, it is still worthless. Hold to the truth; anything and anyone else is accursed.

Pray this prayer with me today:

Father, I pledge my love and allegiance to You, the one true God and Creator of all things. I declare that You are one with Your only begotten Son and the Holy Spirit who dwells within me. I bless You in Jesus' name, amen.

WELCOME TO THE FAMILY BUSINESS

Today's Scripture Reading: Luke 2:41–52 *Key Verse:* Luke 2:49

He said to them, "Why did you seek Me?
Did you not know that I must be about My Father's business?"

In this passage from the gospel of Luke, Jesus wanted to know why Mary and Joseph did not realize that He was about His Father's business. That word *business* is in there for a reason.

What is the Father's business? It is kingdom business, the only business through which you and I can affect our world and its economy today. Business is what God does. We are called to promote our King and His principles in our daily lives—at our jobs, with our friends, and even with our enemies.

Jesus put His total focus upon His Father's business. Then He preached the kingdom and turned our world upside-down—or should I say, right-side-up? By the way, God's business has not changed in two thousand years. Are you in business for yourself, or for Him?

Enter this business contract with the Principle Founder:

In return for an eternity of unspeakable joy and the righteousness I could never afford to purchase or earn on my own, I pledge my life, loyalty, and energies to the promotion of the Ancient of Days, the risen Lord and King, and the Comforter. As for me and my house, we must be about our Father's business.

IT IS TIME TO EVICT THE SQUATTER

Today's Scripture Reading: Ephesians 1:20–23; 1 John 4:4

Key Verses: Ephesians 1:22–23

He put all things under His feet, and gave Him to be head over all things to the church, which is His body, the fullness of Him who fills all in all.

In referring to the fierce competition for customers and market share in nations around the world, businessmen often tell one another, "It is a war out there." But nothing in the secular business world can compare to the level of warfare occurring every moment in the spirit realm.

God has called the people of His kingdom to be fruitful, to multiply, to replenish the earth, to subdue and have dominion over it. Unfortunately, Adam and Eve sinned and gave Satan dominion instead, which is why the Bible calls him "the prince of the power of the air" (Eph. 2:2 NKJV).

That did not alter or annul God's charge; it simply expanded it. Now we must subdue and have dominion over the Prince of the Power of the Air as well as over the earth.

Jesus defeated Satan on the cross; and it is up to us to enforce that defeat. We are to subdue and to have dominion. Now is the season to enforce the kingdom and evict Satan, the squatter. The Father's business includes fulfilling our legal covenants under God. Satan is a defeated foe whose lease God has rescinded. Now it is up to us to implement God's eviction notice and dominate our business territory.

Make this prayer declaration with me before you begin your day:

Father, I thank You for sending Your Son to destroy the works of the enemy in my life and to reclaim my fallen race for Your kingdom. In His name I will speak Your Word of truth and reclaim lost territory and lost souls everywhere I go. I will conduct this territorial cleanup operation not by might or by power, but by Your Spirit for Your glory. In Jesus' name, amen.

THE HUNGRY WILL COME AS THE SON RISES OVER HIS KINGDOM

Today's Scripture Reading: John 12:21–33 *Key Verse:* John 12:32

I, if I am lifted up from the earth, will draw all peoples to Myself.

By all objective criteria, we appear to have an antichrist government running our nation today. Rather than serve as a force for the preservation of religious freedoms, Washington and the courts in particular seem determined to purge all evidence of Christianity from American culture. In the midst of this onslaught, God is not worried about His kingdom; He seems to be concerned about the man-pleasing American church.

"Dig your way back to the true foundation of God," He warns us. "Go back to the ancient ruins of God that have been covered up and lift up the altar and kingdom of God."

Jesus, the King of kings and Lord of God's kingdom, declared, "If I am lifted up . . . " In essence He was saying, "If you lift up the kingdom of God's rule, if you put His order back in its proper place in the earth, then I will draw all people to Myself."

Cult followers around the globe stand ready to commit suicide at the command of their misled leaders, and secular TV networks like the Black Entertainment Network will not play any religious commercials because they generate such a crushing volume of calls. Why? It is because so many people are looking for a spiritual encounter.

These people will come running if we will simply lift up Christ and His kingdom! They are thirsty for the living water that can be found only in Jesus the Christ, the Son of the living God.

Pray this prayer with me:

Lord Jesus, I am digging deep to find the firm foundation. I have covered it up with all the things I have lifted up that have no power to save or transform the lives of others. Please forgive me for my false promotions—now I will lift up only one name, only one cure, only one Savior and cause worth living for. And by Your grace, I will raise up others who will do the same. May You be lifted up and honored for all time in the kingdom of the Son to the Father's glory.

IF YOU KNOW WHO YOU ARE, YOU KNOW GOD'S "NEW THING"

Today's Scripture Reading: Genesis 22:1–19 *Key Verse:* Genesis 22:18

In your seed all the nations of the earth shall be blessed,
because you have obeyed My voice.

Something new will sustain the people of God in the next revival. This "new thing" is not really new to God, but it will be new to most of His people. (If you do not get this, you will be left out, so please pay attention.)

This "new thing" does not focus on shouting, jerking, or speaking in tongues. Generally, it is not found in traditional liturgy or in a high-church mass. You will find it in the God-given inward understanding of who you are as a child of God. This new identity is thoroughly biblical, but it also is thoroughly overlooked. It is the Father's "scepter of the royal seed," if you will, the key authorizing you and me to take our seats of authority in the kingdom.

Does this sound far-fetched? It was Paul who wrote under the inspiration of the Holy Spirit that God "raised us up together, and made us sit together in the heavenly places in Christ Jesus" (Eph. 2:6 NKJV). He also wrote, "If we endure, / We shall also reign with Him" (2 Tim. 2:12 NKJV). This is yet another area where God's Word requires us to revise our viewpoint about spiritual authority, wealth, and riches.

God put this all in place when He promised Abram, "In your seed all the nations of the earth shall be blessed." God's plan for us is that we stay in covenant, sustain families, and pass on generationally the spiritual and material wealth He gives us. That is "kingdom business."

Make this biblical prayer declaration with me:

Heavenly Father, thank You for adopting me into Your family through Jesus Your Son. Because of what Jesus did on the cross, I am now a member of Your royal house, the seed of the righteous, and an heir of all the promises in Christ Jesus. Because I endure with You, I also will reign with You, in Jesus' name, amen.

ARE YOU DOING WHAT YOU WERE CALLED TO DO?

Today's Scripture Reading: Ephesians 4:11–16 *Key Verses:* Ephesians 4:14, 15–16

We should . . . grow up in all things into Him who is the head—Christ—from whom the whole body, joined and knit together by what every joint supplies, according to the effective working by which every part does its share, causes growth of the body for the edifying of itself in love.

Can you describe your calling in Christ? If not, then you may wonder if you have one, and if you do, what it is. The Bible, though, makes it clear that every man, woman, and child in God's kingdom has a "calling" or place of anointed service in His kingdom. This is it: we are all called to build the kingdom in and through our lives. It is that simple.

That may mean that some of us are called to preach and teach God's Word while others are called to serve in the vital ministry of helps or in hundreds of other ways. Even church congregations seem to have specific callings under the main category of "building the kingdom of God."

Many church members seem to believe that their calling is to erect a bigger and better building, but that is not a calling; it is just one activity to support God's main job assignment for the church. My congregation has recently completed construction on a larger worship facility, so I am not against constructing buildings. We know, however, that God will not give us "credit" for building Him a bigger house.

In any case, it all boils down to the individual. The most important question you can ask as a member of God's kingdom is this: *Am I doing what God is doing, or am I doing my own thing?* You also should ask yourself, *Am I doing things the way He directed, or am I merely copying what I see other people doing?*

Pray this prayer with me:

Lord Jesus, I want to make every day count for Your kingdom. Please forgive me for the days and years I have already wasted on things that I have already forgotten. Help me to find my place of service in my local church, and bless its leaders with wisdom as they direct our efforts to build Your kingdom.

IT IS TIME TO BLESS AND BE A BLESSING

Today's Scripture Reading: The book of Esther *Key Verse:* Esther 4:14

Who knows whether you have come to the kingdom for such a time as this?

Queen Esther had no idea that her choices and sacrifice would determine the fate of her people, but they did. When Mordecai spoke this prophetic word to her, he gave us a timeless word as well that applies in a special way because we are the millennium generation. I believe that you and I are living in our season of promise. Every generation that has witnessed a millennial change also has been a strategic generation. We need to think, plan, and act with strategic discernment and accuracy as never before. Now is the time to hear God's voice, move in obedience, and make things happen.

If you are not where you are supposed to be, quickly repent, make all the necessary changes, and follow God. Go where He tells you to go and put yourself in the proper place. This is the season for divine appointments and careful movements under the orchestration of God Himself. We cannot afford to be out of position in this season of transition.

Why? God is positioning you for a blessing. Even more important, He is putting you in place to reign in the kingdom so that you, in turn, can *be* a blessing. You can void the blessings of God and miss your eternal purpose if you do not understand the crucial truth that you are being blessed to be a blessing to others. It is that serious.

Pray this prayer with me:

Lord Jesus, help me to lift my eyes and see beyond my own needs, desires, and limitations. I know I came to Your kingdom for an eternal purpose and that Your blessings are given to me so that I can give them away in Your name. Guide my steps today as I enter my world bearing Your gifts in my heart and on my lips.

YOU WERE CALLED BEFORE TIME BEGAN!

Today's Scripture Reading: 2 Timothy 1:6–11 *Key Verses:* 2 Timothy 1:8–9

Share with me in the sufferings for the gospel according to the power of God, who has saved us and called us with a holy calling, not according to our works, but according to His own purpose and grace which was given to us in Christ Jesus before time began.

The Bible says that God has "saved us and called us with a holy calling." Let that sink into your spirit. Yes, we have already discussed this in our daily devotions, but it is so important that we need to look at it again.

God did not just bring you out of darkness; He did it for a purpose. There is a holy calling on your life, but it will not come about through your own works or effort. It will come according to His own purpose.

Before time began, you received a grace through Christ Jesus to do something wonderful, supernatural, and strategic in God's kingdom. It is all part of the kingdom plan, and your part is crucial. Seek Him to discover that purpose. Return to that holy ground of revelation, if you must. Do everything you can to pursue Him and His calling for you.

Pray this prayer with me:

Father, I want to enter that divine purpose and grace You appointed for me before time began through Christ Jesus. I will no longer live my life as if it is mine to waste on things that do not matter. I will live for You through Christ my Lord. Amen.

FEBRUARY 20

RETURN TO HOLY GROUND AND REMEMBER

Today's Scripture Reading: Psalm 71:5–8 *Key Verse:* Psalm 71:6

By You I have been upheld from birth;
You are He who took me out of my mother's womb.
My praise shall be continually of You.

Go back to the holy ground. Go back to where you had that face-to-face encounter with God and He spoke to you. He wants you to remember the pure experience that you had with Him when He spoke destiny into you. Go back to when it was not mixed with anything that anyone else said.

Return to the pure thing God called you to do and do it. Your ultimate responsibility is to obey God and love others. Perhaps no one knows your name outside of your small circle of friends and associates. You may never be asked to open the mayor's prayer breakfast or to speak at public meetings, but it does not matter. God knew your name before you were formed in your mother's womb. He personally sanctified and ordained you for His holy purposes (and He will *never* forget your name).

Remember the purity of God's original word to you. He wants you to be true to His call, without mixture or compromise. Go back to the holy ground of God's revelation to you, and know beyond a doubt that it is your season.

Pray with me:

Lord, thank You for speaking directly to my heart in such an unforgettable way. I return to that holy place, and I remember how You touched me with destiny and set my feet on a sure path. In the remembering I gain a "knowing." I know that this is my season to produce good fruit in abundance. All I must do is follow You.

February 21

God Is Arranging Some Things

Today's Scripture Reading: Isaiah 54:1–8 *Key Verse:* Isaiah 54:7

For a mere moment I have forsaken you,
But with great mercies I will gather you.

Stop trying to make something happen. The fact that God has not moved on your timetable does not mean that you did not hear from Him or that you missed your time and season.

We often do not understand this passage in Isaiah: "For a mere moment I have forsaken you." God has kept many of us from moving in our destiny because it has not been time for Him to elevate us. He has allowed us to wander for a while so that He can bring us out at the right moment. You need to say, "It is my season." It *is* your season. God has not forgotten you; He is just arranging some things.

He has brought you back on the scene with a fresh anointing. You have a new assignment, and you cannot be denied if you walk in the faith that God has ordained.

Pray this prayer before you start the new day:

Lord Jesus, I forgot what time it is—it is Your time. You called me to follow You, not lead You. Forgive me for trying to impose my timetable on Your eternal purposes. From this day forward, I will follow You, wait upon You, and trust in You to see me safely to destinations You have chosen.

DO YOU SEE HIS HAND IN THIS SEASON?

Today's Scripture Reading: Colossians 1:9–23 *Key Verse:* Colossians 1:13

He has delivered us from the power of darkness and conveyed us into the kingdom of the Son of His love.

You have come out of the world and separated yourself from your old ways and the darkness that ruled over you. Yet in all of that, an aloneness that has settled around you. You just do not feel like yourself. You are in a state of uncertainty.

Take courage; you are not supposed to feel like yourself in your position. Things really are different. God has moved you away from all the things you used to depend upon because you are in a new season.

God pulled you out of the world and into the kingdom. In the world, a lot of things used to thrill you temporarily. Those were plots of the devil. He always will entice your flesh with something that appears to be enjoyable—until he has you hooked. Only then does he expose it for what it really is.

Our "problem" is that we have moved far and away from the devil's kingdom and into God's kingdom where there is only one "ride," and it does not appeal to our flesh.

Only one attraction exists in the kingdom of God, and that is God Himself. Our challenge is to turn away from other attractions to be alone with Him. God does not intend for you to feel close to a lot of people in this season. He does not want people who do not have a clue about eternity or the kingdom speaking into your life. Their godless chatter will only contaminate the word He is speaking to you.

Do not be concerned. Keep your faith in this "in-between" time. God's kingdom purposes will surely be accomplished in your life. Pray this prayer with me right now:

Jesus, I admit that I have not liked feeling alone. But now that I see Your hand in this season, I will trust You to see me through. Let me grow ever closer to You.

FIRST IS NOT ALWAYS BEST

Today's Scripture Reading: Mark 10:28–31 *Key Verse:* Mark 10:31

Many who are first will be last, and the last first.

Sometimes you wrestle with the problem that you were not "first" to tackle a particular task in the kingdom. Do not, because that is not a bad thing. The people who are "first" often get there by cheating. Some of them did not have enough faith to step into what God ordained. Many did not have enough faith to cut unwholesome but profitable relationships, or to give up things that they loved too much. Their baggage kept them from moving into what God ordained.

Perhaps you saw a group ahead of you that appeared to be prospering. It made you feel like a misfit, and you wondered if perhaps God had passed you by. Do not fret, beloved. It is not bad not to be first.

Jesus said that many who are first will be last. Perhaps it will be because they did not step into the season God ordained for their lives. Their season changed, and now you are in your season. God is telling you to step out into what He has ordained for you.

What can we say? It is God's way: you shall be first because you were last.

Pray this prayer with me:

Father, I have worried and wept over my "place" in Your kingdom in days gone by. Today, I choose to rejoice that You know my name, no matter where I stand in the line of faith. I trust the words and leadership of Your Son, Jesus Christ, and I am content to be the last in line as long as it is His line. In Jesus' name, amen.

MOVE BEYOND SAVING FAITH TO KINGDOM FAITH

Today's Scripture Reading: Romans 10:1–13, 12:3 *Key Verse:* Romans 12:3

I say, through the grace given to me, to everyone who is among you, not to think of himself more highly than he ought to think, but to think soberly, as God has dealt to each one a measure of faith.

Most saints (and churches) operate in a "saving faith." You need to get beyond that and grow. It is a new season.

Saving faith is a "given" faith. God said that each person receives a measure of faith. God gives to you the faith to get saved—and it does not require a whole lot. It takes enough only faith to confess with your mouth the Lord Jesus and believe in your heart that God raised Him from the dead. When you do that, the Bible says, "you will be saved" (Rom. 10:9 NKJV). You do not have to foam at the mouth or do cartwheels. Salvation is a simple thing.

Many churches limit their focus to just getting people saved, and this has wrecked many lives. Is it not good to win souls? Absolutely. But lives are wrecked when Christians believe that salvation is "it." Without divine purpose and personal accountability in their lives, they believe they can continue doing whatever they want. They have not moved into the kingdom.

Now is kingdom time. Get beyond saving faith and move into kingdom faith where you stretch and grow continuously for a divine purpose. The harvest is waiting.

Pray with me:

Lord, I sense that this is my season, but I understand now that my season is but one part of Your plan for the kingdom. I give You my measure of faith and ask that You enlarge and strengthen it so I can walk into Your kingdom purposes with boldness and honor Your name. In Jesus' name, amen.

FEBRUARY 25

Do You Believe That God Is Able?

Today's Scripture Reading: Hebrews 5:12–6:3 *Key Verse:* Hebrews 6:1

Leaving the discussion of the elementary principles of Christ, let us go on to perfection, not laying again the foundation of repentance from dead works and of faith toward God.

What does this old song have to do with anything?

Amazing grace! how sweet the sound
That saved a wretch like me!
I once was lost, but now am found
Was blind, but now I see.

The problem with this hymn is that it does not go far enough. You have been saved for twenty years, and yet you are still just celebrating being saved. Without question, salvation is wonderful, but is that all you have to sing about? We need to sing this song:

Amazing grace! how sweet the purpose
That drives a saint like me!
I once was stagnant, but now I am moving,
Had no vision, but now I see.

There is more to the Christian life than just being saved. Our problem is that we do not have vision beyond salvation. We are stagnant because we are not driven by a purpose.

Salvation, your deliverance from darkness, is a gift. You have saving faith, which is a gift. But you do not believe God for anything beyond your heavenly destination. You have not stretched yourself out to see if God is able. You do not have that kind of stretching faith because it requires more than just confessing. It requires walking in it when you cannot see it because God gave you the first line and the last line, and you need to press through.

Pray this prayer with me:

Jesus, forgive me for not using my faith to reach what You have ordained for me. I go back to that holy and pure word You spoke to me. Thank You for saving me. And now I press on.

FEBRUARY 26

DID YOU LIFT YOUR HEAD WHEN YOU HEARD THE CALL?

Today's Scripture Reading: John 10:1–30 *Key Verse:* John 10:27

My sheep hear My voice, and I know them, and they follow Me.

There is a new call in the earth—yet it is an old call.

This nation, and the whole world, is crying out for truth. Unfortunately, they are not finding it in the church. As a result, Christians and non-Christians alike are following an ever-changing conglomeration of lies and nontruth. Yet there is a call, a voice, a word that God is whispering into the innermost parts of people around the world. They cannot tell you where it comes from or repeat it word for word, but whenever they hear somebody stand up and proclaim it, they lift their heads and feel their hearts beat faster.

Does this describe you? Do you hear the call to the true gospel of the kingdom? Does your heart beat faster when you hear the truth? This is the season of the kingdom.

Pray this prayer with me:

Lord, I hear Your voice despite the deafening sound of man's competing slogans, programs, plans, and opinions. The sound of Your voice always causes my head to lift up in expectation and my heart to beat with new life and joy. Grant me the grace to faithfully follow You no matter where You lead me.

IT TAKES A "DIFFERENT" SPIRIT TO FOLLOW HIM FULLY

Today's Scripture Reading: Numbers 14:1–24 *Key Verse:* Numbers 14:24

My servant Caleb, because he has a different spirit in him and has followed Me fully, I will bring into the land where he went, and his descendants shall inherit it.

Caleb and Joshua entered the promised land because they believed God. The Bible says Caleb had a "different" spirit. Do you have a "different" spirit, or do you have the traditional church spirit?

If you are operating in that church spirit, then you need to get a different spirit. This is a new season, and you need to consider your children's children in all that you do. I do not care what kind of job you have or what kind of car you drive; have you made decisions with your descendants in mind? You need to be in place in your kingdom purpose so that they can be in a place where God is moving. No matter what it costs us, we must stop playing church games.

Some people go to church just to play the dating game. Others who attend church and sit in comfortable pews on Sunday have no intention of changing their ways. Are you praying and studying or just taking up space? Get a different spirit. All others will fall, and that fall will be great. When God moves, He always moves with people who have a different spirit.

Be like Caleb and Joshua, and do not quiver like grasshoppers!

Pray this prayer with me:

Lord Jesus, I am tired of dragging around the baggage of "churchianity." I am ready for change; I am determined to get a different spirit and follow You into the fulfillment of Your promises. I may feel like a grasshopper challenging a giant at times, but as long as I follow You, I win.

February 28

New Seasons Require "New" Leaders

Today's Scripture Reading: Deuteronomy 31:1–8; Joshua 1:1–9

Key Verse: Deuteronomy 31:7

Moses called Joshua and said to him in the sight of all Israel, "Be strong and of good courage, for you must go with this people to the land which the Lord has sworn to their fathers to give them, and you shall cause them to inherit it."

This new season requires a whole different type of leader and saint. God needs a fresh breed, people who are free from the patterns and pitfalls of church leaders in the sixties, seventies, eighties, and even the nineties.

This is a major challenge to me, because I am under no illusions. I constantly wonder if I am mature and equipped enough to do what God has called me to do. My ministry is a ministry of total dependence; I make it through each day only by leaning upon the everlasting arms.

The third millennium demands a new kind of leader and saint. Leaders *lead*, and that means they take risks. When you ask God to equip you for this new season, trust Him to take care of it. Do not worry about it, and do not be surprised at what happens.

The Lord takes us through it all to train us. He is developing *trained* leaders among the true saints of God who will possess the land and move in great faith.

Will you answer that call?

Pray this prayer of commitment with me:

Lord Jesus, I want to be part of the new and different leadership in the third millennium. I will undergo the training and trust You no matter what. I hear Your call, and I am answering it!

ONCE YOU KNOW THE "WHO ANSWER," THE "HOW ANSWER" IS OBVIOUS

Today's Scripture Reading: Daniel 11:32–33 *Key Verses:* Daniel 11:32b–33a

The people who know their God shall be strong, and carry out great exploits. And those of the people who understand shall instruct many.

This is the season of promise for God's people, corporately and individually. One of the things this season will bring is a great shift of wealth. Not everybody will get in on the spoils, however.

Many people may be going to church, but only those who understand who the church is will enjoy what God has ordained. Why? They are the ones who will have enough nerve to go into areas that appear to be overwhelming.

When you understand that you and your brethren *are* the church, then you know that everything God has is at your fingertips. When God ordains for you to go somewhere, He goes before you like a fiery blaze to establish the trail. God is a consuming fire, and He burns everything that would hinder you before you get there. All you have to do is walk through the ashes because once God passes through, those things cannot do anything to you.

The catch is that you have to have enough spiritual faith to show up.

Pray this prayer with me:

Father, You have called me to dream, dare, and do things far beyond my natural ability or capacity for accomplishment. Thank You for preparing the way before me. I will follow You, and the exploits will come, but not by might, nor by power, but by Your Spirit. In Jesus' name, amen.

March

Confronting Failure

You Are Not in a Mess; You Are in a Treasure Hunt!

Today's Scripture Reading: Philippians 1:3–6 *Key Verses:* Philippians 1:3, 6

I thank my God upon every remembrance of you . . . being confident of this very thing, that He who has begun a good work in you will complete it until the day of Jesus Christ.

Have you ever made a mistake? Perhaps you thought, *Lord, I did that all wrong, and I am in the middle of a mess!*

I know both of us have, and it does not matter. The important thing is that you are where God led you. If God led you to where you are, then He has something for you there. Do not allow the devil to discourage you and turn your focus toward your failures and shortcomings. This is not the time to dwell on your inadequacies. God, in His sovereignty, loves you so much that He has brought you to where you are—and it is the place of promise.

The Lord says, "Even though it seems you live in a land of famine, I have great blessings and coverings for you. I have hidden your blessings and provision around your enemies. If I put them anywhere else, other people would have gone after them. Yes, you are where are supposed to be."

God knows all about the lazy saints, the ones among us who refuse to dig or pursue anything. They operate by sight and not by faith. God is looking for those who have matured enough to trust Him. They know that if God tells them to enter a lions' den, then He has plans to give the lions lockjaw.

You are not in the middle of a mess; you are in the midst of hidden treasure! Now shut that toothless lion's mouth and dig that treasure out!

Pray this prayer with me:

Lord Jesus, instead of looking somewhere else in times of trouble and saying, "I wish I was there doing that," I will look for You. You have placed treasures and blessings in the midst of my troubles and problems, if only I will look for You. Help me to live by faith and not by sight in the crucial days ahead.

MARCH 2

GOD IS GEARING YOU UP FOR A MIRACLE

Today's Scripture Reading: Numbers 13:1–20 *Key Verse:* Numbers 13:18

[Moses said,] "See what the land is like: whether the people who dwell in it are strong or weak, few or many."

Just as God led the Israelites to the land of promise and told them to "see what it is like," so He will tell you to go to the place He has promised you. He wants you to open your eyes and assess what is going on. Is the land strong, weak, or overwhelming?

God shows you how you are outnumbered and overwhelmed so He can get you geared up for a miracle. He wants you to look at the promise so He can tell you, "I have something for you, but I want to show you what lies in front of it: I have your enemies guarding your blessing."

Are you bold enough to press in? God is setting you up so that no one can get the credit but Him. There was a day when you would not face trouble, but after coming through so much, you now look at trouble and say, "Trouble, you cannot stop me."

God says, "No weapon formed against you shall prosper" (Isa. 54:17 NKJV). That may mean that He will let you see your enemy form the weapon, but it just will not be successful. That is what happened in the lives of Queen Esther and Mordecai—they watched Haman form a gallows for Mordecai and a death decree for Esther and the Jewish people. Yet those weapons went unused. When God shows you the weapon, just pray:

Thank You, Lord, that this weapon is not going to prosper. Thank You for revealing the enemy's plots and plans and for removing their power to hurt me. You are gearing me up for a miracle, for my life is not my own; I have been bought with a price. I bless You, Lord of heaven and earth.

FOCUS ON THE PROMISE, NOT THE PROBLEMS

Today's Scripture Reading: Deuteronomy 5:32–6:12 *Key Verses:* Deuteronomy 5:32–33

You shall not turn aside to the right hand or to the left. You shall walk in all the ways which the Lord your God has commanded you, that you may live and that it may be well with you, and that you may prolong your days in the land which you shall possess.

Ten of the twelve spies Moses sent into the promised land ran into trouble because they were worried about being in the same territory as their enemies. Joshua and Caleb saw the inhabitants of the land, but they kept their focus on the grapes instead. There are blessings in the midst of all your tests and trials, and God does not want you to be distracted. He is there.

Are people talking about you? Let them talk. "Somebody is trying to get me fired." Let him do his best. Your promotion comes from the Lord. "Somebody is trying to take my spouse." Let him try. God ordained you to be where you are. If anybody tries to touch you or your belongings, you should feel sorry for him! Why? Because when he attacks or steals from you, he is attacking and stealing from God.

People who ride with me while I drive usually pray a lot because my driving is much like that of Mr. Magoo, the nearly blind cartoon character who insists he can see just fine. I have had a few fender benders, and they usually happen when I take my eyes off of where I am going to look somewhere else at someone's urging.

When God tells you to go someplace, do not worry about anyone else's presence. You have been ordained to be there, so anyone who tries to distract you must deal with God.

Pray this prayer with me:

Lord, help me to keep my focus upon You and Your promises. There are always distractions awaiting me, and I am all too willing to look aside and feed my fears, my appetites, and my curiosity. Help me to seek You and find the blessings in the midst of every trial. In Jesus' name, amen.

THE FRUIT OF PROMISE IS RIPE AND WAITING

Today's Scripture Reading: Numbers 13:17–20 *Key Verse:* Numbers 13:20

[Moses said], "[See] whether the land is rich or poor; and whether there are forests there or not. Be of good courage. And bring some of the fruit of the land." Now the time was the season of the first ripe grapes.

Never focus on the negative. Move on until you are able to focus on what God sees: "I have good things prepared for you there. The fruit of the land is already ripe and waiting there. Do not pay any attention to the evil reports."

Have you noticed that once we see something that overwhelms us, we get stuck on the negative? God says, "Be of good courage. Do not become afraid; do not get paralyzed. I did not give you the spirit of fear. I do not want to hear prayers about your trouble. Look in the middle of your crisis and see all the rich fruit I have prepared for you. Pick some of it and bring it back as a testimony."

You will see treasure that no one else sees right in the midst of your situation. You will find it right in the middle of your enemies. Be bold and take courage. Now go get that fruit!

Pray with me before you go:

Heavenly Father, thank You for preparing a blessing for me in the midst of my enemies and trials. Help me to be of good courage and to see Your abundance in the midst of my lack. By faith I will take the land and possess its wealth for the kingdom.

YOU DO NOT HAVE TIME FOR A PITY PARTY

Today's Scripture Reading: Jeremiah 1:4–10 *Key Verse:* Jeremiah 1:7

The LORD said to me:
"Do not say, 'I am a youth,'
For you shall go to all to whom I send you,
And whatever I command you, you shall speak."

In this passage Jeremiah was doing the same thing the ten spies did. He was looking at his inability instead of God's ability. God said, "When I talk to you, do not tell Me about your inadequacies. Do not tell Me what you lack. Do not tell Me how nobody loves you. Do not tell Me about all the things stacked up against you. Focus on what you have going for you instead. Tell Me about your gifts and all the things that are going right."

Speak praises and stop focusing on the negative. Do you know why the psalmist said, "From the rising of the sun to its going down / The LORD's name is to be praised" (Ps. 113:3 NKJV)? It is to keep you from talking negatively!

You do not have time for a pity party. God has been too good to you. Every time you look around, God is blessing you, so you should not waste time being negative. Pray this prayer with me right now:

Jesus, I choose to forget the negative things that have happened to me in the past. I choose even to forget what bad things are happening to me now! Instead, I choose to praise You morning, noon, and night. You are so good to me!

MARCH 6

SAY THE WORD AND REAP A HARVEST

Today's Scripture Reading: Matthew 12:22–37 *Key Verse:* Matthew 12:37

By your words you will be justified, and
by your words you will be condemned.

If you are unhappy with the life you live, you have only one person to blame because you built it. Let me put it a different way: you spoke into existence the very situation in which you find yourself right now. Jesus said, "For by your words you will be justified [the Amplified says *and acquitted*], and by your words you will be condemned" (Matt. 12:37 NKJV). That means sentenced. Your own words determine whether you are justified or condemned.

Did you know that God did not let any of Samuel's words fall to the ground (1 Sam. 3:19)? That means they all came to pass. Jesus said that whatever you ask in His name, He will bring to pass (John 14:13–14). Whatever you speak that is not according to God's ways will condemn you.

The common denominator in all this is that results proceed from the words you speak. The writer of Proverbs declared, "Death and life are in the power of the tongue, / And those who love it will eat its fruit" (Prov. 18:21 NKJV). Words are more powerful than we realize. According to the first chapter of Genesis, our universe literally came into being when God simply spoke a word.

If your situation looks dismal at the moment, then start talking differently. Start praising God and watch things change—they have no choice.

Pray this prayer with me:

Lord, I put a guard on my tongue today. I want to speak only good things in alignment with Your Word and the leading of Your Spirit. I speak life, hope, and joy over those You have placed in my life. In Jesus' name, amen.

STEP OUT OF YOUR DOWNWARD SPIRAL WITH FRESH VISION

Today's Scripture Reading: Psalm 119 *Key Verses:* Psalm 119:9–11

How can a young man cleanse his way? / By taking heed according to Your word. / With my whole heart I have sought You; / Oh, let me not wander from Your commandments! / Your word I have hidden in my heart, / That I might not sin against You.

Words create pictures. A simple story can make us smile, cry, or feel a wide range of emotions. This is why you must separate yourself from so many worldly things. It all follows a pattern. We tend to think about the things we hear, then we begin to feel emotions about the things we think. Once the emotions set in, actions almost always follow. In other words, we tend to "do" what we feel.

What you do regularly becomes a habit or pattern in your lifestyle. Your habits determine the direction of your life and eventually your destiny.

Why am I going into all this? Pay attention: if you are having a sin problem, you felt it before you did it. You felt it because you were hearing and picturing it over and over in your mind.

Few of us will readily admit this. Most of us are tempted to act holy and pious, to cover our sin with the claim, "Well, I just 'woke up' in sin. It shocked me. How did I get in this hotel room? Who put that false claim in my tax return? I'm as surprised as anyone."

You were not surprised. You led yourself down that path.

Beginning this moment, you must stop talking about your setbacks, defeats, and disappointments. Stop focusing on your failures and problems. That simply creates feelings that lead to actions and destructive habits. It is a vicious downward spiral, and you cannot afford to stay on this deadly ride. Freedom and a new start are just a prayer away (although your responsibilities do not end after this prayer).

Pray with me right now. Do not put it off or say, "I will do it later, after . . . "

Jesus, forgive me for listening to things and viewing things that are not part of Your kingdom. Forgive me for listening to trash and filling my vision with devilish distractions. I stop the cycle right now! I choose to focus on the positive instead of the negative. I set my eyes upon You and Your Word, and I trust You to put my feet back on a sure path to kingdom living.

March 8

Expect to Be Blessed So You Can Be a Blessing

Today's Scripture Reading: Mark 11:12–14, 23–24; Luke 17:6 *Key Verse:* Mark 11:23

Assuredly, I say to you, whoever says to this mountain, "Be removed and be cast into the sea," and does not doubt in his heart, but believes that those things he says will be done, he will have whatever he says."

Today is the "tomorrow" that you talked about yesterday. Do you ever think, *I wonder what God has for me today?* Do not wonder anymore. God has for you whatever you talked about yesterday. Your tomorrow has come!

If you talked about your lack of joy and your disappointment, heartache, personal pain, loneliness, and poverty, then guess what? You will awake the next day to a fresh load of disappointment, pain, loneliness, and poverty.

Our big God gets excited about people whose faith is strong and with their mouths they confess it. He is thrilled to hear us declare by faith, "God, I am thanking You for divine health. I am going to be spiritually prosperous through your blessings. I will walk in Your favor today. I declare that my house and my heart are yielded to you. I trust You to guide me steps.

Talk about your faith expectations, not your life experiences. Talk about your future, not your past failures. Failure is a natural part of success in God's kingdom. Every home-run king in major league baseball also has a high strikeout average—it is a natural result of swinging at the ball with all his strength and passion.

When you talk about your expectations and bright future in the Lord, you energize the power of God to move in your life. You will wake up every morning with a new joy because you expect to be blessed so you can be a blessing in Jesus' name. Pray this prayer with me:

Lord Jesus, I expect to be blessed. I expect to walk in divine favor. I expect to be healed. I expect the joy of the Lord. I expect to feel the peace of God that surpasses all understanding. I expect my children to be in order. I expect that no weapon formed against me shall prosper. God, these are big things, and I am speaking them out with my faith in You.

HEALING COMES WHEN YOU HEAR AND SPEAK THE WORD

Today's Scripture Reading: Romans 10:17; 1 Peter 2:24 *Key Verse:* Romans 10:17

Faith comes by hearing, and hearing by the word of God.

Do you need healing in your body today? What have you been seeing and saying? Have you focused on God's words? Make sure that you do not read God's Word according to man's limited interpretation. You need to go further back into the Hebrew of Jehovah to know that there is nothing He cannot cure or heal. If you want victory in Jesus, then speak the truth of His Word.

I am talking about more than a positive attitude. The words you speak bring healing and wholeness; they frame your whole world. Once you connect your words with God's, sit back and watch healing be released.

It all begins when you hear the Word, believe it and then speak the truths of the Word. That's the kingdom way. Pray this prayer with me:

Father, I realize that my words have framed my world. When I spoke negatively about myself I often spoke condemnation into my life. My doubt put the Holy Spirit "out of business" because He cannot act on doubt and unbelief.

Lord, I want to walk uprightly in great expectation, and I begin right now. I need Your help, Holy Spirit. I give You permission to arrest anything that starts to come out of my mouth that is unholy, unclean, and contrary to the kingdom. Let me speak only those things that edify and promote the kingdom.

By faith in You, I declare it done now. I speak joy unspeakable in my life, and I speak peace that surpasses all understanding to guard my heart and my mind in Christ Jesus. I speak divine healing in my life and declare that by His stripes I am healed.

MAXIMIZE THE GOOD; MINIMIZE THE BAD

Today's Scripture Reading: Luke 19:15–26; 1 Corinthians 10:13 *Key Verse:* Luke 19:17

[The nobleman] said to him, "Well done, good servant; because you were faithful in a very little, have authority over ten cities."

If we lack energy in our kingdom lives, perhaps it is because we do not focus on the opportunities at hand. We must talk about the blessings that we possess and take time to test and taste our triumphs today. Jesus' parable about the faithful servants in the gospel of Luke illustrates the way God loves to praise and reward us for even the smallest success and obedience.

When something bad happens to you, have you noticed how easy it is to dwell on it? We are far quicker to announce a pity party than we are to declare a victory celebration. How often do you take the time to say, "You know, the devil thought he had me. I did not think I was going to get up, but with God's help, I did! This is a victory. I am just going to bake myself a cake and have a party in Jesus' name."

As parents, we have a bad habit of reinforcing sad habits in our children. When a child comes home with straight A's, we pat him on the back and say, "Good job; I am glad." If the same child brings home lower grades the next semester, we restrict his phone privileges and vividly relive the shame for a month! This is the ideal way to teach a child to remember failure rather than to celebrate victory.

When you encounter a tragedy, you need to say, "God has an opportunity somewhere in this tragedy that He wants me to exploit." Seek out God's blessings in the midst of life's trials and tragedies. God does not want just anyone to benefit from His blessings, so He disguises them as something that no one wants to touch. Then, when you spend time in His presence, He shows you the rich blessings hidden under or behind life's difficulties.

Just stick with God through your trials and He will show you a blessing that is bigger than anybody else could ever believe.

Pray this prayer with me:

Father, I choose to draw close to You in the middle of this mess. I know You have a blessing and divine provision waiting for me in the middle of this fire, and I trust You for it. Show me Your divine opportunity. Grant me the grace and faith to walk through Your door of opportunity and so pass from the fire into Your presence. In Jesus' name, amen.

March 11

Worry Is Not Part of God's Plan for Your Life

Today's Scripture Reading: James 5:13–16; 2 Corinthians 5:7

Key Verse: 2 Corinthians 5:7

We walk by faith, not by sight.

Some of the people who contract cancer do so because they worry about things when they should not.[1] Why? Worry has never been a part of God's plan for man. If you are a worrier, be careful. You can worry yourself right into a hospital bed.

Many worriers are chronically depressed. Depression causes your body to release harmful hormones; it also stops the release of things that your body uses to fight tumorous growths in your body. Sometimes worry stems from our lack of trust in God, which is revealed in the way we talk about our experiences and failures rather than about our expectations in Christ.

Do you get excited about what you *do not* see? James 5:14 tells us to call the elders of the church to pray over the sick and anoint them with oil in the name of Jesus. Why? Elders in the church should be mature enough to avoid worry and embrace faith so the Holy Ghost can flow through them. As a result, when they lay hands on you, the Holy Ghost moves through them and activates the healing power that already resides within you.

Put that old worrier to rest. Walk by faith and not by sight! The power is already in you. Pray this prayer with me:

Lord Jesus, I choose to believe Your promises concerning my healing through the stripes You bore on Your back. I believe the good report in Your Word, and I lay aside every evil report in the natural realm. Thank You for the prayer of unity and faith available through other believers and the leaders in the church.

MARCH 12

WAIT UPON HIM AND THE WEIGHT UPON YOU BECOMES LIGHTER

Today's Scripture Reading: Isaiah 40:27–31 *Key Verses:* Isaiah 40:30–31

Even the youths shall faint and be weary,
And the young men shall utterly fall,
But those who wait on the LORD
Shall renew their strength;
They shall mount up with wings like eagles,
They shall run and not be weary,
They shall walk and not faint.

As men, and especially as fathers, many of us feel that we are about to break as we forge our way into the new millennium. We are under pressure and stress in every arena. If you are at a breaking point, I can tell you why (but you may not like it): somewhere along the way, you parted from God's ordained order.

I know it does not sound fair, but the fact is that God made man to be a foundation (and He did not ask for our opinion or approval). That means He created you to shoulder whatever burden He has ordained in your life.

Examine your life to see if anything you are or are not doing fails to match God's plan as revealed in His Word. Return once again to that pure, holy word He first gave you for you life. Examine the Scriptures and do whatever it takes to step back in line with God. As soon as you do, His strength will flood through your life and you will easily carry what used to knock you to your knees. As the Scriptures say, "Those who wait on the LORD / Shall renew their strength."

Father, I am waiting on You, no matter how heavily life weighs on my soul and my shoulders. I find all my strength in You and in no other. In Jesus' name, I will renew my strength and mount up with wings like an eagle.

Face the Mongrel That Pursues You

Today's Scripture Reading: Joshua 6:1–20 *Key Verse:* Joshua 6:1

Jericho was securely shut up because of the children of Israel; none went out, and none came in.

Do you realize that nobody went out of Canaan's most formidable fortress city because its inhabitants were afraid to face Israel openly? Have you ever noticed that the devil does not deal with you openly? When I was learning about spiritual warfare, I would no sooner figure out where the enemy was coming from, then *bam*—he would hit me from the back. His attacks are never frontal; they never come from where you expect them.

If you have been experiencing a lot of marital problems lately, it is likely that those problems are a smoke screen. The enemy really may be targeting your children. He does not care about your marriage; he wants to get you so tied up and distracted with one another that you ignore your children. He hopes that by the time you figure that out, he can influence them to shoot somebody or contract a fatal disease through premarital sex.

Israel's enemy in Jericho refused to confront the Israelites openly because they feared the God of Israel. The Israelites were the same people who crossed the Jordan walking on dry land. The devil is afraid of the God in you too. You have been running from somebody who is scared of you!

The devil knows that God saved you miraculously. He knows that God has His hand on you in a mighty way, and he knows that God does not waste time saving people who are not worth saving. He saves people for whom He has an eternal plan and purpose. All this time you have been running from a cosmic coward!

Do you not think it is time to turn around and tell the devil to get off your tracks? Any old mongrel dog thinks he is the boss when you run from him. It is when you turn around and face your pursuer that things quickly change! Make this declaration with me:

In Jesus' name, I resist you, Satan. If you wonder why I leave such large footprints in the earth, it is because I follow in the footsteps of the Creator of all things. I stand in the shadow and favor of the King of kings and Lord of lords. I am washed in the blood of the sacrificed Lamb, and no weapon formed against me shall prosper. I can do all things through Christ who strengthens me—and that includes sending you back to hell where you belong!

March 14

All You Have to Do Is Turn Around

Today's Scripture Reading: James 4:6–8; 1 Peter 5:8–9 *Key Verse:* James 4:7

Submit to God. Resist the devil and he will flee from you.

When I was in high school, the bus driver always dropped me off in front of a house that was home to several hellhounds that chased me every day. I tried to talk the bus driver into going to another stop, but he never would. One day I decided to get off at the stop before my regular one, but as soon as I looked around, I saw those panting dogs waiting for me. I could read their minds: *Thought you were going to fool us, didn't you?*

Finally the day came when I had had enough. Have you had enough? Are you tired of the way people push you, mess with you, or generally treat you badly? Have you told yourself, *The next person who even looks at me cross-eyed is going to get it?*

When I got off the bus that day, I refused to run. I made up my mind that it was going to be me or them. When those dogs came after me, I turned around and growled at them. Do you know what happened? They ran away! I grinned and thought, *I have been running from you all this time, and all I had to do was turn around.*

All you have to do is turn around.

Pray this prayer and make this statement with me:

Father, I am tired of running from the hounds from hell. This is the day I take You at Your Word and resist the devil. In Jesus' name, I take my stand, and I will not be moved until you move aside, Satan. I am armed and dangerous with the Word of God, the Spirit of God, and the blood of the Lamb.

NAME YOUR JERICHO AND BRING IT DOWN

Today's Scripture Reading: Numbers 33:50–55 *Key Verse:* Numbers 33:55

If you do not drive out the inhabitants of the land from before you, then it shall be that those whom you let remain shall be irritants in your eyes and thorns in your sides, and they shall harass you in the land where you dwell.

Name your Jericho. Pinpoint the situation you need to correct but have avoided for so long. The longer you let it go, the more it fortifies itself in your soul and becomes an irritant in your eyes and a thorn in your side.

Jericho was a "gateway" city marking the beginning of Canaan. It also was called the "city of palm trees," which implies that it had an abundance of water, making it even more difficult to capture through "waiting" or siege techniques. It marked the first miracle Israel would need from God to possess their promise.

The devil knows that you cannot resolve your problem with Jericho until you face it. It is like a fortress now because you have built it up in your thoughts and imagination. Outward circumstances and problems make its walls look overwhelming to you.

So much time has passed that you have allowed it to become your partner instead of your enemy. Now you are lying with it rather than having victory over it. Wait no longer; it is time to bring those walls down.

March up to that situation and confront your Jericho. It blocks your way into the promised land, so it must come down—all the way down. Once it crumbles, you will experience God's presence in your life as never before!

Pray this prayer with me:

Father, I have an irritant in my eye and a thorn in my side named Jericho. I am tired of walking around it, avoiding it, and pretending that it does not exist. It is an obstacle blocking my progress toward my promise in You. In Jesus' name, I declare that Jericho's walls are coming down!

March 16

With a Shout You Can Take It Out!

Today's Scripture Reading: Joshua 6:15–20 *Key Verse:* Joshua 6:20

It happened when the people heard the sound of the trumpet, and the people shouted with a great shout, that the wall fell down flat. Then the people went up into the city, every man straight before him, and they took the city.

As soon as the Israelites entered the promised land they faced Jericho—a formidable fortified city with massive gates and imposing walls. The Israelites had to deal with Jericho before they could move one step further into the land of promise. This should sound strangely familiar to every follower of Christ. Have you noticed that every time God brings you into some great joy, something seems to crop up to challenge your faith?

You will not move on in your Christian experience if you avoid confronting your Jericho. Is there something that has plagued you for a long time? Do not try to sweep it over to the side and deal only with its minor symptoms. If you bypass your Jericho, you will always have an armed and dangerous enemy dwelling behind you. God has been merciful to you in the past, but now He says, "Where are you going? Get back here. You need to get this out of your life."

Countless leaders in the political and spiritual worlds have bypassed their moral Jerichos, only to have them rise up in all their ugly reality just as these people reach the pinnacle of their careers in public office or in church leadership. It is better to deal with your Jericho now than to wait until later when its very appearance will wreck your life and destroy everything you have worked for.

Jericho may be fortified, but with a shout you can take it out! Do it now, while it is your season.

Pray this prayer with me:

Lord Jesus, others may not see the walls of Jericho looming over my life, but You do. Today I will heed Your warning and begin the march of faith around my Jericho. The battle will not be won by might, nor by power, but by Your Spirit. No matter how high its walls or how great its gates, this monstrosity will come down in Your name!

FIRST THINGS FIRST: BIND THE STRONG MAN

Today's Scripture Reading: Mark 3:23–27 *Key Verse:* Mark 3:27

No one can enter a strong man's house and plunder his goods, unless he first binds the strong man. And then he will plunder his house.

Each year, thousands of teenagers quit high school before they graduate, only to discover how difficult it is to land a good job without a diploma. In the end, many of return to school to earn their GED (general equivalency diploma). Sometimes you have to go back and take care of unfinished business before you can go forward.

Your joy, your peace, your contentment, your victory, your enjoyment of where God has you—these are all locked up in that fortress we have been calling "Jericho." You will never be able to "plunder the goods" and enjoy all that God has provided for you without overcoming your Jericho. You cannot sit back and claim joy and peace until you do what it takes to see those walls fall and pass through the gates to bind whatever binds you!

Pray this prayer with me:

Lord Jesus, I have put things off as long as I can. Now I am ready to do something about the "sin which so easily ensnares" me. Grant me the grace to face the things I fear and the sins I have covered over the years. I bind the ungodly strong man in my life in Your name. Cleanse me with Your blood and set me free forever. Help me to finish this business so I can get on with Your business.

MARCH 18

REMOVE THE SIN AND STAND BEFORE YOUR ENEMIES

Today's Scripture Reading: Joshua 7 *Key Verse:* Joshua 7:13

Thus says the Lord God of Israel: "There is an accursed thing in your midst, O Israel; you cannot stand before your enemies until you take away the accursed thing from among you."

God has ordained that we should be living in the best time of our lives. We should possess more, give more, work more, dream more, and dare to do more in His name than ever before. Why aren't we?

We have, as many older saints would say, "a shame before God." The common thread of this shame is our unbelief. That is the sin that keeps the walls up and keeps us in sin. You are out of your mind if you think you have not sinned, because sin includes the failure to believe what God said.

There are two kinds of sin. Sins of commission include the things you did that you were not supposed to do. Sins of omission are the things you did not do, but should have. Unbelief is the common thread running through them both.

Our unbelief has entertained and maintained a stronghold in our lives and drained us of our anointing. Unbelief has sidetracked us from what God ordained for us to do.

Let's pull out that thread of unbelief from our garments of salvation and robes of righteousness. We have too much to do to allow unbelief to hold us back any longer.

Pray this prayer with me:

Heavenly Father, forgive me for the sins I have committed against You. Forgive me for not believing You enough to do the things You have called me to do. I also ask that You forgive me for doing things You never told me to do. Thank You for removing my shame. Now grant me the grace to do great exploits in Jesus' name, amen.

SEE JERICHO'S DEFEAT BEFORE YOU EVER START THE BATTLE

Today's Scripture Reading: Joshua 5:13–6:5 *Key Verse:* Joshua 6:2

The LORD said to Joshua: "See! I have given Jericho into your hand, its king, and the mighty men of valor."

One of the keys to getting victory over your problems and defeating the Jericho in your life is contained in one word: "*See!*"

You need to get God's Word on your situation and meditate on what He says about it. Continually look at the Word of God's perspective on the challenges in your life. Meditate on and consider it from every angle. I recommend that you do not say a lot about it, however, because it is a private thing.

God told Joshua, "As soon as you can see it, you have won." In God's mind, when you see it, when you grasp it in your spirit, you have it.

Understand that God did not say that Joshua would see it as soon as he started fighting. No, Joshua was to see *before* he began to fight.

Face your Jericho and *see* its walls crumble to the ground!

Pray this prayer with me:

Lord Jesus, I see! I can see the victorious end before I even begin the battle to defeat my Jericho. Thank You for going before me in Your power and might. Thank You for a new beginning and an eternal future in Your presence.

MARCH 20

NATURAL EYES SEE PROBLEMS; SPIRITUAL EYES SEE SOLUTIONS

Today's Scripture Reading: 2 Corinthians 5:1–7 *Key Verse:* 2 Corinthians 5:7

We walk by faith, not by sight.

Our primary problem today is that we cannot see the way we should. Our physical eyes work, but our spiritual eyes are underdeveloped because of neglect. The Bible says we must walk by faith and not by sight, yet most of us walk by sight and not by faith.

If you do not believe me, then take this simple test. When you woke up this morning, what were you worried about? What was the first thing to weigh on your mind? Whatever it was, it may well mark the place where you stopped trusting God and started seeing your problems with your natural eyes instead of your spiritual ones.

When you worry about something, you allow it to put stress on your emotions and physical body. You are walking by sight. If you operate in true faith in God, you will let Him handle the situation. The problem is that when we fail to see a situation through God's eyes, we focus on the problem rather than on the answer. That is not kingdom living!

Turn your walk around. Walk by faith, not by sight. Begin to see your world through God's eyes, not through your physical eyes.

Jesus, forgive me for walking by sight rather than by faith in You. I cannot do anything by myself anyway. Right now I choose to focus on the answer, not the problem. I choose to walk in faith.

March 21

Open My Eyes, Lord

Today's Scripture Reading: 2 Kings 6:12–19 *Key Verses:* 2 Kings 6:16–17

[Elisha said,] "Do not fear, for those who are with us are more than those who are with them." And Elisha prayed, and said, "Lord, I pray, open his eyes that he may see." Then the Lord opened the eyes of the young man, and he saw. And behold, the mountain was full of horses and chariots of fire all around Elisha.

Do you see things as they really are or as they appear to be? God says, "The way your situation looks does not matter. I say that you are more than a conqueror." God calls us to look at things with the eyes of the spirit, not of the flesh. The things we see with our physical eyes can overwhelm us. But when we look at them through the eyes of the spirit, we see them in the light of eternity and the cross. Then we see that we are indeed more than conquerors!

The servant of the prophet Elisha could see only the enemy forces encircling the man of God. When Elisha asked the Lord to open his servant's eyes, the man suddenly saw the fiery army of God waiting for Elisha's command!

If only we can see with our spiritual eyes, we will realize what mighty power God has placed at our command! Pray this prayer with me:

Lord Jesus, forgive me for my lack of faith. Help me to see with the eyes of the spirit the answer that You have waiting in the wings. For You are a faithful God, and You always come through for me.

March 22

Who Do You Think You Are, O Great Mountain?

Today's Scripture Reading: Zechariah 4:6–7 *Key Verses:* Zechariah 4:6–7

This is the word of the Lord to Zerubbabel:
"Not by might nor by power, but by My Spirit,"
Says the Lord of hosts.
"Who are you, O great mountain?
Before Zerubbabel you shall become a plain!
And he shall bring forth the capstone
With shouts of 'Grace, grace to it!'"

What obstacle looms before you today? God says, "Contemplate it by faith and not by sight."

Have you been looking at the problems lined up against your marriage, your relationships, your job, your lifestyle, and your children with your physical eyes? No wonder you feel so defeated and hopeless. Your mind has been contemplating the situation, working at it and analyzing it using the wrong set of eyes.

You can never get all the information you need using your natural eyes. You must use the eyes of your spirit and see from the viewpoint of faith. What has *God* said about your situation? Will you dare to believe Him?

Just as Elisha prayed for his servant to see God's spiritual army, ask the Lord to open your spiritual eyes to see the answer He has already prepared for your situation. Ignore the data collected by your physical eyes and walk by faith!

Pray this prayer with me:

Dear Lord, open my eyes so I can see past my earthbound problems and circumstances and perceive Your divine solutions to them all. May Your will be done on earth as it already exists in heaven. I bless Your name and choose to walk by faith in Your faithfulness, not by sight and dependence on my own limited resources. In Jesus' name, amen.

STAND STILL FOR A CHANGE AND SEE YOUR SALVATION

Today's Scripture Reading: Exodus 14:1–14 *Key Verse:* Exodus 14:13

Moses said to the people, "Do not be afraid. Stand still, and see the salvation of the LORD, which He will accomplish for you today. For the Egyptians whom you see today, you shall see again no more forever."

Things may look bad for you right now, but your situation cannot be any worse than what the Israelites faced when Moses said these words to them.

After suffering for several generations under the cruel power of the Pharaoh of Egypt, the Israelites had a brief moment of freedom when they marched out of Egypt's capital city. Then Pharaoh's army came after them at breakneck speed, and the Israelites realized that they were trapped. The Red Sea lay before them, mountains were on each side, and Pharaoh's elite charioteers and the Egyptian army were massed behind them. When they looked at their options, they thought all was lost.

In that moment of impossible despair, God said something to His people that still rings true in every situation today: "Stand still, and see the salvation of the LORD." He essentially told the Israelites, "Look back again at your enemy, for you are not going to see them anymore!"

It all comes down to walking by faith, not by sight. Stop depending on your physical eyes for information on which to make your decisions. Stake your future on what the Lord told you to do, no matter what blocks your way. It is time to choose which way you will go—choose faith.

Pray this prayer with me:

Lord Jesus, I take this moment to stop my running and my personal efforts to win freedom. I am standing perfectly still physically and spiritually so that I can see the salvation You have already provided. If anything happens, it will happen by Your Spirit, not through my might or power.

March 24

Just Go Forward and Watch What I Will Do

Today's Scripture Reading: Exodus 14:13–18 *Key Verse:* Exodus 14:15

The LORD said to Moses, "Why do you cry to Me?
Tell the children of Israel to go forward."

When the children of Israel stood trapped between the Red Sea and the Egyptian army, they did not see their salvation or deliverance outwardly until they had the faith and obedience to comply with the divine order of God.

The Israelites had to exercise enough faith to obey *before* they could receive their deliverance. God basically said, "I know the sea is there; *just go on*. When you do, look back so you can see Me destroy your enemy."

God had explained everything earlier to Moses. His only requirement was that the Israelites be obedient and act on His word. They had to see their joyous escape in the spirit before God would let them see it in the natural.

Do not look at your circumstances without faith. Just be obedient to God's word to you and keep moving forward. Then watch those situations part before you!

Pray this prayer with me:

Lord, I see Your salvation by faith! I see Your answer to my problem, and I am going to keep moving forward. That obstacle is not a problem anymore; I see it now as a victory about to come forth!

March 25

Encircle Your Jericho with Faith

Today's Scripture Reading: Joshua 6:2–3 *Key Verses:* Joshua 6:2–3a

And the LORD said to Joshua: "See! I have given Jericho into your hand, its king, and the mighty men of valor. You shall march around the city, all you men of war."

Are you still fighting that "Jericho" in your life? Perhaps it reappears week after week because you have been looking at its walls and defenses with your physical eyes. You see how high it is, you have estimated its strength, and you have anticipated how much it could hurt you to assault it. That is the problem. Look through your spiritual eyes instead. See those walls totally crumbled and flattened by faith! See yourself advancing against your enemy with valor as a man or woman of war.

Your Jericho has not come down yet because you cannot see it in the spirit yet. Get the victory in your spirit first. Then, with eyes of faith, you will encircle that city of fear with faith and see the fortress of problems fall down through the power of Almighty God!

Pray this prayer with me today:

Lord Jesus, I have tired of reading about Jericho so many times because I do not want to deal with the very real Jericho in my own life. It is true: I have been building my faith in the strength of the problem instead of building my faith in You, Your Word, and Your supreme power. Today is the day I cross the river of fear and indecision to take the city I have feared for so long. In Your name, I win!

March 26

The Commander Brought His Army for Good Measure

Today's Scripture Reading: Joshua 5:13–15; 2 Kings 6:16 *Key Verse:* Joshua 5:14

He said, ". . . As Commander of the army of the Lord
I have now come." And Joshua fell on his face to the earth and worshiped, and said to Him, "What does my Lord *say to His servant?"*

Do you realize that God has sent you more than the Commander of His army? He also has sent you *an army*. That means you have with you much more than you can see! Elisha's servant had a totally different perspective after God opened his eyes to see heaven's fiery hosts surrounding the puny armies of Elisha's enemies. The prophet told his servant, "Those who are with us are more than those who are with them" (2 Kings 6:16 NKJV).

Let this eternal truth burn deeply into your heart and soul: No matter what challenge rises up in your life, *there are more with you than are with your enemy*, even though it looks to the physical eye that you are overwhelmed.

You will not make it through if you walk by sight, but when you walk in the Spirit, you know there is an angelic host waiting for the Master's slightest command. Best of all, Jesus Christ, the Captain of the army of God, is with you!

Lord Jesus, I look at this challenge today knowing that there are more with me than with it! I have a host, a great army, waiting for my word! Lord Jesus, from now on, I will use my eyes of faith to see what really are the spiritual odds in this fight!

March 27

It Is Time to Take Control

Today's Scripture Reading: Joshua 6:6–21 *Key Verse:* Joshua 6:20

The wall fell down flat. Then the people went up into the city, every man straight before him, and they took the city.

You are almost there.

On this day, at this very hour, whatever remnant is left of the stronghold that has overshadowed your life since you entered into your promise, will come down.

When you hear the trumpet and behold the ark of God, when you obey the command to shout in Jesus' name, you will see the walls come down. Then it will be time to walk straight into the enemy's rubble-strewn city and take it over forever. You will own what Satan once hoped would possess you. It is all part of being the head and not the tail in God's kingdom (Deut. 28:13).

Pray this prayer with me:

Father, thank You for bringing me to this day of freedom and victory over the past. The trumpet of conquest has sounded, a shout has been heard, and the walls of my fears and failures have fallen. Today I take the city and enter my land of promise as conqueror and not as the conquered.

SEEK HIM FIRST AND LEAVE THE REST IN HIS HANDS

Today's Scripture Reading: Matthew 6:33 *Key Verse:* Matthew 6:33

Seek first the kingdom of God and His righteousness,
and all these things shall be added to you.

When God promises you something, He will move heaven and earth to bring it to pass. He will tear down every contrary circumstance, every wall, every obstacle or opposing force that tries to keep you from receiving His promise. The Old Testament is a divine record of God's zeal in fulfilling His covenants with His people.

The Bible says, "Delight yourself also in the LORD, / And He shall give you the desires of your heart" (Ps. 37:4 NKJV). God will give you your heart's desires if you will delight yourself in Him first.

He will give you whatever you have been wanting that is in line with His will and Word. In fact, He will tell you, "You do not have to pay for it or fight for it; I have already handled it." I am not telling you this in a theoretical sense; I have experienced this wonder in my own life and ministry.

If you are going through what seems like a hopeless battle, I advise you to stop for a moment, be still before God, and find out what is on His heart. Then do it. Everything else will work out. Pray with me:

Jesus, right now, I choose to be still and behold Your glory. There is no better time than right now to ask You, "Lord, what do You have to say to me? I promise that I will obey and use my eyes of faith."

YOU ARE NOT ALONE

Today's Scripture Reading: Joshua 5:13–15 *Key Verse:* Joshua 5:14

He said, ". . . As Commander of the army of the LORD I have now come." And Joshua fell on his face to the earth and worshiped, and said to Him, "What does my Lord say to His servant?"

We have looked at the story of Jericho again and again for a reason. Here it is once again, just in case it is not clear: Are you tired of your mess? Are you tired of being pulled out of life by the devil? Are you sick and tired of waking up every day sick and tired? Are you tired of having everything taken from you instead of enjoying the divine favor of God? Are you tired of people pulling you back down? Are you tired of spiritual warfare, of not sleeping at night, or of fighting the schemes of the devil? Are you tired of walking around with all this pain in your mind and body? It is time to *do something about it*.

Once you decide to live by the Scriptures and are secure in the fact that the joy of the Lord is your strength, things will change in your life. When you decide to turn around and stop running, you will not have to fight your enemies alone. The Captain of the Lord's army always shows up to protect His own—you are not alone.

Jesus Christ is waiting for you to turn around. Will you do it? Will you face your Jericho?

Pray this prayer with me:

Lord Jesus, I am weary of running, pretending, and hiding things. I receive Your word as a proclamation of emancipation today. I am free, and as long as You are before me and at my side, I will face my past and my failures head-on, covered by the blood of the Lamb and the Word of God. Thank You for a new life.

March 30

Now Is the Season to Possess the Spoils

Today's Scripture Reading: Joshua 8 *Key Verse:* Joshua 8:2

You shall do to Ai and its king as you did to Jericho and its king.
Only its spoil and its cattle you shall take as booty for yourselves.
Lay an ambush for the city behind it.

After a painful lesson about the dangers of secret sins in the camp, Joshua and the Israelites repented and "cleaned house." Once that was done, God spoke to them in concrete terms about how they would do to Ai what they did to Jericho. Defeat was not even a possibility. Sure enough, Israel won a decisive victory over Jericho's neighboring town of Ai. This time, God allowed the Israelites to take possession of the cattle and any valuable items captured in the conflict.

Victory is yours because you heard the Word and put it into practice. Now openly declare to the enemy of your soul, "This is my time and season to take the spoils of war and reap the blessings of victory!"

The best part of a victory of war is that once you capture and defeat your enemy, he or it cannot rise up in your life anymore. God's power has totally defeated the second city of offense, the place of covetousness and trespass. Now it has no power over you or your future!

Pray this prayer of thanksgiving with me:

Lord Jesus, I am glad You are directing my steps and fighting on my behalf in this drive to possess Your promises in my life. Whether I face a Jericho, a chief sin that has fortified and strengthened its position in my life, or an Ai, a secondary stronghold rooted in secret and concealed sin, I choose this day to confront them at Your word. This is my season to possess the spoils and celebrate Your faithfulness.

SNAP EVERY YOKE FOR GOD'S SAKE!

Today's Scripture Reading: 2 Corinthians 5:16–20 *Key Verse:* 2 Corinthians 5:17

If anyone is in Christ, he is a new creation; old things have passed away; behold, all things have become new.

God wants you to be free in every area of your life, but more is at stake than your freedom. God wants every yoke of bondage snapped in your life for His sake as well.

God needs free people, people who are no longer tied or bound to things in their minds and spirits. He needs people who are not so overwhelmed by life that He cannot move in their lives. He cannot build His kingdom with people who see nothing but the walls in front of them. It is just as hard to work with people who are tied to something they need to leave behind them.

When was the last time you saw your joy? When was the last time you took a deep breath of life?

For God's sake, take your place in victory and conquer every stronghold that dares to stand in your way!

Pray this prayer confession with me:

I am a new creation, a ruler and investor, the head and not the tail. I am new in every way because the old has passed away. In Christ, I can do all things. Every yoke of bondage must go, whether it is great or small, new or old. Nothing can stand between me and the complete fulfillment of my future in Jesus Christ. I am out to snap every yoke for God's sake! In Jesus' name it shall be, amen.

April

Occupation Operations

Take His Light with You into the Kingdom of Darkness

Today's Scripture Reading: Genesis 12:1–3 *Key Verse:* Genesis 12:1

The Lord had said to Abram:
"Get out of your country,
From your family
And from your father's house,
To a land that I will show you."

When God called you and you responded by accepting Jesus as your Savior, you received a new citizenship. Now your citizenship is in heaven, but you still live in the world. Like Abram, you have been called to a new place, but you are residing in another. Why?

God wants you to do something. Your mandate is to represent the kingdom of God, to occupy till He comes. Yet what does that mean?

God's Word makes it clear that God has anointed you and me to walk in the footsteps of Jesus Christ and to do the works that He did on earth. We are called to lay hands on the sick and see them recover, to cast out demons, and even to raise the spiritually dead. We are empowered to destroy the works of the enemy and pull souls from the flames. Together as the church, we are to literally manifest or reveal the will of God to the unsaved world.

That requires us to function as a nation of kings and priests who rule and minister in a land that is not our own. Are you ready to change the old world you left by using your power and authority from the new world?

Pray this prayer with me:

Lord, thank You for translating me out of the kingdom of darkness and into Your kingdom of light. Now help me to be a light set on a hill in Your name. By Your grace and power, I will fulfill the destiny you have decreed over me. Lead me in the way, show me how to transform this world with the gospel of the Cross and life in You.

APRIL 2

KICK OFF YOUR ENTANGLEMENTS; IT IS TIME TO SPRINT FOR THE FINISH

Today's Scripture Reading: Hebrews 12:1–4 *Key Verse:* Hebrews 12:1

Since we are surrounded by so great a cloud of witnesses, let us lay aside every weight, and the sin which so easily ensnares us, and let us run with endurance the race that is set before us.

It is time to bring in the great harvest for God, but you cannot handle the sickle if your hands are tied. You cannot be about God's business if sin has you bound, locked up, and hindered.

God did not send His Son so that you would be bound; He sent Jesus so that you would be set free and delivered and moving in kingdom business! The truth is that Jesus cannot move until *you* move. What has every saint been called to do? We are called to prepare the people of God for His Son's presence.

You cannot afford to let sin block you from your occupation any longer. God's kingdom is to be lived out on this earth before people. God's kingdom needs to be represented in the workplace, in the economy, and in the streets.

Pray this prayer with me:

Lord Jesus, I want to be quick to repent over the slightest sin, disobedience, or breach of faith. I cannot afford to let these things tangle my feet, bind my hands, or cloud my vision. You have too many wonderful things for me to accomplish in this lifetime to waste even one hour by embracing something I should avoid. Cleanse me of my sin so I can honor You in word and deed.

APRIL 3

RELEASE DIVINE CREATIVITY BY WORKING HARD AND WELL

Today's Scripture Reading: Colossians 3:22–25 *Key Verse:* Colossians 3:23

Whatever you do, do it heartily, as to the Lord and not to men.

Do you have trouble keeping a job for longer than just a few weeks? Do you spend your paycheck even before you get it? You may be praying for a miracle, but perhaps you do not need a miracle as much as you need repentance.

The apostle Paul wrote, "He who does wrong will be repaid for what he has done, and there is no partiality" (Col. 3:25 NKJV). This means that if you show up for work a half hour late, or if you take a few extra minutes beyond your allotted lunch break, then you are not living like a saint; you are living the life of a cheater and a time-clock trickster.

The world has its own ever-changing work ethic, while the kingdom has an eternal work ethic rooted in the timeless principles of God. The world says, "Do just enough to get by. Work is only a means to get what you want and to finance your lifestyle." God says, "When I give you a job, do more than you are asked. Work, plan, and steward the resources on the job as if you were working with your own. Do not show up late like everybody else. Show up on time and do it for Me, not to impress men. Remember: work with your whole heart."

When you do these things, God empowers you with a new level of creativity and supernatural ability. If you are wondering why you have not received a raise or promotion in three years, do not blame the Lord. Look a little closer to home. Look at the way you have handled the job God gave you. Is your conduct worthy of a raise? He has placed divinely inspired abilities and creativity within you, but they will not be released until you understand that you are not "working for the man."

Pray this prayer of repentance with me:

Lord Jesus, I confess that I have handled my responsibilities on the job, at church, and in my own home in ways that do not honor You. I had forgotten that You see all things, even though men and women cannot. Please forgive me for my poor stewardship and grant me the grace to make a new start today. Release Your ability and creativity in my life for Your glory.

APRIL 4

YOU HAVE THE BEST JOB SECURITY ON THE PLANET!

Today's Scripture Reading: Colossians 3:22–4:1; Psalm 75:6–7 *Key Verse:* Colossians 3:23

Whatever you do, do it heartily, as to the Lord and not to men.

Do you want to do church work? Are you thinking, *Can I get in the choir, or should I usher? Maybe I should be a deacon.* If you want to do church work, then go to work. Do kingdom work wherever you are. If you are a secretary for the IRS, then you ought to be the best secretary the IRS has ever seen. Why? It is because you demonstrate kingdom principles there just as you do at church. In fact, it does not even matter if your boss is nasty, mean, and unfair. *You do not work for him.* God has no problem turning around an evil heart to favor you.

Your problem may be that you continue to believe that you are working for people—and that is why people find it hard to believe that you go to church. When we think and act as if God does not come to our workplaces, we say and do things that we would never do if "God was watching":

"I was late again this morning, but the supervisor did not see me."

"I was supposed to take only an hour, but I took an hour and a half today."

Who gives you raises and promotions? The Bible says, "For promotion cometh neither from the east, nor from the west, nor from the south. But God is the judge: he putteth down one, and setteth up another" (Ps. 75:6–7 KJV). Wherever you work, serve, or volunteer, you are not there by accident. You work for God Himself. That means you do not need to worry about your boss firing you before "your time." Until God is ready, no one can move you out of the place and job where He placed you—as long as you serve Him with diligence and distinction. If you think about it, you have the best job security on the planet! Your Boss gave His blood to get you, and He laid down His life to keep you. No mere man, devil, or business corporation has a chance against Him.

Pray this prayer from the heart:

Lord Jesus, thank You for planting me in the workforce mission field. Guide my steps as I represent the kingdom of light every minute I am on the job site. I am an executive from the Corporate Office on loan for a season; I have a divine mission to accomplish, and it requires me to be the best employee and worker my supervisors have ever seen. It seems impossible to me, but You specialize in making the impossible possible, using people just like me. Thank You for the promotion and the raises You have in store for me in due time, and thank You for favor on the job.

GET FIRED? HURRY OUT GRINNING!

Today's Scripture Reading: Psalm 105:12–15 *Key Verses:* Psalm 105:14–15

He permitted no one to do them wrong;
Yes, He rebuked kings for their sakes,
Saying, "Do not touch My anointed ones,
And do My prophets no harm."

Suppose you stood up on your job, spoke the truth at the leading of the Holy Spirit, and the management cursed you. By that, I do not mean that they took God's name in vain or swore at you; I mean they *fired* you. You probably would feel badly about that, right?

My question to you would be, "Why are you feeling down?" *Just hurry out grinning.* When they want to know why you are moving so fast, tell them, "Something is about to happen here, and I do not want to be around when it does."

My suggestion should not sound so odd to you. If somebody or some company wrongs, defrauds, or cheats you because of your faithfulness to the King and the righteous principles of the kingdom, God is going to take note of that.

It happened to me. Although I had achieved the position of number-one salesman for a large automotive company, I went to work on a Monday morning to discover that my job was gone. My colleagues had hoodwinked and bamboozled me, and I had to endure a lot of difficulty because of their actions. God took care of me, though, and promoted me to a new position as a shepherd of His sheep. Then, several years later, *all* of my former coworkers lost their jobs. They did not get relocated, retrained, or transferred to another branch—the owner simply closed the entire office and locked the doors.

You are on a mission from God. If you "lose" one job, God has another and better job waiting for you. So why are you feeling down?

Pray with me before you start working on the job or in the home:

Dear Father, thank You for choosing me for Your company of believers. I never have to worry about Your running out of capital, running afoul of the law, or asking me to do unethical and illegal things in the name of profit. I trust You to defend me when necessary and to promote me and reward me when You choose. It is all in Your hands and not in the hands of the people I work with. I understand that You have orchestrated my relationships on the job site, in my neighborhood, in the community, and in my local church fellowship. Help me to live and work in a way that honors and glorifies Your kingdom. In Jesus' name, amen.

APRIL 6

IT IS TIME TO SEE ANOTHER SIDE OF GOD!

Today's Scripture Reading: Genesis 22:1–18 *Key Verse:* Genesis 22:14

Abraham called the name of the place, The-LORD-Will-Provide; as it is said to this day, "In the Mount of the LORD it shall be provided."

God, why did that so-and-so take that position from me? Why did You let that happen?"

Have you ever said something like that? Do not get sad or angry when people take everything away from you. Get glad! Say, "It looks like God is about to show me another side of His glory. I am about to discover why He calls Himself 'Jehovah-Jireh,' or 'the Lord Will Provide.'"

Above all, do not pray against people who misuse or abuse you. Do not rebuke the situation; just hang on to see what the end will be. Your prayer should be, "I want to see another side of God." He loves to surprise us with His glory, power, and beauty. Whatever trap you think you are in right now, rejoice! It is just another opportunity to see God come through for you.

Pray this prayer of declaration with me:

Lord Jesus, this situation is getting me down, but now I see it should lift me up. I rejoice because I know that You are about to show me another side of Yourself. I refuse to worry about it any longer. Show Yourself strong, Lord!

WILL YOU PASS THE TEST AND CONFESS HIS NAME?

Today's Scripture Reading: Hebrews 11; Matthew 10:33 *Key Verse:* Hebrews 11:17

By faith Abraham, when he was tested, offered up Isaac, and he who had received the promises offered up his only begotten son.

Many preachers read only the first part of Hebrews 11, where the writer talks about those who were faithful. Have you noticed that none of the people in that chapter's "faith hall of fame" were there because they received a split-level house, two cars, and a job promotion? Their faith had nothing to do with what they received; rather it had everything to do with the kingdom.

When you follow the King into His kingdom, God works with you. If you do not follow the King in the kingdom way, God will not go with you.

Most of the suffering and persecution we experience have nothing to do with God's kingdom. (In other words, most of the things we label "persecution" are simply the results of our own mistakes.) But if you face harassment because of your work for Jesus, if you lose your job because you honor the Lord, then the Bible and the God of the Bible will stand for you. Do not expect that to happen if you say, "Well, I know I am saved, but I am just going to be quiet about it at the office." How can you be quiet about something that saved your life?

If you cannot say anything about Jesus at work, then maybe you are in the wrong place. There is something about this gospel of the kingdom that causes people to speak up when no one else dares to say something. The God of power rises up and gives us supernatural courage to do things we never would do on our own. If you follow Jesus into the streets and job site and represent Him the way He instructs you, then all the power and resources of God Himself are at your disposal. All you have to do is pass the faith test.

Pray this prayer with me:

Father, I understand now that I possess the promises after I pass the test of faith. Faith and obedience are my investments in Your kingdom inheritance. Help me to openly confess Your Son before men so He can freely and openly confess my name before Your throne. I bless You and honor You in the name of Jesus, amen.

APRIL 8

YOU ARE GOD'S MESSENGER—NOW DELIVER THE MESSAGE

Today's Scripture Reading: Matthew 3:1–6; Mark 1:1–8; Luke 7:24–28 *Key Verses:* Mark 1:1–3

The beginning of the gospel of Jesus Christ, the Son of God.
As it is written in the Prophets:
"Behold, I send My messenger before Your face,
Who will prepare Your way before You."
"The voice of one crying in the wilderness:
'Prepare the way of the LORD;
Make His paths straight.'"

Do you know where you are in the time line of God? You are in the *beginning*. In fact, as long as the earth remains and men and women have not heard the good news, we will always be in the beginning of God's time line.

He has started a new thing in you and in many others around the nation and the world. He is raising up men and women to be like John the Baptist, the forerunner of the Savior of the world. You and I, with all the others He is calling, have the anointing of John resting upon us. Something within us compels us to cry out and awaken the people of God to return to God, and to reach out to the lost and bring them in.

John the Baptist also appeared "in the beginning." The gospel of Mark introduces John with the words, "The *beginning* of the gospel of Jesus Christ, the Son of God. As it is written in the Prophets: / 'Behold, *I send My messenger*.'" You, too, are a *sent messenger* armed with the good news of a new beginning—the beginning of Jesus in the lives of your hearers. Like John the Baptist, you have a mandate to call people back to Him. Will you answer the call and dare to proclaim Him to your generation?

Pray this prayer of consecration with me:

Heavenly Father, forgive me for thinking everything was done in the first century. You are still sending out messengers to prepare the way for Jesus to enter the hearts of people—and now I understand that I am one of those messengers. Grant me a supernatural boldness to declare the good news with joy and faith. An entire generation awaits our message of hope. In Jesus' name, amen.

You Have a Heart-Turning Anointing and Ministry

Today's Scripture Reading: Malachi 4:5–6; Luke 1:11–17 *Key Verse:* Luke 1:17

He will also go before Him in the spirit and power of Elijah, "to turn the hearts of the fathers to the children," and the disobedient to the wisdom of the just, to make ready a people prepared for the Lord.

The anointed ministry of John the Baptist took up where Elijah left off generations earlier. An angel told John's father, Zacharias, before his son's birth, "He will turn many of the children of Israel to the Lord their God" (Luke 1:16 NKJV).

Look closely at these passages in Malachi and Luke again, because they describe what your life is going to be like from now on! Our mission from God right now is to make ready the people and prepare them for Jesus.

No, I am not talking about preparing them for the Second Coming. We must prepare the people so the Holy Spirit can move among us and reveal Christ right now. That is the only way we will see the miraculous power of God move in this generation of harvest. Only then will God manifest His glory before the world. It is my opinion that if we seek first the kingdom of God and His righteousness in absolute obedience to His Word, then the events of the end times will take care of themselves in God's perfect time.

Pray this prayer with me:

Lord Jesus, I accept Your calling to proclaim Your name in every place You take me. Guide my steps and anoint my way as I speak the truth and urge everyone I meet to seek You and to yield to the gentle voice of the Holy Spirit of God. May You be revealed in everything I do and in every word I say.

Do Not Worry About Popularity; Tell the Truth Anyway

Today's Scripture Reading: Matthew 10:7–42 *Key Verses:* Matthew 10:32–33

Whoever confesses Me before men, him I will also confess before My Father who is in heaven. But whoever denies Me before men, him I will also deny before My Father who is in heaven.

We know that God called us to be like John the Baptist and to set the kingdom in order. We understand that He has anointed us to become voices crying in the wilderness. We know and we understand, but why are not more of us *doing* it?

Sad to say, the church seems to be too busy trying to please its members so they will be sure to come in on Sunday and pay their tithes. We find very few preachers telling us to go out and "make a way in the wilderness."

Regardless of what others are doing, you know the truth. That means you must make a decision. Will you obey? If the spirit of John the Baptist is resting on you, then know that some people will not want to hear what you have to say.

Some of your friends, work associates, and family members will not treat you the way they used to if you dare to tell them the truth in love. If you cannot handle that rejection, then go on to hell along with them so you will be accepted. (I have to be blunt and to the point because this is an important point. I am merely echoing Jesus, who said in Matthew 10:33 that if you deny Him before men, then He will deny you before the Father in heaven. Now *that* is blunt.)

God is looking for people who have holy words in their mouths and the authority to speak them. In other words, He is looking for kingdom people. Are you ready to deliver the message of heaven?

Pray this prayer with me:

Lord Jesus, I am beginning to understand what it means to follow You. It also means leaving other things behind—things that resist You and Your kingdom. It means leaving certain relationships, comfort zones, and preconceived ideas so I can follow You without hindrance or hesitation. Grant me the grace to pick up the cross of a messenger and follow You faithfully without looking back.

You Are Called to Root Out

Today's Scripture Reading: Jeremiah 1:9–10 *Key Verse:* Jeremiah 1:10

See, I have this day set you over the nations and over the kingdoms,
To root out and to pull down, To destroy and to throw down, To build and to plant.

We Christians like to talk about the "reigning" part of our inheritance in Christ. But have we taken seriously the responsibilities of reigning that God outlined to Jeremiah? What about the process of "rooting out"?

The Lord must think we are ridiculous at times. We stand up and say, "Devil, wherever you are, I bind you in the name of Jesus. Come up and show yourself." It sounds silly, doesn't it? You see, when you "root out" something, you uncover that which is hidden, disguised, or intermingled with other things. Most of Satan's devices are cunning strategies. We must root out and discern them before we can deal with them.

We also say, "I am praying that God will clean up the neighborhood, fix the schools, and fix the government." Meanwhile, God is shaking His head and saying, "I put *you* over them. Now you need to root them out."

The only way to "root out" something that wants to stay hidden is to go after it. You take everything He has given you and dig deep. Invest some real time in the Word, in prayer, *and* in the problem. Be willing to get your hands dirty, because it is hard work.

Once you root out the problem, you cannot just say, "I am going to pull you down," and then do nothing. Figuratively speaking, you have to reach up with your hands and stretch to pull someting down. If it does not come easily, you should not be surprised. God told you to go further and "destroy and throw down." Do not leave anything uncovered, for you are going to build and plant. This is what it means to "possess the land" of God's promises.

Jesus Christ defeated, stripped, and humiliated the chief rebel almost two millennia ago. This means that in many cases, our first and most difficult battles take place within our own hearts; and the weapon of preference is called *repentance*.

Then our battles move into the heavenlies where our weapons of warfare include fervent prayer, the blood of the Lamb, and the Word of God.

Pray this prayer with me today:

Lord Jesus, I know you expect to see fruit growing from the "branches" of my life this year. That means some hoeing, rooting, clearing, and soil preparing must happen. Have Your way with me, Lord; I humble myself before You and yield to the Holy Spirit. I confess my sin and repent of any and all things that bring dishonor to You or grieve Your Spirit. I destroy and cast down every area of my life that refuses to acknowledge that You are Lord of all. Now build me up in Your image and plant Your purposes deep in the soil of my heart for a record harvest in due season.

April 12

Is Your Life a Determined Declaration or Just a Cheap Bumper Sticker?

Today's Scripture Reading: Philippians 1:19–30 *Key Verse:* Philippians 1:29

To you it has been granted on behalf of Christ, not only to believe in Him, but also to suffer for His sake.

Perhaps you have noticed that the church today lacks staying power. This passage from Paul's epistle to the Philippians must be one of the least-quoted verses in the Bible. The gospel message of the first century echoed Paul's determined statement, "To me, to live is Christ, and to die is gain" (Phil. 1:21). The gospel message preached today sounds like a cheap bumper sticker on a luxury car: "Just be happy." Christians obviously believe—and practice—the philosophy: "If you are not happy in one place, then go somewhere else." It is clear that the devil continues to perpetuate tricks and schemes against us despite thousands of years of advance warning in God's Word.

God gets interested when you get down to the real stuff—feeding the hungry, clothing the naked, and visiting the sick. Why? That is kingdom gospel. It is what God ordained for us do in His Word. Real Christians should *declare* the Word and *demonstrate* the works of God equally well. James the apostle put it this way: "Show me your faith without your works, and I will show you my faith by my works" (James 2:18 NKJV).

We do not want to hear about doing, touching, sharing, and stretching for others. We prefer to hear about faith, believing, getting, and moving. We really hate to hear God ask us to make the ultimate sacrifice so that our children's children can be warriors and walk as kings and queens on this earth.

He has called you to make a sacrifice. Lay down what you want in order to do what He requires. That is just another way of saying, "Seek first the kingdom of God . . . and all these things shall be added to you" (Matt. 6:33 NKJV).

Pray this prayer with me:

Lord Jesus, deliver me from flesh-friendly appetites and bumper-sticker Christianity. Teach me how to stand and keep on standing for You and the kingdom. Holy Spirit, help me to declare and demonstrate the true works of the kingdom today. In Jesus' name I pray, amen.

APRIL 13

DOES THE SIGN ON YOUR DOOR SAY, "GONE FISHING . . . FOR MEN"?

Today's Scripture Reading: Mark 1:16–20 *Key Verses:* Mark 1:17–18

Jesus said to them, "Follow Me, and I will make you become fishers of men." They immediately left their nets and followed Him.

Parents of teenagers pray for the day their teens "wake up" to discover and accept their responsibilities as adults. For late bloomers, the discovery of that hard reality can really shake their world. I think God is looking forward to the day we wake up to our responsibility as His body in the earth.

The world next door is full of hurting people, but the church has become selfish and self-centered. All we are concerned about is what goes on in "our house." We gather for meetings—but never mobilize. That is one of the differences between a social club and an army. I think we have become a religious social organization because nothing happens after we leave our four walls on Sunday mornings.

In many of our churches, if you do not work in the local "evangelism ministry" or are not part of the "evangelism team," then you do not try to save anybody. I believe that "fishers of men" are supposed to be out there *fishing*. How many "fish" did you pass today whom you know were saved? How many "fish" did you leave home in bed last Sunday who cannot call on the name of Jesus because they do not know Him?

If you have been praying for somebody to get saved, keep it up! God says that now is the season of his salvation. Now is the time to open your mouth again and start pouring out your passion for his situation: "Jesus is Lord. Repent, for the kingdom of heaven is at hand. I have come to tell you that God has given me an assignment: to save your soul."

I will never forget one of the most convicting things in my life. My mother's unsaved brother, Uncle Tom, lay dying in a local hospital, and he wanted to see me. Things just kept happening, and I never got there until after he died. By the time I arrived, the season had changed. While I was standing by that bedside, God said, "What was more important? He sent for you, but you were too busy being a preacher." Do not let that happen to you.

Pray this prayer with me:

Lord, I repent for the times I have become so busy that I relinquished my job as a kingdom representative. I will stay on assignment and fish for souls at every opportunity through the power of the Holy Spirit. In Jesus' name, amen.

Where Are the Signs of Belief?

Today's Scripture Reading: Mark 16:15–18 *Key Verses:* Mark 16:17–18

These signs will follow those who believe: In My name they will cast out demons; they will speak with new tongues; they will take up serpents; and if they drink anything deadly, it will by no means hurt them; they will lay hands on the sick, and they will recover.

How bold are you?

We need saints who walk in great boldness. I am not talking about the boldness that comes from your mouth. I am talking about the boldness that wrecks the works of darkness everywhere it goes. You are bold when you walk along a parkway and your shadow cast by the sun heals the person it touches. That's Holy Ghost boldness.

You will not get that kind of boldness just by sitting in church. You have to want God. You have to take the kingdom to the people and be willing to be among them. True boldness has no false pride or self-glorying to contaminate it. Jesus said that supernatural signs would follow "those who believe." If there are no signs, does that say something about our ability to believe?

Pray this prayer with me:

Lord Jesus, I do not know why the signs You described in Mark's gospel are not visible in my life. I know this much: If You said it, then it is my duty to believe and walk in it. Holy Spirit, I yield to You. Conform me to Christ's image so people will see supernatural signs of boldness in my life and give God glory.

April 15

Welcome to "Christ's Called-Out Rulers" Fellowship

Today's Scripture Reading: Deuteronomy 15:6; Revelation 5:10

Key Verse: Revelation 5:10

[You] have made us kings and priests to our God;
And we shall reign on the earth.

The Greek word *ekklesia,* usually translated "church," literally means "elected and called out." It comes from a political term that described people who ruled. The *ekklesia* included public officials, business managers, and entrepreneurs of Greek culture.

One of the problems with kingdom people today is that we have a very narrow view of what being "called out" means. We are the *church*, the *ekklesia*, the rulers. We should be the world's leading entrepreneurs and business managers, the chief controllers of wealth.

The Holy Spirit did not use this word lightly. Paul was inspired to use *ekklesia* as his term for rulership. When we begin to understand and operate in that mind-set, then we as the church will be the kingdom people God is looking for—kings *and* priests; rulers *and* worshipers.

Pray this prayer with me:

Lord Jesus, I am beginning to catch on to my true identity in the kingdom. You described Your people as the ekklesia, *the "called-out rulers." Help me—help us—live up to Your high calling by revealing Your strength in our weakness.*

APRIL 16

YOU WILL REIGN AS YOU GIVE

Today's Scripture Reading: Deuteronomy 15:5–6 *Key Verses:* Deuteronomy 15:5–6

Carefully obey the voice of the LORD your God, to observe with care all these commandments which I command you today. For the LORD your God will bless you just as He promised you; you shall lend to many nations, but you shall not borrow; you shall reign over many nations, but they shall not reign over you.

God has called out and assembled the church, the *ekklesia*, to rule. That leadership mandate has not changed since Genesis. The Old Testament promise God made to Israel, the descendants of Abraham, in Deuteronomy 15 also applies to the church today through the finished work of Christ.

The local church is to play a primary part in the community where God places it. It must always make an impact locally before it goes abroad. Understand that capitalism is part of the system that God set up in this nation, and He has ordained for the church to have an impact on it. Tithes and giving are much more important than most of us perceive. Money, wealth, and economic influence are one of the major thrusts we must make in this world.

God's plan to change this world involves one thing: Him—His kingdom ways and principles. There is no other plan but "Him." He created this world, and He will change it through His people whom He calls the church, the *ekklesia*, the called-out rulers. This is the reason your giving is so important.

Pray this prayer with me:

Father, everything works together for good in Your economy. Even my faithful and liberal giving in tithes and offerings helps manifest Your kingdom on earth as it is in heaven. Grant me the grace and faith to increase my giving and my impact on my community in Jesus' name.

PUT YOUR MONEY WHERE YOUR HEART IS

Today's Scripture Reading: Deuteronomy 28 *Key Verse:* Deuteronomy 28:13

The Lord will make you the head and not the tail; you shall be above only, and not be beneath, if you heed the commandments of the Lord your God, which I command you today, and are careful to observe them.

Did you know that you were to be a ruler? If you shook your head and mumbled "No," then perhaps you have just illustrated why your community has not changed. God calls us the church—those called out to rule—but we do not manage or rule anything.

It is time to wake up. God called you to rule! When you say you belong to the church, you are saying that you are called to be a manager, a businessperson. You are someone who knows how to transact business and make an honest profit.

The church is supposed to be an army of rulers in the process of taking control of that which God ordained. You do not have to be a superspiritual person to understand who really controls the nation. The world controls the economy because we do not understand economics. We are still living under the curse earned by Adam and Eve instead of the blessings won by Christ Jesus.

We are consumers instead of producers. As soon as our children make a dollar, they want to spend it on the latest basketball shoe manufactured in another country. Where is your investment? Compare the number of shoes in your children's closets with the number of books in their rooms. It is time to put your money where your heart is.

The world is profiting from our runaway appetite to consume, but this is not what God planned. We are to take rulership over all that God has called us to rule—including the wealth of the nations.

Pray this prayer with me:

Lord Jesus, I repent of living in a permanent slave mentality. It is time to shake off the chains of poverty, servitude, and lack in Your name. Today is the day I stand up in freedom and dare to take hold of my inheritance in You.

YOU ARE THE EVIDENCE OF GOD'S WISDOM

Today's Scripture Reading: Ephesians 3 *Key Verses:* Ephesians 3:8, 10–11

This grace was given, that I should preach . . . to the intent that now the manifold wisdom of God might be made known by the church to the principalities and powers in the heavenly places, according to the eternal purpose which He accomplished in Christ Jesus our Lord.

God gave Himself to us in Christ Jesus. Then He "gave us" to the world. He commanded us to change our world in His name. It is vitally important to understand that no other plan exists to transform this world.

We have joined many fine groups and organizations, but if they are not connected with Jesus Christ, they are powerless to change the world! The best that man's institutions can offer is a temporary fix to "dull the pain."

The psalmist wrote, "The earth is the LORD'S, and all its fullness, / The world and those who dwell therein" (Ps. 24:1 NKJV). God created this world, and only He can reform it. The way He has chosen to change it is through the church! That should tell you how important your kingdom work is in the earth.

Pray this prayer with me:

Lord Jesus, thank You for investing so much in me. Now I invest everything I am and ever hope to be in Your kingdom. Let Your will be done in me on this earth as it is in heaven. May my life lived by divine grace provide absolute evidence of Your wisdom to my neighbors, associates, and community.

The Spirit Is upon You to Do What Jesus Did

Today's Scripture Reading: Luke 4:18–19 *Key Verse:* Luke 4:18

The Spirit of the Lord is upon Me,
Because He has anointed Me
To preach the gospel to the poor;
He has sent Me to heal the brokenhearted,
To proclaim liberty to the captives
And recovery of sight to the blind,
To set at liberty those who are oppressed.

The gospel is the "good news" of God's plan in Christ for those who listen and obey Him to actively rule and reign with Him.

The church is the workforce God charged to implement this plan. The Chief Executive Officer is the Holy Ghost. Jesus said, "The Spirit of the Lord . . . has anointed Me / To preach the gospel to the poor." What kind of good news should the poor hear? They do not need to learn how to speak in tongues, shout, or do a little dance. Jesus did not tell the poor of His day how to join a choir or usher board. He told them how to leave their poverty behind and become rulers in God's kingdom! You are anointed to spread the same message to the same people!

Pray this prayer with me:

Lord, where I am poor You have made me rich. Where I have been a slave, You have made me a king. Grant me the courage to invade the darkness of my neighbor's bondage with the light of Your good news. It is time to set even more captives free so they can rule in Your name.

YOU CAN "RETIRE" LATER—YOU HAVE WORK TO DO!

Today's Scripture Reading: Luke 4:18–19 *Key Verse:* Luke 4:18

The Spirit of the LORD *is upon Me,*
Because He has anointed Me
To preach the gospel to the poor.

Jesus said that the Spirit had anointed Him first of all to preach the good news to the poor. We are supposed to follow in His footsteps, but we have not made it through the first level of His anointing.

Why not? The major problem is with us, His workforce. We do not understand our assignment or the anointing of God. We like to focus on our "retirement program" in heaven when we should be *working* right now. We are preaching our way into heaven rather than taking the good news beyond our church walls to the halls of the poor!

If you sing too long about the golden streets in heaven and your misery on this earth, your "good news" will turn sour. The poor do not want to hear about "the sweet by and by." They want to hear about hope for the gritty here and now!

God is calling for a changed mind-set in the church. We need to know God's kingdom agenda. Then we need to get to work, preaching the good news to the poor!

Pray this prayer with me:

Lord Jesus, forgive me for any obsession with possessions and for my blindness toward the lost. Today I turn my gaze from my own things and the things of the local church toward the needs of the lost. Today I choose to give away the good news You shared with me.

ARE YOU PURSUING THE ABUNDANT LIFE OR THE SECURE DEATH?

Today's Scripture Reading: John 10:7–11 *Key Verse:* John 10:10

The thief does not come except to steal, and to kill,
and to destroy. I have come that they may have life,
and that they may have it more abundantly.

Jesus was not just making small talk when He said these words.

If Jesus came to give us the abundant life, then why do we allow His death, burial, and resurrection to be in vain? It is for the same reason that Christianity does not really attract ambitious folks. It explains why the devil can essentially ignore us. Why should the adversary bother us? We are just lazying around. We pose no danger to his dark kingdom! He hits college campuses and high schools to recruit those guys and girls who are sharp go-getters.

When I sought my first job, I did not want to hear about the retirement package or the pension plan. I wanted to know how to get promoted and exploit every opportunity for advancement.

People do not want to hear about *later;* they want to know about *now.* Tell people the truth: "Jesus came so that we could have life, and have it more abundantly." God is looking for people who want to stretch, dream, achieve, and rule in this life (as well as in the life to come).

What kind of person are you? Are you interested more in God's retirement package or in His "corporate goals and strategies" in this life? Do you want the abundant life or a secure death? (You can have *both.*) Do you "seek first the kingdom" or do you focus on security in the "sweet by and by" while letting every precious day slip away? Pray this prayer with me:

Jesus, forgive me for focusing on the later rewards. That's really spiritual laziness and an excuse for not following You in my daily life here. I want to live for You to the fullest. You are good news! And I will proclaim it to the poor around me.

April 22

We Have the Power; All We Need Is a Plan

Today's Scripture Reading: Matthew 11:11–15 *Key Verse:* Matthew 11:12

From the days of John the Baptist until now the kingdom of heaven suffers violence, and the violent take it by force.

What is your job description as a Christian? What does God look for when He reviews applicants? Look closely at Matthew 11:12 once again: "The kingdom of heaven suffers violence, and the violent take it by force."

God is looking for some sharp people who want to get into kingdom business. He is searching for people who do not mind being tough, who understand that they are rulers. These believers are go-getters. "Let's get up and start," they say. They can look at a troubled community and see renovation and reconstruction, not hopelessness and defeat. All they need is a plan.

They know that they already have a bank account in heaven, so they do not have to figure out where the money will come from. God made them rulers. So they just pray to their Father and let Him support what He has already ordained. All they need is an idea.

Does this description fit you? It can if you start thinking God's way.

Pray this prayer with me now:

Lord Jesus, You have provided everything we need to rule and reign in this life. All we need is Your plan and strategy for the specific project at hand. Thank You for providing the power, the will, and the plan to establish Your kingdom on earth as it is in heaven.

ARE YOU READY TO SETTLE ACCOUNTS?

Today's Scripture Reading: Matthew 25:14–30 *Key Verse:* Matthew 25:19

After a long time the lord of those servants came
and settled accounts with them.

God is establishing a kingdom, and He has called us to be rulers and exercise dominion. He expects us to be ambitious self-starters who come to an acknowledgment of His business. We must go and do what He has ordained.

Study the parables. When God gives working capital, building materials, and directions on how to use them, He always *comes back* to see if we have obeyed and multiplied His investment. If we have not, He is not happy.

"Well, God has not given me anything." What about your good health? What about your children? God expects you to prove yourself with whatever you have. As soon as you prove yourself with what you have, God will give you more.

Our problem is that many of us have never tried Him. We have never reached the point where we really operate in kingdom principles. Take stock of what God has given to you. Then go and multiply it.

Pray this prayer with me:

Lord Jesus, I want to hear You say to me, "Well done, faithful servant." I want to invest everything You have given me for a rich return in the kingdom. Help me to stretch out by faith and put Your Word to the test for an abundant harvest.

APRIL 24

HE CALLED YOU OUT TO SET YOU UP

Today's Scripture Reading: 2 Corinthians 6:14–7:1 *Key Verses:* 2 Corinthians 6:16–17

You are the temple of the living God. As God has said:
"I will dwell in them
And walk among them.
I will be their God,
And they shall be My people."
Therefore
"Come out from among them
And be separate."

Another requirement for you, as an elected and called-out member of the *ekklesia,* is that you "come out from" the world and separate yourself from its lusts and evil desires. That demands a change of actions, associations, and thought patterns.

We have already noted that the *ekklesia* in New Testament times were the rulers and business managers of their culture. You need to operate with the understanding that God has called you out to set you up as a ruler and manager on this earth.

Understanding comes with proper thinking and accurate speaking. Begin by saying, "My Master is King of kings and Lord of lords, and there is no other higher than Him." You literally serve as a colaborer with God, the supreme Ruler.

Pray this prayer with me:

Jesus, I recognize today that I am a ruler of the earth, according to Father God, who owns this earth. And right now I determine to walk in that understanding in my home and at my job, to Your glory!

RESCUE YOUR TIME; PRESERVE YOUR CALLING

Today's Scripture Reading: Ephesians 5:8–20 *Key Verses:* Ephesians 5:15–16

See then that you walk circumspectly, not as fools but as wise, redeeming the time, because the days are evil.

Do you know your calling? Not too many people in the church do. I am so driven by my calling that some people feel called to hold me down. Sometimes I must get away from my "Peters" to answer my call. Peter loved God through Jesus so much that he almost interfered with His will. Jesus had to go to the cross, and Peter tried to show his love for Him by sparing Him from the pain and humiliation of crucifixion. Yet Jesus was determined to fulfill His divine destiny.

Watch out for those who love you so much that they will love you "out of your purpose." The language of loving hindrance sounds like this: "You are working too hard. You are going too much." If God put eternity in your heart, then you know that you must work while it is still day. When God says that you can take a break, then you will; but you and I know that we have a charge to keep.

Pray this prayer with me:

Father, it is my delight to do Your will all day long, and even into the night at times. I know You have a perfect balance for me, but I will not find it by listening to the warnings and urgings of those around me. Show me Your balance, Lord, and I will follow You.

IS IT TIME FOR A TUNE-UP?

Today's Scripture Reading: Ephesians 1:22–23; Galatians 3:1

Key Verses: Ephesians 1:22–23

He put all things under His feet, and gave Him to be head over all things to the church, which is His body, the fullness of Him who fills all in all.

God will change the world only as the church begins to understand and operate in His call to rule the earth. He planned it that way. If He wanted to rule the earth Himself, He could do it anytime He chose, including the moment of truth on the cross. Instead, He decided to operate in the earth and transform nations *through the church.* That can happen, however, only as the church obeys His will and fulfills its preordained destiny.

This is the gospel, the good news. It is a plan for rulership, a strategy to bring everything into order under the authority and name of our risen King.

Why is the plan not working the way it should? It is because one key component of the plan is not functioning as it should. That defective component is us. The church and its individual workers/members are the only components that are out of line in God's redemption process.

We are the rulers, the managers, but we do not understand this job assignment or teach it in our pulpits. It is no wonder that we have failed to pass on our responsibilities and duties to our children. We must reclaim our holy destiny and deliver it to our children in all its power and glory.

Pray this prayer with me:

Jesus, I repent for failing to see and pursue my calling in You. I step up to the line and accept my call and anointing to rule. I will pass on this good news to my children and my children's children as well. Thank You for "tuning us up" in the things that really matter.

Roll Up Your Spiritual Sleeves and Get Radically Violent

Today's Scripture Reading: Matthew 8:26; James 4:7 *Key Verse:* Matthew 8:26

He said to them, "Why are you fearful,
O you of little faith?" Then He arose and rebuked the
winds and the sea, and there was a great calm.

We have another problem that may explain why we are not ruling the way God ordained that we should. It also may explain why we are not attractive to the world.

God is looking for people with radical faith. He wants people who are willing to roll up their sleeves, who will not be denied, and who walk around like mighty warriors in the earth. These people understand that the devil has no power when he tries to get in their way. They do not have pity parties for themselves because they understand that Jesus has empowered them to overcome every scheme of the enemy. They go against his schemes with great violence in the Spirit.

Are you a ruler? Do you understand your ownership in the kingdom? Whatever you take, you own; so do not take any junk. Whatever you own, you must protect and preserve so no one can steal it. Would you let me walk into your house and walk off with your brand-new stereo? No, I think you would have a fit!

Why don't you have a fit and get violent with the devil? Do you not know that he intends to walk into your house and steal your children? You are a ruler! Is it not time to violently protect what is yours?

Pray this prayer and make this declaration with me:

Lord Jesus, You are right. Enough is enough! I am fighting mad and righteously violent in my spirit. I am the servant of the most high God, the redeemed of the Lord, washed in the blood and carrier of the name.

In Jesus' name, I resist you, Satan, and I declare that you are a defeated foe and the father of liars. Get out of my home, out of my children's lives, out of my financial affairs. In fact, just get out of my life, in Jesus' name.

Thank You, Lord, for the peace that passes all understanding; amen.

April 28

Saint: It Is Not How You Feel; It Is Who You Are!

Today's Scripture Reading: 1 Corinthians 1:2–3; 2 Corinthians 6:17–18

Key Verses: 1 Corinthians 1:2–3

To those who are sanctified in Christ Jesus, called to be saints, with all who in every place call on the name of Jesus Christ our Lord, both theirs and ours: Grace to you and peace from God our Father and the Lord Jesus Christ.

The church has the sad mind set that *saintly* is something believers should *feel*. It is not. It is something we *do* because God says it is what we *are*. Unfortunately we tend to just stop being saints of God if we do not "feel" like it.

That is why children are dying, people are crying, and multitudes are without help. We wait on welfare to clean up the community. We wait on the government to renew and reconstruct the things that have fallen down. If you ask many of us about our job descriptions, we say, "We are waiting."

Sad to say, the entire kingdom of God is waiting because God's people are "waiting." God wants to know what we are waiting on.

We have given up the kingdom for a lie, and the devil has taken our ruling seat. That is a shame, and that is why we need to be aggressive and take back what God ordained for us to rule. The world will not change until God's people step up to their kingdom responsibilities.

The solution begins with you and me. You are a king's child, a son or daughter of God Himself and of His kingdom. You are the answer; will you answer the call to the throne of rulership?

Pray this prayer with me:

Father, I am waiting no longer. Now is the day of salvation, and today is the day for action. You have called, anointed, and appointed me to rule, so I will rule. Use me to glorify Your name and build Your kingdom. In Jesus' name I pray, amen.

Are You a Kingdom Employee or a World Ruler in the Kingdom?

Today's Scripture Reading: 2 Timothy 2:12; Romans 5:17 *Key Verse:* Romans 5:17

If by the one man's offense death reigned through the one, much more those who receive abundance of grace and of the gift of righteousness will reign in life through the One, Jesus Christ.

How many business owners do not really care about their business or their profit margin? Not too many, I am sure. (Those who do not care quickly go broke.)

One of the problems with the church is that too many of God's rulers have an employee mentality. Everyone in the body of Christ should have an *employer* mentality. I do not "have a job," because I am not an employee of the kingdom. What I do is my life; there is no separation.

I am a ruler of the kingdom; my family and my Father own the kingdom and everything else as well. That means that I will do whatever it takes to get something done—even if I have to stay up all Saturday night. That is something my wife had to deal with when we got married.

That does not make sense to most people because they believe that they are employees of the kingdom. They think that when they attend Sunday service, it is the same as punching a cosmic time clock. They just "punch out" again two hours later and go about *their own business* the rest of the week because, after all, they are just employees with no ownership stake in the kingdom.

Those believers with an employer mentality, however, will do whatever they have to to advance God's kingdom. Their lives are no longer their own; they have been bought with a price. They are "on call" day and night, every day of their lives. Why? They are representing the kingdom.

Are you a kingdom employee or a kingdom ruler? Here is a quick and simple test: when you walk into the bathroom of your local church and see pieces of paper lying on the floor, do you pick them up or leave them for the janitor? If you have an ownership stake in the kingdom, you will pick up those pieces of paper because you want everything to be right and to represent the kingdom of light.

Pray this prayer with me:

Lord Jesus, thank You for calling me into world management. You paid the supreme price for me. So the least I can do is remain on call for the kingdom all the days of my life.

TAKE CARE OF WHAT COUNTS AND GOD WILL TAKE CARE OF YOU

Today's Scripture Reading: 1 Corinthians 1:26–29 *Key Verses:* 1 Corinthians 1:26–27, 29

For you see your calling, brethren, that not many wise according to the flesh, not many mighty, not many noble, are called. But God has chosen the foolish things of the world to put to shame the wise, and God has chosen the weak things of the world to put to shame the things which are mighty . . . that no flesh should glory in His presence.

When God says, "All this is yours," do not get frustrated because you do not have it. Go and possess it. How? You simply walk in the kingdom.

This means that once you see and understand a kingdom principle, then start *doing* it. Live it out in your life, and watch God show up. The best thing about God's Word is that it does not depend upon our educational level, personal abilities, or resources!

Education is important in our culture, but in the kingdom, it is not what counts. I know many people in the kingdom who do not even have high school diplomas, yet they make more money than other people who earned master's degrees or doctorates! This is nothing but God's favor and grace in operation. God can use anyone who dares to believe Him and possess the inheritance.

Let God promote you and raise you up. You just walk in the kingdom. Pray this prayer with me:

Lord Jesus, I know that I have let Your kingdom principles fall by the wayside in my life. Forgive me. I pick up Your kingdom ways, Jesus, and I trust You with the results.

Lay the Foundation of Praise

May 1

We Have Too Much to Do to Whine About the Past

Today's Scripture Reading: Numbers 11; Luke 9:62 *Key Verse:* Luke 9:62

Jesus said to him, "No one, having put his hand to the plow, and looking back, is fit for the kingdom of God."

God is not impressed with people who are not thankful for what they have. In fact, I have noticed that these people tend to slip into sin faster than most.

When the children of Israel did not get what they wanted, they tended to whine about what they left behind back in "good ol' Egypt." It was a classic case of slip-sliding into sin. It happens when people complain to God about how their lives were "better" back in the situation where they came from. Trouble starts quickly when we begin resenting our move into the kingdom.

The children of Israel failed to realize that while they were complaining about not getting new shoes, their old shoes had not worn out. They whined for a new wardrobe while wearing clothes that were still whole! They were in the middle of miraculous provision and were too blind to perceive it.

Do not slip back to the bondage of Egypt. Adopt an attitude of gratitude and praise God for what He has given you. That qualifies you for even more blessings and abundant provision. Anything less qualifies you to handle life on your own without God's blessings, favor, provision, protection, or guidance. After a while, He will just lift His hand from your life and let you enjoy all the blessings of your "Egypt," including the bondage, brutality, and other "benefits" of life apart from God's provision.

Trust me: your *worst day* in the kingdom is far better than the best day *outside* the kingdom. Guard your tongue and be thankful for what you have so you will be qualified to receive God's best for your life. He entrusts His treasures only with the trustworthy and the thankful.

Pray this prayer with me:

Lord Jesus, thank You. Thank You for life, hope, freedom, and an incredible reason to live—Your kingdom. I have no interest in returning to the past. I have set my face toward Your throne and the building of Your kingdom. I have too much to do to whine about something I used to have. All that is only garbage to me compared to what I have in You.

MAY 2

GOD SAYS YOU ARE MORE, NOT LESS

Today's Scripture Reading: Romans 8 *Key Verse:* Romans 8:37

In all these things we are more than conquerors through Him who loved us.

Do you battle low self-esteem? The cure is to stop relying on what *you or other people* say about you. Above all, do not believe a thing that the devil says about you. Instead, discover the truth about God and the things He says about you. I promise that you will be surprised.

Low self-esteem is rooted in the lies you heard as a child and as an adult. Do not believe the people who said you were nothing. They lied, but if you believed them, their words have bound and harassed you since childhood. Take courage; I promise there is a relief and cure!

Millions of women, in particular, let some skin-and-bones nobody on some magazine say, "If you do not look like me, then you are not a woman." God says they lie. He says, "Do not even think about holding your head down. I thought so much of you that I will never make anyone else quite like you! You are unique and precious to Me. I personally preordained your birth. You were not an afterthought; you are the product of My grand design. I created you so that anyone who sees you is viewing an original design of God. When you leave this world, they will never see you anymore because I want you back with Me for eternity."

Do not hesitate to dismiss, disregard, and separate yourself from any foolish liar who says you are ugly. When God completed you and the rest of His creation, He said, "It is good." If God says you are good-looking, why should you believe a liar who is blind in one eye and cannot see out of the other?

Too many of us allow the devil to blind us so we forget or fail to understand God's sovereignty and absolute power. The devil says we cannot, but God says we can. We need to understand that we are more than conquerors and that we are dealing with Satan, the master deceiver and the father of lies. Resist his lies with the truth, and remember the power of your God. Then give God a shout of thanksgiving and praise, for He has made everything beautiful in its time!

Pray this prayer with me:

Father, I choose to believe You. From this day on, the only opinions I am interested in are the eternal truths revealed in Your Word. You say I am more than a conqueror, that I am forgiven, redeemed, made new, and am Your child. That settles it for me, once and for all, in Jesus' name.

MIRACLES START WHERE THE "BLESS ME" MENTALITY ENDS

Today's Scripture Reading: Ezekiel 43:1–5, 44:1–4 *Key Verse:* Ezekiel 44:4

I looked, and behold, the glory of the LORD filled the house of the LORD; and I fell on my face.

Do you know what the missing element is in church? God asked me that one day, but I did not know the answer. He said, "The missing element in the church is that My glory is not being manifested." Somehow I get the feeling that when God's glory fills a place, everyone in the vicinity *knows it.*

Is that not amazing? Most of us have to admit that we go to church to get blessed. We come to "consume" instead of to give God glory. That is why we do not see the demonstrations of power that should be common in a truly supernatural church.

We do not seem to understand what God is about. Why are we not saving the world the way we should? Why does the unsaved population continue to grow at an overwhelming rate while the church seems to shrink? The unsaved are not seeing the demonstration of power that we claim should be happening. They do not see God showing up in our meetings, so they follow the devil. They are looking for power, and they will latch on to any kind of spiritual experience in the process.

It is time for the church to be supernaturally alive instead of unnaturally dead. Miracles should be part of our everyday experience instead of religious hypocrisy, hype, and pretense. Once the unsaved see the real thing, once the hurting see evidence that God is alive and well and still working miracles among us, we will not be able to handle the crush of hungry souls at our doors!

The miracles start where the "bless me" mentality ends (because that is when God shows up). Go to church to bless the Lord and expect to see Him show up in His power and glory. Pray this prayer with me:

Lord Jesus, You are the King of glory. Reveal Yourself to the world through Your people. Begin with Your ability to change me from a religious person into a radically changed and motivated kingdom person. Help me exercise the faith to expect miracles every day of my life and in every place You lead me!

May 4

Win the Unwon with Inexpressible Joy and Glory!

Today's Scripture Reading: 1 Peter 1

Key Verses: 1 Peter 1:6–8, emphasis mine

For a little while, if need be, you have been grieved by various trials, that the genuineness of your faith, being much more precious than gold that perishes, though it is tested by fire, may be found to praise, honor, and glory at the revelation of Jesus Christ, whom having not seen you love. Though now you do not see Him, yet believing, you rejoice with joy inexpressible and full of glory.

You and I are glory makers; yet we don't operate in the power of God. Why? We let the devil snatch our joy before we can give glory to God. Instead of coming together to bless Him by creating such a joyful noise that we shake the doorposts, we come to church weary, worn, and overloaded with sadness.

I understand that everybody has those days or seasons of weariness—but should it happen to *all of us* at once? If only a few in the church were weary and the rest of us glad, then that gladness would get on the sadness and the sadness would become gladness!

The Holy Ghost is outrageously contagious. If someone who does not know Jesus Christ gets anywhere close to a joyful, Spirit-filled Christian, anything might happen. If the Spirit of God dwelling inside a true believer starts to rise up and "bubble out," even a hard-core unsaved person will feel something and know that God is near. This kind of "Holy Ghost volcano" starts boiling when we give Him glory, honor, and praise with all our being. He cannot help but respond and draw near to us! Shouldn't it be that way all the time?

Pray this prayer with me:

Lord, I have made up my mind and set my heart in motion. My lips have no choice but to follow through and honor You. I love to praise You, and I long to worship and adore You as I stand, when I bow, and especially when I lie on my face before You. I give You glory and honor You as Lord of all, worthy of all praise. Reveal Yourself among us in all Your beauty and glory.

MAY 5

GOD IS NEITHER DEAF NOR IMPRESSED

Today's Scripture Reading: Matthew 6:5–15 *Key Verse:* Matthew 6:6

When you pray, go into your room, and when you have shut your door, pray to your Father who is in the secret place; and your Father who sees in secret will reward you openly.

Excuse me, but the anointing has nothing to do with volume.

Some people must think that they get more results if they pray loud. I wonder if they think God is growing hard of hearing after thousands of years of listening to man's prayers. No, He is not deaf; and no, the power in prayer does not come from your vocal cords; it comes from deep within your spirit. Many silent prayers get more results than the earsplitting versions we rocket toward the heavens.

You can say it softly and Jesus will still manage to hear it. Have you ever found yourself in a serious situation where you could not talk loudly, so you whispered, "Jesus"? The Lord still heard your prayer, did He not? He probably intervened because your virtually inaudible prayer catapulted from the very depths of your sanctified soul and pierced the heavens.

Now if the Holy Spirit speaks to your heart about shouting your prayer from the rooftops, then do it with all your strength. The keys are motivation, purpose, and knowledge. Pray to God, not to man. Know that He knows the very thoughts and intents of your heart, whether you shout them or simply allow them to move silently from heart to mind.

Pray this prayer with me (but you do not have to pray loudly):

Lord Jesus, thank You for listening. I know that You know about my needs before I ever put them into words. I also know that You can hear me whether I pray without spoken words, simply whisper, or shout them as loudly as I can. Teach me how to pray effectively so I can better serve You and those in need of Your grace. Show me the difference between "fervent prayer" and "feverish prayer." Thank You, Lord.

May 6

I Am Glad God Knows Me

Today's Scripture Reading: John 10:2–10 *Key Verses:* John 10:2–3

He who enters by the door is the shepherd of the sheep.
To him the doorkeeper opens, and the sheep hear his voice;
and he calls his own sheep by name and leads them out.

We need to shake the modern myth that we have to go to conventions to get blessed. I think it is much more effective and biblical to get up in the morning and shout a good prayer confession into the heavenlies! Try this one:

I thank God that I am blessed to be a Christian. Now let me tell you something, devil. Because God has blessed me, I have the joy of the Lord and you cannot steal it away! Wait, there is more: I also have the peace of God, and you cannot have that either! In fact, you might as well go someplace else because I have everything I need in Christ Jesus. I am going to walk and talk about my Jesus. I am going to be a blessing, and naturally, people are going to bless me too.

Now that you brought it up, I do feel that pain, but in a little while God is going to move this pain. Yes, I have a little arthritis here and there, but I am still moving forward because in Him I live, move, and have my being. You cannot discourage me because Jesus Christ has encouraged me! I am out to snatch some people out of your kingdom and put them in God's marvelous light. In fact, I am looking for somebody who is unsaved. I am looking for somebody to whom I can witness. I do not have time for you anymore; I have to get busy with my Father's business.

Next time you feel less than blessed, and you sense that old convention compulsion coming on, ask yourself three questions: *Did I wake up looking for a blessing or looking to be a blessing? What do I shout in the morning? Is God telling me to attend a convention to get blessed or is it just my flesh man?*

Pray this prayer with me:

Thank You, Jesus. I have a feeling that everything is going to be just fine because You are walking with me. Your rod and staff comfort me. You never leave me, even when I stay at home or hide myself away in my prayer closet to spend some precious time with You. You do not need to look at my name tag to know who I am, and you do not need to know my credentials to love me. That is the greatest comfort in the world. I know that I am blessed because You have called me into Your presence by name.

MAY 7

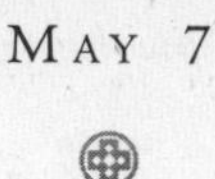

ARE YOU A PART-TIMER OR A FULL-TIMER?

Today's Scripture Reading: Philippians 4:4–9; 1 Thessalonians 5:16–18

Key Verse: Philippians 4:4

Rejoice in the Lord always. Again I will say, rejoice!

God will see to it that you always will have to deal with something in your life. (We should all realize that by now.) That is why the Lord commanded us to give Him thanks in everything. He said it *twice* through the apostle Paul: "Rejoice in the Lord always. Again I will say, rejoice!" This means praise God unceasingly.

You might as well step over into the rejoicing mode and stay there. Whether we like it or not, rejoicing is our full-time profession, no matter what comes our way in this life. It is even more central to our life in God *after* this life. This means that you are in the middle of a training time right now, and the most difficult task is to offer Him thanksgiving, praise, and worship in the midst of difficulties and trials. (That makes it "high praise.")

Do not let your circumstances worry you. Just praise Him! Now praise Him some more. The Bible makes it clear from cover to cover that God most often shows up in the middle of our praises!

Father, I praise You in Jesus' name. I lift up the name of Jesus, and I honor the Holy Spirit who dwells within me. I bless You, my God, and offer my body, soul, and spirit to You as a living sacrifice. You are worthy to be praised and honored, for there is no one like You. I give You thanks right now, no matter what thoughts or worries hammer at my mind's door. You are my Rock and sure Foundation. You are my Fortress and Protector in the time of storms. Blessed be the name of the Lord. In Jesus' name I offer this praise, amen.

May 8

It Is Time to Raise a Holy Uproar of Praise

Today's Scripture Reading: Isaiah 6:1–3; Habakkuk 2:14 *Key Verse:* Isaiah 6:3

One cried to another and said:
"Holy, holy, holy is the LORD of hosts;
The whole earth is full of His glory!"

Isaiah the prophet gave us a heavenly view of what should be going on in earth right now. Did you notice that the seraphim weren't crying to God? Look again: they were crying to one another.

Think about it: the seraphim in Isaiah's vision had a sectional thing going on. On one side, an angelic worshiper cried, "Holy," and then the angelic counterpart on the other side responded with another, "Holy." Then somebody in the back cried out, "Holy," and that started the whole cycle up again. Soon they were crying out to one another, "The Lord of hosts!"

It became so holy when those angelic worshipers cried out to one another in worship and adoration to God that the whole earth was filled with His glory! This is how it happened: as one section rose up in pure worship and adoration to the Lord, it inspired another section to do the same or better. It just kept going until all of heaven was in a holy uproar of worship and praise, and naturally the Lord enthroned Himself in that atmosphere of holiness. That is how the whole earth was filled with His glory.

It is time to bring that holy uproar down to earth, and the praise party begins with us! Pray this prayer with me:

Holy Lord, join me together with other worshipers who share Your vision of a holy uproar of praise and worship. Let Your worshipers around the world band together in a symphony of unrestrained, uninhibited worship and praise to Your holiness. May we see You high and lifted up once again, and may Your glory fill the earth as we sing Your high praises back and forth to one another! In Jesus' name we pray and praise, amen.

MEET ME AT THE SMOKEHOUSE

Today's Scripture Reading: Isaiah 6:1–4 *Key Verse:* Isaiah 6:4

The posts of the door were shaken by the voice of him who cried out, and the house was filled with smoke.

Isaiah saw so much glory being manifested that he said, "The posts of the door were shaken." When you compare Isaiah's worship experience with ours, you have to admit that we do not really have church. The reason is clear: there is not enough "holy" going on.

Admit it: We are too preoccupied our problems. That explains why none of the church doorposts are shaking during the praise service. Nothing happens and nothing gets filled with God's glory because no one is crying "Holy!"

The Bible says that the doorposts of the temple started shaking when the seraphim began to cry "Holy" to one another. Why? I think it was because what was *inside* was trying to get *out*. My friend, if you consider everything Jesus gave us on the cross, on resurrection day, and on pentecost, we should have the Holy Ghost inside us trying to get out all the time!

My daddy said something to me one time that I am just now beginning to appreciate. At the time, I foolishly believed that I knew more than he did because I went to seminary and he went to Bible school. He turned to me and asked, "Will you be preaching?" When I told him yes, he said, "Do you see smoke when the Holy Ghost comes?"

I told him, "Daddy, I do not know what you are talking about. I have not seen any smoke."

Then he said it: "Boy, when the Holy Ghost comes, when the power of the Lord comes, I am going to tell you, *everything gets smoky*."

I did not understand what Daddy was saying then, but I want to see some smoke now.

Pray this prayer with me:

Mighty God, in Jesus' name we worship and praise You. We set aside every longing but one—we long to see You in all Your glory. We lay down our burdens to lift You up in praise and adoration, for You alone are worthy of glory, honor, power, and praise forever. We empty ourselves of our concerns and worries. Fill us with Your glory. Fill Your church to overflowing with Your glory. Fill the earth with Your glory, but let it begin with us.

MAY 10

YOU HAVE THE POWER TO PRODUCE GLORY

Today's Scripture Reading: Habakkuk 2:14; Isaiah 6:2–3 *Key Verse:* Habakkuk 2:14

The earth will be filled
With the knowledge of the glory of the LORD,
As the waters cover the sea.

In the Hebrew, the word for "glory" is *kabod*. Its basic meaning is "heavy in weight," but in the Scriptures, it refers to both "the weighty importance and shining majesty which accompany God's presence," and something more. It also refers to the act of *creating* or *giving weight* to something or someone innately worthy of such honor.

I want you to get a glimpse of what Isaiah saw. We traditionally have limited our thinking to define God's glory exclusively as His presence around us. That is not the case. In Isaiah 6, God gave us a glimpse of the length, breadth, and width of that heavenly thing called glory.

Isaiah saw God in the temple, but he also heard the seraphim calling to one another, "Holy, holy, the earth is full of His glory." Remember that they were not crying to God; they were crying to one another back and forth, "Holy, holy, holy, He is holy."

What would happen if you tried that in church? If one section of redeemed worshipers cried out, "Holy," and another responded, "Holy, He is Holy!" in succession, then something supernatural would occur. You see, when you do that, *you are producing glory*.

Not only does God bring His glory with Him when He enters our presence, but we have the power and privilege to produce glory and offer it to Him! It is our destiny to help bring to pass the ancient prophecies that declare the whole earth will be filled with His glory! Pray this prayer with me:

Holy, holy, holy! Lord God Almighty, You are holy and worthy to be praised. We worship You in one mind and one accord as a people cleansed, redeemed, and united under the blood of the Lamb. Blessed be His name forever. Receive the glory due Your name and dwell among us, Holy One. In Jesus' name we pray and worship, amen.

Create Glory and God Will Move

Today's Scripture Reading: Genesis 1:1–3 *Key Verse:* Genesis 1:1

In the beginning God created the heavens and the earth.

In the beginning God created what? The heavens and the earth. Do you know why God created the heavens first? Because He had to have glory produced before producing anything else.

Let me explain. Before God said, "Let there be light," He had to have somebody—the angels—who would create glory. While they were creating glory, God sat on His throne and said, "Light, be."

Perhaps the reason nothing is working in your life or in the church is because you do not understand the purpose and source of glory. On the one hand, God has His own glory by virtue of who He is. On the other hand, God never does anything before He has glory generated by others through praise, worship, adoration, and faith. If no one is producing glory, God is not going to do anything.

We have glorious work to do. Pray this prayer with me:

Heavenly Father, I give You glory and honor Your name. May Your kingdom come and Your will be done on earth as it is in heaven. I magnify You in the earth and give You glory. Now I ask You to move over the face of the earth again in glory and power and manifest Your light in darkness through me as I praise You. In Jesus' name I pray, amen.

Man-Made Materials Created This Mess

Today's Scripture Reading: 1 Corinthians 1:26–29 *Key Verse:* 1 Corinthians 1:27, 29

God has chosen the weak things of the world to put to shame the things which are mighty; . . . that no flesh should glory in His presence.

What has happened to power in America? I think we gradually took God off the throne and replaced Him with gods made in our own image.

The devil appears to rule the earth because the Lord is not on His earthly throne. The only reason the Lord is not on His earthly throne is because the church has had mostly private "bless me" meetings where we produce virtually no glory.

There is no door shaking or earth quaking associated with our members-only meetings because nothing is happening! We come together in private gatherings week after week with "me" on our hearts and minds. Then we go out and face flak from the devil and wonder why he has so much power.

We act more like the First Church of the God Who *Was* than the Living Church of the God Who *Is!* Why? It is because we never allow God to come and "tabernacle" or dwell with us. We do not produce glory, and we do not allow Him to sit on His throne of praise. The problem is not with God; it is with us. This means that the solution also begins with us. It is time to look up from our self-absorption and see God high and lifted up as we cry to one another, "Holy, holy, holy is the Lord God Almighty!"

Pray this prayer with me:

Mighty God, You are the only God in my life and the only King on the throne of my life. I have abdicated my own throne, and I have thrown off everyone else who presumed to sit there as well. I have taken my eyes off of myself and other people. I have eyes only for You, and I give glory only to the King of kings and Lord of lords. I worship and praise You, and give You thanksgiving continually. In Jesus' name, amen.

DO YOU DARE TO WORSHIP LIKE A SERAPHIM?

Today's Scripture Reading: Matthew 6:6–10; Isaiah 6:1–3 *Key Verses:* Matthew 6:9–10

In this manner, therefore, pray:
Our Father in heaven,
Hallowed be Your name.
Your kingdom come.
Your will be done
On earth as it is in heaven.

Are you tired of artificial, flaky religion? We ought to be tired of endlessly going through the motions of reading about the miraculous works of God but never witnessing His power in our lives. Why do we not see miracles like those "they used to have" in the old days?

This is a good question because God says the same things that are happening in heaven should happen for us on earth.

According to Isaiah's eyewitness report in the Bible, the seraphim were producing so much glory in the temple that the doorposts shook. Those doorposts moved because angels "overfilled" the temple of God with glory by crying out to one another, "Holy, He is holy!"

When you dare to do the same thing those seraphim did in Isaiah's vision, when the members of your local church body begin to cry out to one another in selfless worship, "Holy, He is holy," then they create glory and offer it as a sweet sacrifice to God. That is when He comes suddenly to take up residence or "tabernacle" among the praises of His people! Amen and so be it!

Pray this prayer with me:

Our Father in heaven, hallowed be Your name. Your kingdom come. Your will be done on earth as it is in heaven. May we fill Your dwelling place to overflowing with glory, honor, and praise until You are pleased to take Your seat in our throne of adoration. For You are holy, glorious, and wonderful in all of Your ways. In Jesus' name we pray and give You honor, amen.

May 14

Give Him Glory and Enthrone Your God

Today's Scripture Reading: Isaiah 6:1–3 *Key Verse:* Isaiah 6:1

In the year that King Uzziah died, I saw the Lord sitting on a throne, high and lifted up, and the train of His robe filled the temple.

The only time God sits on His throne is when He has generated glory from those whom He created to give Him glory. Now God does not sit on His throne to be comfortable. I have a chair on the platform of my church, but I do not sit in that chair to be comfortable; it is the most uncomfortable chair up there. I sit in that chair because of the authority given to me. It is there that I execute the authority God has bestowed upon me.

When you create glory, God sits in His throne. It is from that throne of glory that He looks out and executes what He said. If you need healing, then when God is on His throne, He will heal you. If you need to be delivered, when God is seated on His throne, He will deliver you. Whatever you need, whatever you want, God will give when He is seated in His throne.

Create glory and seat Him on His throne. Praise and bless His name!

Pray this prayer with me:

Lord of all creation, I worship and honor You as Creator, Master, Lord, and the only true God. Holy Father, blessed Son, beloved Holy Spirit, mighty God—take Your place of supreme authority and power in Your throne of praise, glory, and honor. We await You, in Jesus' name.

What in the World Is Going On?

Today's Scripture Reading: Acts 16:25–26 *Key Verses:* Acts 16:25–26

At midnight Paul and Silas were praying and singing hymns to God, and the prisoners were listening to them. Suddenly there was a great earthquake, so that the foundations of the prison were shaken; and immediately all the doors were opened and everyone's chains were loosed.

We have a problem in the church. By the time our preachers arise to preach, we should already be delivered. We should already be healed. By the time our ministers preach their messages, our sadness should have been turned to gladness!

Paul and Silas simply did what the seraphim did in Isaiah's day: they created glory and gave it to God. Then He showed up, and His footsteps rocked the prison they had turned into a temple.

Your problems should not be as nearly as big by the end of a true worship service. Why? You already should have enthroned God with glory! And when He shows up, darkness has to flee.

If we were really to bless Him in our church services, I am convinced that the doors would start shaking. If we were really to bless Him, the angels in heaven would have to peek down and say, "What in the world is going on? Why is the Almighty standing up? Now He is taking a seat among them!"

Just praise Him and give Him the glory due His name!

Lord, I repent of waiting for a man or woman to stand before releasing my faith for healing, deliverance, or relief from the troubles of life. Your best for me is found in You! I will worship and honor You continually, and I trust that You will respond to the glory I give You by joining me in sweet communion. It is there in Your presence that I will find all that I need.

May 16

God Is on His Throne and All Is Well

Today's Scripture Reading: Psalm 22 *Key Verses:* Psalm 22:3–5, emphasis mine

You are holy, Enthroned in the praises of Israel.
Our fathers trusted in You; They trusted, and You delivered them. They cried to You, and were delivered; They trusted in You, and were not ashamed.

One day while I was meditating, God said to me, "Do you remember how your family grew up poor, yet you were rich?" The Lord showed me how much we didn't have (although I did not know it at the time). Then He showed me all the stuff that He took us through (and we didn't even know that we were going through it then). "What do you think happened?" He asked. "Your mama had a sixth-grade education, and she cleaned folks' houses for only sixteen dollars a week. Your daddy was on a preacher's pay, and the money did not add up. Yet you were clothed, your plates were full, and you lived in a nice house."

I said, "Lord, how did all that happen?"

"Do you remember when you used to hear your mama singing every day when you came home from school?" He asked.

That triggered thousands of memories. We used to tease Mama at times, saying, "Why do you always sing those songs? Why do you go around with tears in your eyes, saying, 'Thank You, Jesus'?" Sometimes we thought she was crazy because she would walk around the house speaking praise and holding up her hands. Then we would nearly come unglued when she would suddenly shout, "Hallelujah! Thank You, Lord. Bless Your name, Lord."

Then the Lord interrupted my thoughts and said, "Your mama created glory. I kept My throne in her presence. I took My seat in that house because she created glory for Me. When anyone or anything came to do something evil, I told them, 'Get away from here; you can't do that!'"

Finally He told me, "You don't realize that the glory of God is between your two lips." Pray this prayer with me:

Holy Father, I open my mouth for conversations, requests, and discussions of every kind. Today I open them for a holy purpose: to lift up Your holy name and create glory for Your pleasure and blessing. Come dwell with me as I build a throne with the fruit of my lips. In Jesus' name I pray and praise You, amen.

LORD, CLEAN ME UP SO I CAN LIFT YOU UP

Today's Scripture Reading: Isaiah 6:5–7 *Key Verse:* Isaiah 6:5

I said: "Woe is me, for I am undone!
Because I am a man of unclean lips,
And I dwell in the midst of a people of unclean lips;
For my eyes have seen the King,
The LORD of hosts."

What did Isaiah say once he got a heavenly view of God on the throne? He gasped, "I am a man with unclean lips!" He understood that he had to produce glory with his lips, but they were unclean.

The prophet also said, "And I dwell in the midst of a people of unclean lips." He was saying, "Everywhere I go—on the job and even in my house—they are all unclean. Everybody is talking down and acting up, telling dirty jokes, cussing, and profaning everything that is holy."

What happened next? One of the seraphim flew to Isaiah and said, "I'm going to teach you what to do." The Bible says that the angel touched Isaiah's lips with a hot coal! It had to burn, because it was a coal from the fires of heaven.

If you do not have the Spirit of God inside you, you have unclean lips and you will not be able to bless God. When the Spirit of God dwells inside you, a cleansing fire burns in your heart that purifies your lips and releases the glory so the angels can hear their cue: "Holy!"

Look at your life this week. To what CDs are you listening? What kind of TV programs, movies, and video games are coming into your house? Do you think God wants to enthrone Himself in the midst of that mess? It is like asking Him to take a seat in a sewer. Do not wait another minute. Just cry out, "He is holy; He is holy." God has a hot coal prepared for your lips and your life so you can create glory with them.

Pray this prayer with me:

Lord, I feel "undone" too. I know my lips are unclean, and I have to associate with people who are unclean in their language, lifestyles, actions, and thoughts. Holy Spirit, cleanse me with the fire of Your holiness so I can once again create glory for the Father with my lips. In Jesus' name, amen.

May 18

Is That Seat for Me?

Today's Scripture Reading: Psalm 22:19–28 *Key Verse:* Psalm 22:22

I will declare Your name to My brethren;
In the midst of the assembly I will praise You.

Do you realize what happens when you create glory?

When you produce glory by declaring the holiness of God and by praising and worshiping Him with your lips from the heart, God comes and *sits* in the middle of it all! The Scriptures say that He dwells in the middle of our praise because our praise and worship becomes His throne (Ps. 22:3). When God sits on His throne, He goes to work on our behalf.

Imagine a pair of children shivering in a cold wind at a football stadium. You watch as they busy themselves preparing a stadium seat and a cushion as if someone is coming to join them. From time to time they have to stop and tuck their cold fingers into their pockets, but they keep working at that seat while they look up the aisle between the stadium benches.

Then you see a tall man in a large overcoat walk down the aisle and hug the children. He points to the seat as if to say, "Is that seat for me?" When the children eagerly nod yes, he gives them a big smile and steps in front of the seat they prepared.

To the children's delight, the man who is obviously their father opens his great coat and spreads it wide before he sits down. Then he gathers his children together inside the coat and draws them in under his arms so they can watch the game together in absolute warmth.

This is a picture of the way we create glory and prepare a seat for God with our lips.

The reason most of us do not operate in the power that God promised us is because we do not produce enough glory from our lips for God to show up and make it come to pass. We must create glory for power to work.

Pray this prayer with me:

Lord, this seat is for You and only You. No one else is holy like You are. There is no other name under heaven or on earth that can save and deliver like Your name. No one else could create the earth, moon, and stars with a word like You did. I bless You and glorify Your holy, holy name. Come sit with me a while. In Jesus' name.

IT IS TIME TO PLUG IN

Today's Scripture Reading: Acts 4; 2 Timothy 3:5 *Key Verse:* Acts 4:7

When they had set [Peter and John] in the midst, they asked, "By what power or by what name have you done this?"

Do you know what we as the church are supposed to be when we come together and worship? We are supposed to be a power generator. In fact, when people walk in they should immediately feel the power!

When you were small, did you want to know how the light worked? Did you want to know the answer so badly that you ignored every warning and stuck your finger or your mother's butter knife into that little slot in the wall socket? It took me three times to learn not to do that.

When I stuck my finger in the socket, I suddenly felt the power. When a sinner walks into your church service, he should feel the power too! He should feel like he just stuck his entire body into a power receptacle. He should be shouting, "Wow—I feel something!"

If Satan does not seem worried, it is because he knows that sinners will not ever feel anything in a church that does not manifest the power of God! Paul the apostle talked about people "having a form of godliness but denying its power" (2 Tim. 3:5 NKJV). The original Greek term implied that these people "turned off the flow" of power. It is time for us to turn on the power. We must assemble and cry out to one another, "Holy! He is holy and worthy to be praised!"

Pray this prayer with me:

Lord Jesus, You never intended to us to live in a perpetual "brownout" condition where we are always short of power. Today I have made up my mind to stick my finger, my hand, and my entire body in Your power outlet. I choose to glorify and honor You so Your flow of power and anointing will flow freely through me to those in need.

NEVER TRY TO MANIPULATE GOD— SIMPLY GIVE HIM GLORY

Today's Scripture Reading: Romans 12 *Key Verses:* Romans 12:1, 21

I beseech you therefore, brethren, by the mercies of God, that you present your bodies a living sacrifice, holy, acceptable to God, which is your reasonable service . . . Do not be overcome by evil, but overcome evil with good.

Most of us in the church make noise, but few of us produce glory. What little glory we do produce has strings attached. We tend to give God glory only when we feel blessed. If we happen to go to a church service where we do not get what we think we deserve, we clamp our lips (as least as far as glory is concerned).

We basically say, "God, if You bless me, I will bless You. If You do not bless me, then I am going to be depressed and You will not get any blessing." In other words, many of us seem to view God as we do Santa Claus. Children often do the same thing to their parents. If their parents buy them something, they heap blessings on them. If they dare to say no to a request or purchase, the kids get depressed. That is not love; that is manipulation.

Local congregations sometimes hinge their praise levels on what God does for them in a service. That is not love; that is manipulation, and it never works with God. He deserves our worship and praise regardless of the changing situations, circumstances, and attitudes on earth. He deserves everything we are and everything we possess—it is our "reasonable service," in Paul's words.

Another reason we fail to produce glory is that we allow Satan's attacks to overcome us. We let things go until it is difficult to part our lips. When we finally open them, we speak death instead of life: "I feel so bad . . . It is so wrong . . . I have so much bad luck . . . I am not going to get the job . . . He is going to leave . . . I just know the worst is going to happen . . . Woe is me."

The highest of all praise and worship is that which we give Him regardless of circumstances, with no strings attached, simply because He is God and He is worthy. That is what it means to give Him glory, and that is what it means to be a true Christian.

Lord, You are worthy of praise and worship simply because You are the one true God. You are holy, righteous, all-wise, all-knowing, and full of mercy and grace. I bless Your name in this moment, regardless of what has happened in my life, or what will happen in the days to come. Blessed be the name of the Lord.

Feeling Sad and Beat Up? He Will Make You Glad and Upbeat!

Today's Scripture Reading: Psalm 92 *Key Verses:* Psalm 92:1, 4

It is good to give thanks to the Lord,
And to sing praises to Your name, O Most High; . . .
For You, Lord, have made me glad through Your work;
I will triumph in the works of Your hands.

It all comes down to this: the devil messes with you so that you will not create glory. It is in his best interests to keep you tired, weary, worn, and sad. The reason is simple: if you create glory, then God manifests His power.

The enemy knows that sad, beat-up saints who cannot say "holy" or praise and bless God will not produce any glory. Thus there is no power of God revealed in the church. This is the season for change, transformation, and the restoration of glory and manifested power to the church! In difficult times, focus your attention on the "work" Jesus Christ did on the cross. Consider the "works" God did for Abraham, Joseph, Moses, David, and the apostles. Remember the "work" He did in your life when He saved you and set you free! Like the psalmist before you, your song will be, "Lord, You have made me glad through Your work!"

I tell you, He is holy! He is worthy to be praised!

Pray this prayer with me:

Lord Jesus, no matter how bad things may seem in my life today, I know everything is going to be all right because I am going Your way. It may be cloudy, gloomy, and sad where I stand at the moment, but glory and light still flow from Your throne on high, and that is where I am seated with You! You are holy and worthy to be praised! I give You glory and honor today.

May 22

Let Us Shout About the Blesser, Not Just the Blessings!

Today's Scripture Reading: Matthew 6:25–34 *Key Verse:* Matthew 6:33

Seek first the kingdom of God and His righteousness,
and all these things [the Gentiles seek] shall be added to you.

Many of us in the modern church seem to shout about God's "benefit package" more than about our adoption as members of His royal family. Our status as members of God's kingdom family means that we have direct access to His throne room along with specific jobs to do and responsibilities to fulfill as members of the King's court.

When you get a good job, the company provides you with everything you need to get the job done. You also may receive a benefits package that includes a medical plan, a retirement plan, and perhaps free access to counseling services. It is all part of the package.

When you go to work, does your boss have to remind you about your benefits every day? No, your main responsibility is to do the work you were hired to do, not sit around reading your benefits brochures and dreaming about what you will have at retirement.

God wants you to walk in your blessings as you do your kingdom work. He provides for our needs so we can work and serve without worrying about the "stuff" of life. We should not need to be reminded that He is our great Physician and Jehovah-Jireh, the "God who provides" for all our needs. God should not have to remind us that we are the head and not the tail, or that we are blessed in our going and coming.

How long are we going to focus exclusively on God's benefit program? We need to wake up every day and know that we are blessed. We are the redeemed of the Lord. Now let us act and work like we know it.

Pray this prayer with me:

Heavenly Father, You are my chief joy, not the countless blessings You provide for me. I bless You and call You holy. Thank You for supplying for all of my needs so that I can do Your will without hindrance or delay. In Jesus' name I pray, amen.

FIRST WE WORSHIP IN SPIRIT

Today's Scripture Reading: John 4:24; Acts 9:17; Ephesians 5:18 *Key Verse:* John 4:24

God is Spirit, and those who worship Him must worship in spirit and truth.

Look closely at Jesus' words in John 4:24. He said we must worship God "in spirit and truth." Did you notice that Jesus did not say we must worship God "in truth and spirit"? His statement reveals a divine order that is no accident. We must be filled with the Spirit to effectively walk in the Spirit and to properly worship God.

You cannot even speak to God without the Spirit. God is not human; He is Spirit, so your spirit must talk to Him "spirit to Spirit."

Isaiah the prophet said the temple in his vision was so filled with the glory of God that the doorposts began to move. This is a view into the spiritual realm, and it is an accurate description of what should be happening among us today! But it will never happen unless we yield to the Holy Spirit of God and allow Him to fill, overflow, and permeate our lives with heavenly influence.

In the book of Ephesians, Paul commanded us to be filled with the Spirit and directly linked that condition with the singing of psalms, hymns, and spiritual songs to one another. (It sounds like the seraphim Isaiah described, doesn't it?)

First we worship in spirit; then we worship in truth. First comes worship from the heart and spirit of man; then comes the revelation and knowledge from God to the human mind. Divine results come when we follow the divine pattern.

Pray this prayer with me:

Holy Father, I confess that at times I have done things backward. I have tried to worship You with my head and my knowledge first, and then presumed to move into the things of the Spirit. Your Word makes it clear that I must begin with worship in spirit and then move on into truth and knowledge. I love You, Lord. You are holy and worthy to be praised.

May 24

Create Glory Like a River

Today's Scripture Reading: John 7:37–39 *Key Verse:* John 7:38

He who believes in Me, as the Scripture has said,
out of his heart will flow rivers of living water.

Most churches today are not praising God and creating glory; they are making noise. It may sound spiritual, but it is noise.

The only way you can give God glory is to receive the Spirit of God. It comes in as Spirit and goes out as glory. That is why the Bible talks many times about "the fruit of your lips." When you open your life to the continual flow of the Holy Spirit, the cycle is completed when glory flows out of your life in the form of prayer, praise, and works of holy service.

When you speak of the holiness of God and express your longing for Him to "tabernacle" or dwell within you, He does just that. Then He begins to freely execute His power and activate the "full benefits package" as a "side benefit" to His presence.

Pray this prayer with me:

Lord Jesus, teach me the difference between mere noise and true worship and glory. I want to offer You the firstfruits of my lips—my very best glory for Your good pleasure. Bless You, Lord. I love You.

IS THE POWER ON?

Today's Scripture Reading: Acts 1–2 *Key Verse:* Acts 1:8

You shall receive power when the Holy Spirit has come upon you;
and you shall be witnesses to Me in Jerusalem,
and in all Judea and Samaria, and to the end of the earth.

Receiving the Spirit is not the end or ultimate goal in the Christian life; it is just the beginning. Jesus said in Acts 1:8, "You shall receive power." What is the power? The power is your ability to communicate spirit to Spirit. When you do that, you start producing glory so that God can invade your situation and make things happen.

That is why many "quiet" churches are closing up. They have already been dead for a long time. Many people use these excuses: "I like to worship quietly. Everybody has his own way of worshiping God, you know." I know. That is why they are broke, busted, and disgusted.

Your Christian life will not demonstrate any power unless you open your mouth and start producing some glory! An electrical socket has power, but it will not help you unless you stick something in it. In the same way, you have the power of God residing in you, but the only way to make the power work is to *speak it out*.

Before you tell me, "I have the power," I want to see some fruit. Show me how your power has changed lives. I want to see how you put the devil on the run through the power of God in your life. Let me see the power you received from the living God. When you are first filled with the Spirit, you only have reached the first stage. Keep going and keep producing glory for God!

Pray this prayer with me:

Lord, my prayer is this: I want You—and everything that means. I want to be filled with Your Spirit, Your presence, Your power, Your love, Your anointing, Your favor, Your peace, and far more. Above all, I want to honor and please You with the fruit of my life and my lips. I bless You and honor You in Jesus' name, amen.

May 26

It Is Time for an Overflow

Today's Scripture Reading: Ezekiel 43:1–4 *Key Verse:* Ezekiel 43:2

Behold, the glory of the God of Israel came from the way of the east. His voice was like the sound of many waters; and the earth shone with His glory.

Isaiah helped us see what went on inside God's temple. Ezekiel offered a vision of what went on outside the temple. When Ezekiel witnessed the glory of God, he said he heard a voice sounding like "many waters." If you remember, Jesus said, "Out of his heart will flow rivers of living water" (John 7:38 NKJV).

This means that as you speak, you produce "water" or glory for God. That, in turn, opens the way for God to manifest or reveal Himself. The prophet added, "The glory of the LORD came into the temple by way of the gate which faces toward the east" (Ezek. 43:4 NKJV). This is yet another glimpse of the glory, the Spirit of God, being moved.

Finally the prophet wrote, "Then he brought me back to the door of the temple; and there was water, flowing from under the threshold of the temple toward the east, for the front of the temple faced east; the water was flowing from under the right side of the temple, south of the altar" (Ezek. 47:1 NKJV).

Again the water or glory of God overflowed and flooded outside the temple walls. That means that once we create so much glory that the church cannot contain it, it will start overflowing to the people outside the church. This is a good picture of God's plan and purpose for the church in the earth.

Pray this prayer with me:

Father, we love and worship You as holy and true. You are worthy. May Your train fill this temple once again, and may Your glory fill and overflow our place of worship until it spills out into our community and touches the lives of the people around us. In Jesus' name, amen.

May 27

Are You Ankle-Deep Yet?

Today's Scripture Reading: Ezekiel 47:2–6 *Key Verse:* Ezekiel 47:3

When the man went out to the east with the line in his hand, he measured one thousand cubits, and he brought me through the waters; the water came up to my ankles.

Ezekiel gave a prophetic picture of the Spirit-filled church in action. It created so much glory that the house of God couldn't contain the presence of God. It made God so big (by creating glory) that the church/temple couldn't contain it.

The overflowing flood of glory rose up to the people's ankles, then to their knees, then to their loins, and then it passed flood stage. If this is what could and should be, then what is wrong with the blood-bought church today?

We are in the "water," and we are walking biblically. Why, then, do we have so many problems in life? I noticed that in Ezekiel's vision, the first stage of overflow produced enough water or glory to reach the ankle. That means that the worshipers produced so much glory that they were able to *walk* in it. That speaks of enough power and glory to walk in holiness and power on a daily basis.

Most of us cannot walk in this glory, and that has convinced the people outside the church that we are more talk than walk. If you have not produced glory, then you cannot walk in the Spirit. Most of us create our own spiritual anemia by limiting our spiritual encounters to one two-hour session on Sunday. We do not really pray, praise, or worship Him any other time. We do not talk much about Jesus all week either. Then we wonder why we cannot walk "in the Spirit." The answer is that we are too busy walking in the flesh.

We need to get busy blessing the Lord and producing glory with our lives every day of the week. Then the power will begin to flow.

Pray this prayer with me:

Lord Jesus, my power-failure problems have nothing to do with You and everything to do with me. You gave me the power, but it is up to me to hook up, plug in, and turn on the power. It is up to me to create glory through the fruit of my lips, and I accept the challenge. I bless You, and I declare that You are holy and worthy to be praised. There is none like You.

DO YOU HINDER THE GLORY OR CREATE IT?

Today's Scripture Reading: Ezekiel 47:2–6 *Key Verse:* Ezekiel 47:4

Again he measured one thousand and brought me through the waters; the water came up to my knees.

Some people complain that just when they get the "water" of the Spirit past their ankles where they can halfway walk in it, it goes up to their knees. That is not a problem; that is God's glory. If it reaches to your knees, that means you can get down and pray in it.

Half of the time we complain, "Oh, I just can't pray. Every time I get out there in the middle of something, I just cannot say anything. I cannot get it out."

Have you created an atmosphere of glory where God likes to dwell? Have you prepared a place of glory where it is easy to get on your knees in the peace of God and pray with power and effectiveness?

Perhaps you need to burn up some of the CDs in your music collection, those devil-inspired audio tracks that hinder the glory of God in your home. Were you raised in a Christian home? Did you ever notice how your mama did not allow you to listen to certain kinds of music? Your parents would not let you watch certain programs on TV.

Were your parents always singing? They did not hinder the glory of God; they created a presence. They did not have any problems praying, either. They knew the key: everything they did was focused on Jesus. Where is your focus?

Pray this prayer with me:

Father, thank You for raising the level of Your anointing so much that my sin floated to the top. I repent of my sinful ways and appetites. Cleanse me and help me to start clean and fresh in Your presence right now. Let Your glory flow as I magnify Your name and rehearse Your mighty works, in Jesus' name, amen.

SPEAKING OF SPIRITUAL INFERTILITY . . .

Today's Scripture Reading: Ezekiel 47:2–6 *Key Verse:* Ezekiel 47:4

Again he measured one thousand and brought me through;
the water came up to my waist.

Any individual believer or corporate church body that lacks the power to walk in the Spirit will most likely lack the power to pray in the Spirit as well. Sad to say, that almost guarantees that there will be no power to reproduce.

According to Ezekiel 47:4, the prophet saw the overflowing water from God's temple come up to his waist or loins. In the Bible, the "loins" always connote the ability to procreate or reproduce. Individuals who are unable to reproduce were doomed to see their line die out after one generation. Ancient Israelite society went to great lengths to avoid that tragedy. The growing number of dying churches and our failure to bring the young into the church speak volumes about our spiritual infertility.

Have you been thinking about a project for years, but never started it? Have you noticed that there is not anything really big, exciting, or challenging going on in your life? Perhaps it is because you are not producing enough glory to make it happen. The ability to create glory and offer it to God is central to everything in the Christian life. There is simply no substitute for it.

Pray this prayer with me:

Father, You are waiting for me to "produce children" in my Christian walk. I should be producing dreams, the fulfillment of dreams, and the fruit of spiritual offspring, but I am not. That changes today. This is the day I begin to create glory and life with the fruit of my lips. I praise You and honor You as the fountain of my life—holy, righteous, all-powerful, and true. You are holy and worthy to be praised, O Lord. In Jesus' name I praise You, amen.

May 30

Have You Used Daniel's Prayer Hammer?

Today's Scripture Reading: Daniel 10 *Key Verse:* Daniel 10:12

Do not fear, Daniel, for from the first day that you set your heart to understand, and to humble yourself before your God, your words were heard; and I have come because of your words.

Think about Daniel. We know him as one of the greatest prophets in the Old Testament, but God knew him first and foremost as a man of fervent and faithful prayer. When he got on his knees and prayed, God heard him the instant he opened his lips. In that same moment, God sent this prayer warrior his answer. Yet Daniel kept praying for twenty-one days. Why?

It was not because Daniel did not think God's answer would come. He understood that there was warfare in the air. I am convinced that Daniel *produced so much glory* in three weeks that God had to dispatch warring angels to do battle with the enemy and remove the hindrances so Daniel's answer could get through. It is almost as if Daniel used a "hammer of prayer" to drive the answer through.

Where is that vision God gave you? It is not in heaven, and it is not in the earth. It is suspended in battle between the first heaven and the second heaven. All you need to do is get down on your knees and create enough glory to push the answer through Satan's hindrances. Pray this prayer with me by faith:

Lord, I know I have it, I know You sent it, and I know it is coming. Now, Satan, get off, get out, and get lost. I bless You, Lord. You are holy, You are holy, and You are worthy to be praised. I am not giving up, and I refuse to give in because I know You are faithful. I know the answer will come because of the glory I give to You in Jesus' name!

HE IS ON THE THRONE—A FLOOD IS COMING!

Today's Scripture Reading: Psalm 29 *Key Verse:* Psalm 29:1

Give unto the LORD, O you mighty ones, Give unto the LORD glory and strength.

Remember the principle of glory and the Spirit: When you receive the Holy Spirit in your life, He flows through and out again in the form of glory. Paul said that God "is able to do exceedingly abundantly above all that we ask or think, *according to the power that works in us*" (Eph. 3:20 NKJV, emphasis mine). That is the power we receive through the Spirit. This power does not "come out" silently; it has to come out through your mouth as well as through your deeds.

Today's Scripture reading is filled with references to the glory: "Give unto the LORD the glory due to His name" (Ps. 29:2 NKJV). That is all God asks you to do. Get in position and give Him what is His. "The voice of the LORD is over the waters" (Ps. 29:3 NKJV). Where is the water coming from? It comes through our mouths from our hearts.

The writer went on to say, "The LORD sat enthroned at the Flood, / And the LORD sits as King forever. / The LORD will give strength to His people; / The LORD will bless His people with peace" (Ps. 29:10–11 NKJV).

Do you live in depression? Are you suicidal? Hopeless? Lonely? He will give strength to you and bless you with peace. Give Him glory and He will give you strength and peace. If you create an overflow of glory for Him, He will flood your life with His presence and establish His throne in your home.

Ezekiel the prophet said the river flowing from God's temple became so big that it went to the sea and healed everything it touched (see Ezek. 47). God wants us to produce so much living water with our lips that it can't be contained within the four walls of our churches! It will flow down our streets and transform drug addicts and draw them to church. It will flood your neighborhood and schools with glory. Wherever God's glory flows, healing and transformed lives surely follow!

Pray this prayer with me:

Holy Father, I have set my heart to join with my brothers and sisters to enthrone You on a flood of glory created with our lips! You are worthy, and we are needy. The answer is obvious to me at last: I must glorify You and entrust the rest to You as well. I want nothing less than a flood of Your glory to flow through my life, my home, my church, my community, and my city. May You be glorified and honored above every name. In Jesus' name I pray, amen.

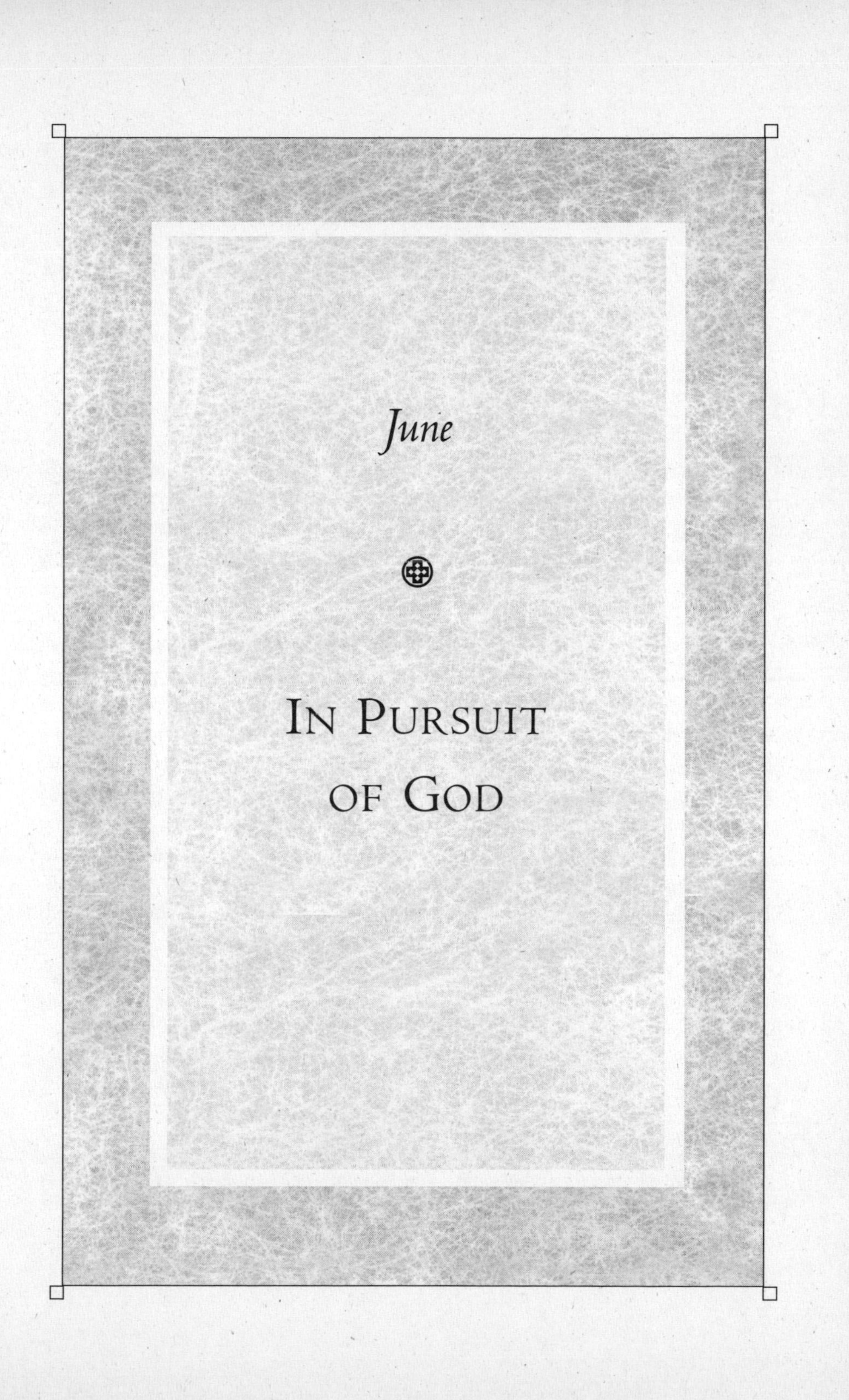

June

In Pursuit of God

RELIGIOUS PEOPLE NEED NOT APPLY

Today's Scripture Reading: Mark 2 *Key Verse:* Mark 2:4

When they could not come near Him because of the crowd, they uncovered the roof where He was. So when they had broken through, they let down the bed on which the paralytic was lying.

The desperate persistence in this story from Mark's gospel seems almost embarrassing to some people because of its intensity. It highlights one of the clearest aspects of Jesus' earthly ministry. God has something special for His church today, *but it is not for religious people;* it is for hungry people. There is a big difference between the two.

Religious people care about who is going to preach on Sunday, what the choir sings, and whether the sanctuary is too hot or too cold. A religious person knows when to put his hands up and when to put them down. Religious people know how to say, "Hallelujah, thank You, Jesus!" inside—then cuss while they speed out of the church parking lot. Religious people are slow to give you a shoulder to cry on; some of them will not touch you at all. (They prefer to give you a Scripture verse—from a safe distance, of course.) Basically, religious people tend to be so locked up in their religiosity that they do not have any joy.

Hungry people, on the other hand, do not care who is preaching, what the choir is singing, or if frost is forming on the pews. They just come to see Jesus. They will search, ask, beg, and crawl, if necessary, until they touch the hem of His garment. Hungry people do not care what you think, what you say, or how much you do not like them. That is your problem because they come to church to get something that God promised them. They will not be mean about it, but no one is going to get in their way. They do not care if you talk about them because they have been delivered from people. Their pain transcends everything else. All they want is to find Jesus.

Are you religious or hungry? Either way, pray this prayer with me:

Jesus, I have been guilty of religiosity, and I do not want that. I want to be hungry for You. I want to know You more.

June 2

He Satisfies the Hungry and Aggravates the Satisfied

Today's Scripture Reading: Matthew 5:1–8 *Key Verse:* Matthew 5:6

Blessed are those who hunger and thirst for righteousness,
For they shall be filled.

The idea that God reserves His blessings for the hungry instead of for the religious did not originate with me. It did not come from a modern revivalist or a disgruntled pastor somewhere. It came from the lips of Jesus. He told His disciples that those who hunger for righteousness will be filled. Jesus said it, so if this upsets you, take it up with Him. He satisfies the hungry (and aggravates the satisfied).

For those of us who are just religious, our problem is really just a serious case of laziness. We can get so caught up with outward performance and religious protocol that we miss the move of God!

While religious people complain about standing too long during a worship service, hungry people do not even want to sit down. In fact, they usually do not even know how long the service went, and they really do not care how long they stood as long as they somehow touched Him.

Which group do you think walks out of a worship service satisfied?

Pray with me:

Lord, deliver me from religiosity! Holy Spirit, keep me hungry for more and desperate for the Master's touch. Holy God, cause my appetite to shift from the sweet things that bless my flesh to the deep things that feed my spirit and leave me panting for more of You. In Jesus' name I pray, amen.

ARE YOU HUNGRY ENOUGH TO LOSE EVERYTHING FOR HIM?

Today's Scripture Reading: Psalm 8; Matthew 10:39 *Key Verses:* Psalm 8:3–4

When I consider Your heavens, the work of Your fingers,
The moon and the stars, which You have ordained,
What is man that You are mindful of him,
And the son of man that You visit him?

If it makes you uncomfortable to take limits off of God, to not control Him, why are you pursuing Him? (What makes you think you could control Him, anyway?) The problem is that you are suffering from "religion withdrawal." You actually think religion makes God safe, tame, and predictable. If that is what you really want, then go back to a church that (thinks it) controls God.

I do not want to control God (and I have enough sense to know I could not if I wanted to). I do not want to limit His power in my life. When God wants to move, I am hungry enough to follow Him. I am not going to tell Him to stop, even if the destination frightens me. How can I say that? It is because I trust Him who gave me life in the first place.

How hungry are you? Are you hungry enough to stop trying to control the One who spun the stars into place with a word? Are you desperate enough to "throw your life away" by giving yourself to Him without limitation, condition, or hesitation?

If you dare to believe that you will gain everything by losing everything for His sake (Matt. 10:39), then you *are* hungry. Here is your cross . . . now follow Him.

Pray this prayer with me:

Lord Jesus, somehow, somewhere, a politically correct church diluted, antisepticized, and popularized Your gospel. You are larger, greater, and more powerful than any of us knows. All I know is that I am desperate for You. I must be with You, no matter what it costs me in this life. I trust Your Word; if I lose all to follow You, then I will gain everything!

June 4

You Are Well Able to Overcome

Today's Scripture Reading: Numbers 13:26–33   *Key Verse:* Numbers 13:30

Caleb quieted the people before Moses, and said, "Let us go up at once and take possession, for we are well able to overcome it."

It is not about what we can see or feel. It is about what God said. Remember the twelve spies Moses sent into Canaan to check out the land? Most of them talked themselves—and everyone who listened to them—out of the blessing.

Twelve spies went into the land. Ten focused on the problem; two—Joshua and Caleb—focused on God and His promises. Ten had faith in the problem; two had faith in God. The two who had faith in God also had an attitude that said, "I do not care what we see; we are well able to go up there and do what God said we can do."

It is not about what we see. It is about what God said. Most of our problems arise because we act like the Bible does not exist, or that the things God says in it are mere myths, fairy tales, and sound bytes for a sermon or speech. We are in grave error. Jesus told the religious types of His day, "You are mistaken, not knowing the Scriptures nor the power of God" (Matt. 22:29 NKJV). That sums up the problem in our day too.

How much do you want to follow God? Ignore what you see and just do what He said.

Pray this prayer with me:

Holy Father, by Your grace and mercy I will look past the towering obstacles and the entrenched strongholds before me. I will see the Rock of my salvation towering above all things. I will see Your enemies scatter when You arise in Your might and power. I will see Your promise as an unfailing bridge to my destiny, for You are faithful.

SPEND TIME ALONE WITH JESUS

Today's Scripture Reading: Luke 12:32–34 *Key Verse:* Luke 12:34

Where your treasure is, there your heart will be also.

I have some potentially devastating news for you: that five-minute devotion you did while you sat on the toilet this morning did not make you "spiritually deep."

You must spend some serious time with Jesus. No substitute for it exists. You may even have to take time off from work and sit with Jesus. It takes desire and devotion to put Him above all the other things clamoring for your time.

Jesus said, "For where your treasure is, there your heart will be also." A modern adaptation might also say, "Where you spend your time is where you invest your heart." God wants to give us His kingdom, but we have to make a life investment first.

If you want to be deep, spend time with Him. Allow Jesus to pour into you the authentic gospel that transforms lives, sets the captives free, and overturns entire nations. After you receive His Word, then do what He says. Pray with me:

Jesus, forgive me for not spending time with You—and I mean time that really counts. Lord Jesus, I commit today to spend time with You alone. It may be one hour; it may be two—I do not care. All I want is You.

Stop. Sit. Wait. Hear.

Today's Scripture Reading: Matthew 26:36; Psalm 46:10 *Key Verse:* Psalm 46:10

Be still, and know that I am God;
I will be exalted among the nations,
I will be exalted in the earth!

Do you want to hear from God? Then you must quiet yourself. Go to a place where you can quiet your spirit. This means you need to find a place where there are no distractions—no phones, no beepers, no children, no spouse, no whatever. Then make yourself sit down and quiet your spirit before God.

(Note: It is good and proper to love our spouses and children, to spend time with them, and to do things for them. The worst error we can commit, however, is make them idols by putting them ahead of God in our priority list. Seek God first; then bless your spouse, your children, and your friends.)

We race a lot in this society. Have you noticed that when you sit down and become still, your thoughts are still spinning at high speed? That is because your soul is running. You are not sitting down on the inside. You must be *still* to hear from God, and the ability to hear from God is the greatest asset any saint can have! (It is also the asset most lacking in our lives.)

It amazes me to see how many books and manuals we have to help us hear the voice of God. When I was born, I had no problem discerning the voice of my daddy. Throughout my years in his domain, I knew my father's voice. I did not go to school to learn how to discern his voice, and I did not go to the library or buy books to learn how to recognize Daddy's voice. I knew my daddy's voice because I knew him.

If you want to know God's voice, all you have to do is *know Him*. And in knowing Him, you also will know when He is speaking to you. God says in His Word that you must quiet yourself to hear His voice. *Slow down.*

Pray this prayer with me:

Heavenly Father, forgive me for my foolish schedules and racing lifestyle. I need You too much to miss our appointments in stillness. I will stop, sit, and quiet myself before You because I want to hear what You have to say . . . and I have some things to say to You as well. I am waiting on You in Jesus' name. Amen.

June 7

Be a Doer, Not a Forgetter

Today's Scripture Reading: James 1:23–25 *Key Verse:* James 1:25

He who looks into the perfect law of liberty and continues in it,
and is not a forgetful hearer but a doer of the work,
this one will be blessed in what he does.

What is the cry of your heart? I want to be led by the Spirit of God. Is that your greatest desire?

Let me tell you the first criteria for being led by the Spirit of God. It is *obedience*. You must be obedient to what He says, or He will not waste the effort to speak to you.

Think about it. If someone does not listen to you, how often will you talk to that person? Not very often. It is annoying.

Listening to the Spirit involves more than merely hearing words and getting goose bumps. It means *doing* what the Spirit says. You cannot be a hearer without being a doer. Thousands of people heard the words of Jesus in person. They even saw the miracles and ate the bread and fish He miraculously provided. Yet only a few followed through by dedicating their lives to Him.

Millions of Christians file into church services and hear God's Word preached every weekend. Then they file back out and climb into their cars having forgotten nearly everything they heard. When hard times come, they forget who they are. They forget their inheritance in the kingdom, and they have no foundation for recovery from life's hard knocks. Those who hear God's voice in prayer, in the Word, or by direct revelation, and then *do* what they hear, are blessed.

Father, I do not want people to say of me in my old age, "He has forgotten more of God's Word than you have ever heard." I want it said, "He was a doer of the Word. He changed lives and made a difference in the kingdom—and God blessed him for it." So be it, in Jesus' name. Amen.

IF YOU SAY IT, I WILL DO IT

Today's Scripture Reading: John 15:12–18 *Key Verses:* John 15:13–14

Greater love has no one than this, than to lay down one's life for his friends. You are My friends if you do whatever I command you.

Have you ever been in a play? When I walked onstage as a child, I sometimes felt nervous. My stomach tightened up whenever I looked out from the stage and saw the audience. Then I saw the teacher directing me where to stand and what to do, and I was not nervous anymore.

The Holy Ghost is directing you in the play of life. He will lead you into all truth. He will confront and transform weak personality traits in your life, such as shyness or selfishness, so that you can do what God has ordained for you to do.

Remember that God always requires an account of what has passed. He holds us responsible, and He is coming back to see if we did what He told us to do. The Bible teaches that we will be judged and rewarded according to whether or not we did the things God told us to do (see Matt. 25:31–46).

All God says we can do for Him is to be obedient to Him. The Holy Spirit does the guiding and directing; all you have to do is obey. It is a simple scenario, so start today.

Pray this prayer with me:

Lord Jesus, I have made things too complex and difficult. You did the work on the cross to deliver me from the debt of sin and death. Now it is up to me to do Your Word. Forgive me for making endless excuses and justifications and for avoiding the obvious. If You say it, I will do it without excuse, delay, or hesitation. Thank You for the mercy and grace You have extended to me.

JUNE 9

WHOSE KINGDOM ARE YOU BUILDING?

Today's Scripture Reading: Romans 6:16, 16:19–20 *Key Verses:* Romans 16:19–20a

Your obedience has become known to all. Therefore I am glad on your behalf; but I want you to be wise in what is good, and simple concerning evil. And the God of peace will crush Satan under your feet shortly.

If you are not obedient to God, then whom or what are you obeying? Whose ministry are you building—His or yours?

Obedience gets God's attention. It excites Him because He knows He has found someone with whom He can build a kingdom! When we are obedient to Him, He moves on our behalf to crush our enemy and wave aside impossible obstacles. He challenges us to obey His Word above everything else, even if it means trouble for us. No matter what it costs you, obey Him with joy.

The Bible commands us to "rejoice always" (1 Thess. 5:16 NKJV). A joy comes when you move into the things of God, even when it inconveniences you or means you will go through hardship. The eternal purpose of God always brings joy to you.

If you are not full of joy over what you are doing, you have good reason to examine your life and your motives. Whose ministry are you building? If you have veered away from God's eternal purpose, change; obey Him so joy will return to your life. Pray this prayer with me:

Lord Jesus, at times disobedience marks my life more than obedience. Please forgive me for my sin. Today, right now, I change directions and motivations. Every area of my life that is "out of joint" with Your purposes must be brought back into alignment. With the help of the Holy Spirit, I will obey and follow You wherever You lead me.

What Can You Do for Me?

Today's Scripture Reading: Psalm 50 *Key Verses:* Psalm 50:10–12

Every beast of the forest is Mine,
And the cattle on a thousand hills.
I know all the birds of the mountains,
And the wild beasts of the field are Mine.
If I were hungry, I would not tell you;
For the world is Mine, and all its fullness.

God has a question for you. Are you ready for it?

"*What do you think you can do for Me?* With all that I have done and created—the very thing you are sitting on, the molecules in the clothes you wear, the galaxy, and all the stars—what do you think you can do for a God like Me?"

We are too arrogant in the church. We even have the nerve to sit up and be proud of "what we have done" for the kingdom.

There is one thing, and one thing only, that we can do for God: *obey Him*.

We must return to a holy and reverent fear of God. We have presumed too much, and we pretend that He needs us and all the things we do for Him. God does not need us, but He does want and love us.

He is our heavenly Father, but He is also the almighty God, Lord of heaven and earth. He has no interest in a "spiritual one-night stand" with people; He wants a lifetime commitment or nothing. Commitment in the form of obedience is the *only* thing we can offer Him. Obedience then takes the form of our prayers, praise, worship, and good deeds in obedience to the Spirit.

God is looking for an obedient people who will do what He asks without question. What can you do for God today? You know the answer.

Father, in Jesus' name I obey. Yes, Lord. Yes, Lord. Without question, without excuse, without delay, I will do whatever You say.

June 11

What Will God Say to You?

Today's Scripture Reading: 1 Samuel 15 *Key Verse:* 1 Samuel 15:22

Behold, to obey is better than sacrifice.

You should probably know that God does not get as excited as you do when you complete a great spiritual fast. He does not even get as excited as you do when you fulfill some great deed, because He is more interested in the deeds of the heart than the deeds of the hand.

Have you ever had a conversation like this:

"Lord, You do not understand! I just spent all that I had to feed the hungry!"

"No, you do not understand. I did not call you to feed the hungry. I called you to obey Me. If I called you to devote your life to feeding the hungry and you obeyed, I would be pleased. However, I did not call you to that, but you did it anyway."

Any "good deed" apart from God's direction is a dead work. It may have some value among men as a charitable act, but it is only another instance of disobedience in God's eyes.

The thing that excites God is obedience. If God calls us to do only one thing, and we do that one thing well, then God will say, "Well done, good and faithful servant," and He will give us an abundant reward (Matt. 25:21 NKJV).

What will He say to you? Are you doing what He asked you to do, or are you doing your own thing in His name? One is obedience worthy of reward; the other is disobedience worthy of another response . . .

Lord Jesus, forgive me for all of the times I passed over the thing You asked me to do and then offered You something You never asked me to do. I choose to obey today and to do that thing which You told me to do—nothing more and nothing less. I want to hear You say, "Well done."

June 12

Obey God No Matter What It Costs You

Today's Scripture Reading: Acts 1; 1 Corinthians 15:6 *Key Verse:* Acts 1:4

Being assembled together with them, He commanded them not to depart from Jerusalem, but to wait for the Promise of the Father, "which," He said, "you have heard from Me."

After the resurrection, Jesus appeared to five hundred people, yet there were only 120 in the Upper Room on the day of pentecost. Why did the number decrease when it should have increased? Why did He appear to only five hundred, and where were the other 380 people on the day of pentecost?

Jesus told them, "Do not depart from Jerusalem." Those were His orders. "Do not depart, but wait for the promise of God the Father." It is probable that many of the five hundred people listening to His command did not live in Jerusalem. They would have to sacrifice to obey Him. Once He disappeared from their sight, they were left to obey on faith alone.

If somebody pushes you to go out and march when God told you to wait, do not budge. Do not get anxious to do anything. As long as God says wait, then wait. On the other hand, if God says, "March!" and your naturally conservative counselors say, "Wait," just obey God.

Did God tell you to do something that you have not done? Are you thinking about taking action on something you know you should wait for? In every situation, obey God no matter what it costs. None of us can afford to step outside His will and favor, and no one can bless us like He can!

Pray this prayer with me:

Lord Jesus, I have made mistakes and committed sins in the past. Today is a new day, and I choose to wait where You say wait. I will charge in when You say "Charge in and take the land." In all things, lead me in the way everlasting, the path of Your perfect will. As for me and my house, we will follow.

GLORIFY HIM THROUGH YOUR OBEDIENCE

Today's Scripture Reading: Romans 10:17; James 1:25 *Key Verse:* Romans 10:17

Faith comes by hearing, and hearing by the word of God.

Hearing the Word of God means that you hear *and* you obey. Faith grows only when you do what you hear. If you are not doing what you hear, then you are not growing in faith. You should just throw away the teaching tapes because as long as you fail to *do* what you have heard, they will not help you.

God does not want you to just ride in your car and listen to something spiritual. He wants you to listen to it, yes, but He also wants you to get out of your car and do what you heard. You might be able to quote the Bible from Genesis to Revelation, but if you cannot do what you heard God say, then you do not have enough faith to get out of a wet paper bag!

On the other hand, if you move in obedience, you will experience a continual degree of excitement in your life. Every day you will rise in faith and lovingly "dare" God to show you something else to do for His glory.

Pray with me:

Heavenly Father, I want to be a doer of Your Word, not a hearer only. Grant me the grace and courage to do the things I hear You saying to me. Show me how I can glorify and please You through obedience. In Jesus' name I pray, amen.

June 14

Grow from Faith to Faith, Not Fake to Fake

Today's Scripture Reading: 1 Corinthians 4:20; Romans 1:17 *Key Verse:* Romans 1:17

The righteousness of God is revealed from faith to faith;
as it is written, "The just shall live by faith."

Moses sent the twelve spies into Canaan to spy out the land and bring back evidence that God was true to His word. That did exactly that—they found a land flowing with milk and honey and brought back some grapes that were so large that two men were required to carry one cluster of them.

Understand that God will allow you to see the grapes, but He will not put them in your mouth. He will allow you to see the blessings, but you have to stretch out on faith in some way to get what God has. He will not just lay it in your hands. Do not rub your Bible and wish that God would do something. You must reach out to attain what God has ordained.

You have to grow your faith because God's righteousness is revealed from faith to faith. That is what keeps you excited about God.

If you meet someone who is not excited about God, I can tell you that person is not growing in his faith. It probably has been a long time since he witnessed or experienced anything new about God. People who are being stretched in their faith are always excited about God. They constantly see new sides of God's glory because He is revealed from faith to faith (not from fake to fake). Are you excited or nearly comatose in the Spirit?

Pray this prayer with me:

Lord Jesus, I am tired of delayed growth and the joyless life. I am turning my eyes back to You, which is where they should have been all along. I am stretching out my faith to reach for something bigger than I am—I am seeking to do Your will and attain what You ordained.

God Is at Work in You; Are You at Work in Him?

Today's Scripture Reading: Philippians 2:12–16 *Key Verses:* Philippians 2:12–13

Work out your own salvation with fear and trembling; for it is God who works in you both to will and to do for His good pleasure.

Do you realize that there are two kinds of faith? One faith you are awarded as a gift of God. That is called "saving faith." The Bible describes it: "God has dealt to each one a measure of faith" (Rom. 12:3 NKJV). Most churches today work only in saving faith. That secures their eternal destination but little else. That is why most Christians are spiritually sick and not seeing any fruit in their lives. They never move on in their faith.

The second kind of faith has the capacity to grow. This is the faith God gets excited about when we demonstrate it in our lives. I call this "stretching faith." God says that without faith it is impossible to please Him (Heb. 11:6).

It takes more faith to please Him after you enter the kingdom through the cross than it does to enter the kingdom. Jesus did everything for you then. Now that you are a Christian, He expects you to "work out your own salvation." This verse is not talking about "working" your way into heaven; it is talking about "walking out" your salvation on earth as an ambassador of God's kingdom. That requires you to walk in a greater dimension of faith.

Some people preach that the greater dimension of faith is to believe for "stuff." I am sorry, but God gives the greater dimension of faith to us to use for the journey—to get us where we are supposed to go and to help us do what we are supposed to do.

Paul said, "I have fought the good fight, I have finished the race, I have kept the faith" (2 Tim. 4:7 NKJV). Why do you think he said at the end that he had kept his faith? He had to mention faith because that is what excites God.

Do you want to excite God? Then get moving with your faith!

Father, I am ready to walk in a greater dimension of faith and to stretch out to do Your will. I trust You to get me where I must be and to help me do what I must do in Your kingdom. I put all my trust in You—in Your strength, wisdom, power, and faithful provision. In Jesus' name I pray. Amen.

WHO PUT THAT RIVER THERE?

Today's Scripture Reading: Genesis 12:1–3 *Key Verse:* Genesis 12:2

I will make you a great nation;
I will bless you
And make your name great;
And you shall be a blessing.

God commanded Abram to "get out" in Genesis 12:1. God's commands rarely come with reasons, but they always include promises. After the command, the Lord told Abram that He would make him a great nation and bless him so he could become a blessing.

Even God's promise to Abram would ultimately test his faith because the Lord revealed only the first and the last step in the process. The rest of the way could be called "the journey of faith."

Go back to the "holy ground experience" in which God spoke directly to your heart. He did not give a reason, did He? Yet there was some promise spoken or understood. Everything in His command and promise to you is calculated to test your faith—not your saving faith but your stretching faith.

God's call always stretches you in new dimensions because He reveals Himself "from faith to faith." He gives you enough to come after Him, and then He gives you enough for you to catch up to Him again for the next piece of the puzzle. Through it all, you grow and are "conformed to the image" of Christ (Rom. 8:29 NKJV).

God speaks to us in part, not in whole. He gives us just enough to get to Point B. But He rarely tells us in advance that the river Jordan separates Point A from Point B. The Jordan represents a death experience we must go through, a risk that we must take, a gamble that we go for. Faith reveals God. It allows us to move in a greater dimension and allows us to see God in a different way.

Are you in the middle of a faith journey today? Are you staring at the boiling waters of a river obstacle you never expected? Pray this prayer with me:

Lord, I admit that I am confused and discouraged. I just did not expect this kind of trouble when I said yes to You. I am convinced in my heart that it does not matter because I know I heard Your voice, and I know I am going in the direction You told me to go. I trust You to lead me through and over every obstacle between where I was and where You want me to be. Blessed be Your name forever. In Jesus' name I pray. Amen.

June 17

Get Out, Give Up, and See the Promise

Today's Scripture Reading: Genesis 12:1–3 *Key Verse:* Genesis 12:1

The Lord had said to Abram:
"Get out of your country,
From your family
And from your father's house,
To a land that I will show you."

First came the command in verse 1, then the promise in verse 2: "I will make you a great nation" (Gen. 12:2 NKJV). God gave Abram a proposition. "If you do this, I will do this." If he would leave his country, his family, and his father's house, God would show him a land.

Look closely at Genesis 12:1. God did not say He would *give* Abram something; He said that He would *show* him something.

You need faith to break camp without the promise of everything else. You need to be deep in love with God to do what He tells you without knowing for sure that you will be rewarded.

Now, do not confuse faith with mercy. Most of the time you do not have faith enough to get the job done; rather, God simply has mercy on you. Abram, though, moved in such a dynamic level of faith that God compensated him for the loss of his country. That is why God said He would make Abram great nation.

My friend, the blessings of God always make up for the cost of the things you leave behind to obey Him. The real question is this: Would you leave them even without any promise?

Pray this prayer with me:

Thank You, Lord, for all the things You have done and for all the things You have promised to do. Above all, thank You for being You—the almighty God who was, and is, and always shall be. You are worthy of praise, worship, honor, and obedience simply because You are the only true God. I bless You in Jesus' name. Amen.

June 18

Establish a Dividing Line

Today's Scripture Reading: Genesis 12:1; Matthew 12:46–50; John 4:44 *Key Verse:* Genesis 12:1

The Lord had said to Abram: / "Get out of your country, / From your family / And from your father's house, / To a land that I will show you."

The first requirement for the walk of faith is separation from the world and from the human nature of your family. This is a picture of the way the church must join with her Husband, Jesus Christ. God does not call us literally to hate our family members; rather we are to put them into proper perspective and priority. It is part of growing up spiritually.

Some of us have not separated from our kinfolk. A lack of separation will hinder your "marriage" to the King of the kingdom. Newly married couples that fail to establish a dividing line around their marriage usually suffer from the intrusions of well-meaning family members.

Sometimes the family and friends you love most can contaminate the pureness of the word God gave you on holy ground. They have known you from birth, and they often become the "hometown naysayers" who doubt your ability to do a supernatural task at God's command.

It happened to Jesus, so why couldn't it happen to you? He had to establish a dividing line the day his mother and brothers showed up to "pull Him out of His madness." Only later did they understand and appreciate His divine mandate as the Lamb of God. On the day they showed up at one of His meetings, He said, "Whoever does the will of My Father in heaven is My brother and sister and mother" (Matt. 12:50 NKJV).

Before God makes a major move in your life, He will separate you from the old so you can receive the new. He called Abram to leave his family as well as his country. God will not do any less with you.

Pray this prayer with me:

Lord Jesus, You separated Yourself from Your throne on high and from the Father of lights so You could take my place on the cross and redeem me with Your blood. The least I can do is separate myself unto You.

I love my family and thank You for them, but I must never allow them to turn my heart away from the things You said to me in the secret place. The best thing I can do for You, for myself, and for them, is to put You first. Then we all will be blessed through my obedience.

SEPARATE YOURSELF FROM DELAYS, DISTRACTIONS, AND HINDRANCES

Today's Scripture Reading: Genesis 11:26–12:5 *Key Verse:* Genesis 12:1

The Lord had said to Abram: "Get out of your country,
From your family And from your father's house,
To a land that I will show you."

God told Abram to do three things: leave his country, separate himself from his family, and go to a land that God promised to show him. Abram followed through on the first requirement, but he failed to do the last two. He left Ur of the Chaldees, but instead of separating himself from his family, he took along Terah his father and Lot his nephew.

Terah means "delay." Allowing his father to accompany him resulted in a delay of five years in Haran. *Haran* means "parched, dry place, extremely dry place." Are you in a dry place spiritually? If you are, perhaps you have someone with you whom God told you to leave behind.

Abram delayed his own destiny because he took with him those whom God said not to take. He endured a five-year dry period in his life and never even made it to Canaan. He stopped and stayed in Haran until his father's death finally broke the link that bound Abram to Haran. Only then did he enter Canaan.

Lot's name means "covering or veil," and it comes from a verb meaning "to wrap up." Lot wrapped up and entangled Abraham in all kinds of problems. Abraham actually divided his inheritance to provide land for Lot (in the region of Sodom and Gomorrah). That was when he finally said to Lot what he should have said a lot earlier, "Please separate from me" (Gen. 13:9 NKJV).

Have kinfolk unintentionally or intentionally delayed and hindered your pursuit of God's will? It is time to move on and separate yourself so you can do what God told you to do.[1] It may not make sense, but you must enter Canaan.

Pray this prayer with me:

Lord Jesus, I love You. You are my Life, my Light, and my Salvation. Grant me the grace, the courage, and the determination to obey You and separate myself from every hindering and delaying influence. Bless my family and give them the grace to see Your hand at work in my life. If, however, they refuse to see, I will still follow You.

June 20

What (or Who) Is the Holdup in Your Life?

Today's Scripture Reading: Isaiah 6:1; 2 Chronicles 26 *Key Verse:* Isaiah 6:1a

In the year that King Uzziah died, I saw the Lord.

Anytime you disobey God's direction concerning a relationship, you risk delaying your destiny.

For instance, if you know that guy is no good, why do you say, "But he is so nice"? If that woman has no interest in the kingdom, I do not care how nice she is. If God did not send him or her into your life, then tell that person good-bye.

We do not have time to be casual about this. Do not allow wrong relationships to hinder your relationship with God. They will hold back your promise.

Abram was delayed for five years because he failed to separate from his father, and he gave up half of the land God promised him to gain freedom from Lot after he finally reached Canaan. Isaiah had to deal with this as well. He said, "In the year that King Uzziah died, I saw the LORD sitting on a throne, high and lifted up" (Isa. 6:1a NKJV).

King Uzziah was good for Israel and for Isaiah for nearly fifty-two years, but late in his reign, he presumptuously entered the temple to burn incense at the altar of incense—something God reserved only for priests under the old covenant. God struck Uzziah with leprosy, and he died a leper. God did not speak again until the contaminating relationship was removed.

I do not care how much you love your pastor; do not get so caught up with a spiritual leader that you give him the glory and honor reserved only for God. There is a better way: get caught up, tied up, tangled up, and wrapped up in Jesus!

Pray this prayer with me:

Lord Jesus, I have eyes only for You. My ears are tuned to Your voice above all others. I give my heart without measure to You alone, for You are my Life and my Salvation. Wrap me up, entangle and tie me up in Your will and Your way.

June 21

Seek Me More Than Any Other

Today's Scripture Reading: Matthew 6:24–34 *Key Verse:* Matthew 6:33

Seek first the kingdom of God and His righteousness,
and all these things shall be added to you.

To seek means to search for and go after. Most of us read the words "seek first" and start thinking about first, second, and third in terms of priorities. We say, "Put God first, family second, and job third," and we try to do all those things. I think we are missing the point. God is saying that He is first, above all else.

The author of Proverbs wrote, "In all your ways acknowledge Him, / And He shall direct your paths" (Prov. 3:6 NKJV). When He says, "seek first," that means your relationship with Him should be so close that you check with Him before you move to the next place.

If you do that, you will experience one of the most wonderful relationships in your life, and it will be with the Holy Ghost. After a while you will not even have to ask! You will be able to sense whether or not a particular direction is right. Your spirit will automatically acknowledge Him, and you will not have to check your priorities. When God is your guide, He will tell you when to invest time in the family and when to focus on the job. He will tell you when you are spending too much time at work and need to be home. He will warn you if you have not done enough with your children. He even will let you know when you need to get off of that sofa and go exercise.

When you search for and prize your time with Him more than any other, He will show you how to live. In the process, He also will keep you healthy and thinking and experiencing wholesome things that enrich your life. This is the life of a lamb under the guidance of the Good Shepherd.

Jesus, I want to acknowledge You in all that I do. I know that You will direct my paths. I do not want it to be a "religious" thing where I always "check my priorities." I want it to be as natural as breathing. Lord. I am seeking after You.

JUNE 22

I LOVE THE PILOT MORE

Today's Scripture Reading: John 21:1–19 *Key Verse:* John 21:15

Jesus said to Simon Peter, "Simon, son of Jonah, do you love Me more than these?"

What does it mean to diligently seek God? More than anything else, it means, "I am pursuing Him." When Jesus spoke to Peter after the failures in the garden of Gethsemane and the high priest's house, He did not ask Peter to promise he would never make another mistake. He had only one question, and He repeated it three times: "Do you love Me?"

I have settled the matter in my life. Jesus is my Life, my Sustainer, my Savior, my Lord, my Director. He does not have anything to do with copiloting; He is the Pilot who alone gives me instruction. In Him I live and move and have my being (Acts 17:28). God is my all and all. I acknowledge Him in all my ways (Prov. 3:6).

This is the kind of God we serve, and that is the kind of faith it takes to serve and honor Him.

It takes God *in you* to believe *what He wants to do in you*. You must allow God in you so that when He speaks to you, you will obey and not delay what He has ordained.

God is all that matters.

Pray this prayer with me:

Lord, You know that I love You. You also know how many times I have denied and failed You. You know about everything I have said in public and in secret, yet You still love me. Yes, Lord; I love You more.

ARE YOU FLEXIBLE ENOUGH FOR TOMORROW?

Today's Scripture Reading: John 21:17; Luke 19:10 *Key Verse:* John 21:17b

And [Peter] said to Him, "Lord, You know all things; You know that I love You." Jesus said to him, "Feed My sheep."

How much do you want to walk with God?

God is looking for those with great faith, for people He can stretch beyond where they are today. He is looking for people who are so dedicated to Him that they will carry on—no matter what comes in the "in-between" times.

Can you ignore pain? Can you sail through struggle? Will you walk through unprepared-for events in life while keeping your eyes on Him alone? If you can, then God wants you!

This is His mandate: in His name, serve the present generation for which He died. Pick up His cross and follow in His footsteps, seeking "to save that which was lost" (Luke 19:10 NKJV).

Pray this prayer with me:

God, give me great faith to better serve You and represent Your kingdom. Send me, Lord; use me to fulfill Your will among men. Where You lead, I will follow. In Jesus' name I pray. Amen.

June 24

Do Not Quit Now!

Today's Scripture Reading: Luke 9:62; Deuteronomy 7:9 *Key Verse:* Deuteronomy 7:9

Know that the L*ORD your God, He is God, the faithful God who keeps covenant and mercy for a thousand generations with those who love Him and keep His commandments.*

Get ready. Critical things are taking place, and you need to prepare yourself for them. You need to be strong and grow in faith.

What happens in the "in between" requires you to have so much faith that you follow God *regardless* of what happens. You keep going because you know that God will get you where He ordained.

Why does the "wilderness" in our lives exist anyway? Why does He allow things to happen that would take out the average saint, much less a worldly person? God wants to demonstrate that He is able to keep us.

His whole purpose with the children of Israel was to show all other nations that He was able to provide for His people. They were to be a living testimony. God wanted to show mankind that the Israelites could go through everything that came their way because He personally kept them.

Do not quit now. Do not put your hand to the plow of faith and look back (Luke 9:62). Let God show Himself strong on your behalf. Then make sure that you give Him all the glory. Pray this prayer before you go "out there" again:

Lord, the pressure seems unbearable, but I can bear it in You. The heat of criticism and conflict almost threatens to burn me, but I will prevail in Your name. The goal seems too far away for me to ever reach it, yet I will because You said so. I refuse to give up on You because You refuse to give up on me. I bless Your name and thank You in advance for victory.

Stuck in the Sand with Hope in Hand

Today's Scripture Reading: Hebrews 11:6, 8–19 *Key Verse:* Hebrews 11:6

Without faith it is impossible to please Him, for he who comes to God must believe that He is, and that He is a rewarder of those who diligently seek Him.

To seek something *diligently* means hard work—and lots of it. It means staying with a project even though God did not explain what would happen. Diligence means following through with God's plan even though adversities or trials catch you off guard. It means continuing to seek Him no matter what happens or does not happen.

The problem with the children of Israel in the wilderness was that they stopped seeking God as soon as He delivered them from Pharaoh's shadow. They got caught up in the moment, the now, the "in between." Trust me, the "in between" does not matter when compared to the far greater destination God has ordained for you.

Are you stuck right now in the "in between"? Are you saying, "God, You did not tell me about this!" If God had forewarned you about what you would face in the "in between," you would have said "no." Do not die in the wilderness. Do what Abraham did when he took his son, Isaac, to make a sacrifice in the land of Moriah: get diligent faith that pushes forward even when you cannot see any sense in it.

Pray this prayer with me:

Lord, here I am, "in between" the problem and the promise. I am stuck in the sands of adversity with the bondage of the past behind me and nothing but the distant hope of Your promise before me. Yet I will trust You, for You are faithful. I will bless You, for You are worthy. I will worship You, for the only freedom I have ever known has come from You alone.

JUNE 26

WHAT IS HAPPENING TO ME?

Today's Scripture Reading: Psalm 23 *Key Verse:* Psalm 23:4

Yea, though I walk through the valley of the shadow of death,
I will fear no evil;
For You are with me;
Your rod and Your staff, they comfort me.

Does the idea of facing the "in between" scare you? Do not let it intimidate you. God is the God of the "in between" as well! David knew this truth and wrote about it in the Twenty-third Psalm. He called it *tsalmaveth*, "the shadow of death." So did Job, Jeremiah, Isaiah, and Amos. Death is mentioned in the term, but it refers even more to the *fear* of death.

Sometimes, in the middle of one of your most satisfying times with the Lord, you sense that you do not really feel like yourself. Unless it clearly stems from a physical problem, and assuming that you have been taking care of the basics in your Christian walk, nothing is wrong with you. You have just raised your commitment level.

You heard the voice of God directing you to come up higher, and you obeyed. You became a tither, or perhaps you became more faithful in keeping your word. Maybe you started witnessing and became unashamed of the gospel of Jesus Christ. Things started happening, and life began to change. It is no wonder that you are not feeling like you used to. You are a new person in a different place.

I have good and bad news for you, depending on how you react to it: you are simply in the "in-between" time. Keep going. The promised land is straight ahead!

Pray this prayer with me:

Lord Jesus, I was not prepared for the jet lag of my spiritual journey. One moment I was in a pit crying out to You. The next moment I was free and on my way to the paradise You promised. Then I woke up in the desert with a dry mouth and an aching heart. What is happening to me? I know—it is the "in-between" time, the wilderness again. I will keep walking and hoping in You, even in the middle of the valley of the shadow. I know You are with me—even here.

REMOVE THE "MIGHT" IN THE "IN BETWEEN"

Today's Scripture Reading: Deuteronomy 6:20–25 *Key Verse:* Deuteronomy 6:23

Then He brought us out from there, that He might bring us in, to give us the land of which He swore to our fathers.

What a testimony! "Then God brought us out." There is no doubt that God brought us out, and nobody else gets the glory. God brought us out—not Mama, Daddy, Moses, or even Pastor Jones.

The scary part for us should be the place where God says He brought them out so that He "might" bring them in. God rescues us and brings us out with His mighty hand so that He "might" bring us in.

Since God can do whatever He wants to do, there must be something tied up in this "might." The problem where the "might" comes in is found in the "in between." You can go out of Egypt and head straight for the promised land, or you can get sidetracked in doubt and disbelief and die in the wilderness. The "might" has more to do with you than with Him. God is faithful to keep His promises; it is your part that is in doubt.

The solution is simple: press through that wilderness. Remove the "might" in the "in-between" place. Push on to the other side of "in between" and give God all the glory.

Pray this prayer with me:

> *Lord God, things do not look very good right now, but I know You brought me out so You could bring me in. I know You will keep Your word if I will keep mine, so I will keep going until You see me through. Bless You, Lord, in Jesus' name I pray. Amen.*

June 28

I Am Glad You Made Me for More Than This

Today's Scripture Reading: Matthew 8:23–27 *Key Verse:* Matthew 8:24

Suddenly a great tempest arose on the sea, so that the boat was covered with the waves. But He was asleep.

Going through the "in between" really is not a problem—if you obey all the commandments and observe all the statutes. When the disciples took a short boat ride with Jesus, they knew there was something special about Him, but experience also told them they were in real trouble when a wild storm began to swamp their boat. They were "in between" a crisis and a miracle while Jesus slept in the boat, but fear got the best of them.

It is like going on a roller-coaster ride. The only rides I trust at amusement parks are merry-go-rounds because I can see where I am going. They are more predictable. I do not get on things that go up and down and propel me into a blind zone with violent force.

Once upon a time I thought I would like a roller-coaster ride. I foolishly believed the things claimed on the sign that stood at the front of the line: first, if you had a good heart and were taller than a certain height, then you could take this ride; second, it was guaranteed that you would get to the end, and you would have the experience of a lifetime. The problem is that the sign said nothing about what happened "in between" those two claims.

I took the ride and thought that I was going to die! I thought my insides were going to come out, but I survived nevertheless. Why? Because I knew when I got on the ride that an end would follow that naive beginning.

Now I am guaranteeing you that if you follow instructions, regardless of what happens or what you see and feel, *you will get through*. Your wilderness may turn into the roller-coaster ride of your life. Just hang on, and you will get through! Jesus is riding right next to you, and He is no more worried there than He was in the rocking boat in the middle of a storm two thousand years ago.

Pray this prayer with me:

Lord Jesus, my world seems ready to explode. Down seems up, and up seems down, and I do not feel like I am up to anything. I really would be worried except for two all-important facts: I know You are with me and will never leave me; and You created me for more than this "in-between" place. Thank You for taking me through this.

JUNE 29

THERE IS NO BETTER PRAISE TIME THAN WILDERNESS TIME

Today's Scripture Reading: Acts 16:20–34 *Key Verses:* Acts 16:23, 25

When they had laid many stripes on them, they threw them into prison, commanding the jailer to keep them securely . . . But at midnight Paul and Silas were praying and singing hymns to God, and the prisoners were listening to them.

Do you feel that everything in your life has come to a complete stop? I assure you that God has a reason for it. Reason had nothing to do with the prayers and hymns Paul and Silas offered to God. Everything looked bad and like it was getting worse for them. Reason walked out the door when they were unlawfully beaten and imprisoned, but the Spirit of praise was just warming up.

God's ultimate purpose for putting you "in check" is to see if you are concerned about what He originally told you in the secret place. Are you still focused on the pure word He gave you about His destiny for you? Are you still determined to accomplish His will above all others?

God's chief concern is the purpose to which He called you. He wants you to stay on track. Are you running a one-hundred-yard dash or a marathon? Even more important, which one did He tell you to run? God wants you to be close to Him. "The closer you are to Me, the less you will mess up," says the Father. Once you fall deeply in love with Him, you will not want to hurt or grieve God in any way.

Take advantage of this delay to fall more in love with Jesus. It will do your heart good.

Pray this prayer with me:

Lord Jesus, is my life over? Did all my usefulness in the kingdom suddenly evaporate? No, You made me for a divine purpose, and it will come to pass. I love You more than ever, Lord. I will use this wilderness time to lift up Your name out loud. I will shout Your praises from every windswept cliff and recount Your mighty acts from every deep valley. By the time I pass through this dry place, Your name will echo in every corner of its expanse!

I LOVE YOU FOR YOU, NOT FOR WHAT YOU DO

Today's Scripture Reading: Romans 5:5–10 *Key Verse:* Romans 5:8

God demonstrates His own love toward us,
in that while we were still sinners, Christ died for us.

In the days when I did a lot of premarital counseling, I used to ask every couple, "Can you marry this person and be reasonably happy if he or she does not make another change in his or her life? Do not marry this person with that hope. Do not marry him because 'he's got potential.' Can you be happy if he or she stays just the way he or she is?" I told them bluntly that if their answer was no, then it was not time to marry.

We have a similar problem in the church. Jesus laid down His life for us when we had no potential at all. What is the nature of your love for Him? Can you say to God right now, "Father, I will love You even if You do not give me a better position and my life stays the same until I die. I will still love and serve You"?

Have you humbled yourself to the point that you will serve Him even if you are called to clean toilets the rest of your days?

God has a big problem: most of us are trying to be something we are not. We have too many people with high aspirations and a very short timetable. "But God sent me here to fulfill a ministry." Well, if God sent you, then the timing and plan are in His hands. Whenever God wants to release you, He will do just that.

Pray this prayer with me:

Lord, I appreciate all the things You have done for me, and I appreciate the new beginning and the bright future You have given me. Yet most of all, I just love You. If nothing spectacular or exciting happens the rest of my life, it will not change a thing. I love You because of who You are, not simply because of what You do for me. I bless, praise, and worship You in Jesus' name, amen.

July

Understanding Authority

JULY 1

EXCUSE ME, DEVIL; IT'S DINNERTIME

Today's Scripture Reading: Psalm 23 *Key Verse:* Psalm 23:1

The LORD is my shepherd;
I shall not want.

Everybody loves this verse. "I shall not want" means that God gives you not only what you need, but also what you want.

Most people forget, however, that a shepherd is a leader. If you are not letting Jesus lead you, then you will not get what you want.

Everybody wants the anointing: "You prepare a table before me in the presence of my enemies; / You anoint my head with oil; / My cup runs over" (Ps. 23:5 NKJV). Yes, everyone wants the anointing, but the anointing comes only when you are able to face your enemy at the table God has prepared. Let me put it another way: He will not anoint you until you get in your enemy's face. Even then, the Lord will not anoint you until you smile at your enemy and say, "I am in charge."

You have the authority. Your Good Shepherd led you here and prepared a table for you right in front of your enemies. Now it is your turn. Stand up in the name of the Lord and declare:

I do not care how you got here, enemy; and I do not care what you think you are doing. I expected you to come here. I knew I was going to have tribulations in this world, so you are no surprise. Guess what? You cannot hinder what God has ordained for me because He is my Shepherd. I am supposed to be here because He led me here. Now I am going to enjoy a heavenly feast right before your eyes, and there is nothing you can do about it. In Jesus' name, I am in control.

Thank You, Lord, for leading and guiding me into all righteousness. You are my Light and my Salvation. Amen.

July 2

I Am Coming Out to Take My Seat

Today's Scripture Reading: Psalm 23; Isaiah 54:11–17 *Key Verse:* Isaiah 54:17

"No weapon formed against you shall prosper,
And every tongue which rises against you in judgment
You shall condemn.
This is the heritage of the servants of the LORD,
And their righteousness is from Me," says the LORD.

God, why have You not taken care of this enemy?"

God is not going to move your enemies out of your way for you. He has already given you authority and power over them. He prepared a table before you in the presence of your enemies.

God does not move your enemy because He wants your enemy to see you blessed. Your job is to concentrate on Him. If you focus on your enemy, then you will miss your blessing.

God prepared your daily bread even before you got up. If you are worried about your enemy, however, you will miss the fresh provision and refreshment your God has prepared.

You must see and understand that there is no enemy on earth that can rule you, and there is no weapon formed against you that can prosper—unless you let them. God would rather see you sit down and eat His feast right in front of your enemies than cower under the table. He has given you authority. Do you have the faith and courage to walk in it?

Pray this prayer with me:

Lord, I am coming out from under the table. I do not care how many enemies, obstacles, fears, or bondages from the past surround me; as long as You are with me, I will confront them face-to-face. Thank You for this victory meal. In Jesus' name, let us feast together!

July 3

My Aim Is to Be Lead Servant

Today's Scripture Reading: Philippians 2:12–13 *Key Verses:* Philippians 2:12–13

Work out your own salvation with fear and trembling; for it is God who works in you both to will and to do for His good pleasure.

The leaders in industry, education, politics, sports, and technical achievement reach their positions of leadership only through personal sacrifice and a significant investment of their abilities and resources.

In the same manner, you cannot sit in a seat of authority next to Jesus without paying a price. You must lay down your life for the Lord before you can put your foot on the neck of the enemy. Leadership always costs.

All across this nation, people are preaching popular messages that say we can come to God and get what we want or need without making a deposit or an investment. They claim that there is no price to pay to be a ruler in the kingdom. They are preaching some book other than the Bible.

On one hand, it is true that Jesus "paid it all." He did pay the supreme price so you would not have to bear the penalties for your sins. Yet there is still another price *you* must pay to ascend into the mountain of God. Jesus paid the price of redemption to get you through the gate. Now, according to Paul the apostle, it is up to you to work out or "walk out" your own salvation with fear and trembling.

Kingdom leadership requires faith, obedience, diligence, and a humble servant's heart. No one listens to a ruler in authority who has not paid the price. You must earn the right to speak by serving others. You earn the right to lead by submitting to those who lead you; you earn the right to exercise authority by submitting to those in authority over you. In obvious contrast to popular American culture, there are no shortcuts or "fast tracks" in God's kingdom. Jesus said it all when He told His disciples, "If anyone desires to be first, he shall be last of all and servant of all" (Mark 9:35 NKJV).

Pray this prayer with me:

Father, grant me the grace to serve with a pure heart that I may be qualified to lead in humble righteousness. Wherever I end up, I know that You are working within me both to desire and to do Your perfect will. Let Your will be done in Jesus' name. Amen.

ARE YOU A JUDGE OR A TRUE FRIEND?

Today's Scripture Reading: Matthew 7:1–5; Ephesians 4   *Key Verse:* Matthew 7:1

Judge not, that you be not judged.

The King who sits on the throne has given us the right and the authority to judge. Yet this Scripture passage appears to say that we are not to judge. The context or surrounding discussion tells us this is not a contradiction, but a clarification. We do have the right to judge, but we are not to judge one another. We are to judge the world and the world system.

There is a place for exercising discernment in the body of Christ, however. The prerequisite is this: you must remove the beam or wooden plank from your own eye before you presume to point out a splinter in someone else's. This rule tends to bring us all back to reality quickly. Examine and judge yourself first, and step in line with God.

Once you do that, you are responsible to look after the welfare of your spiritual brothers and sisters. That does not mean you should make yourself a busybody, a self-appointed "God cop," or a gossip practicing under the guise of "sharing caring prayer requests." Anyone who does this will reap exactly what he sows.

When we see those we love falling into sin or struggling with a difficult burden in their walk, we are authorized to "speak the truth in love" with a pure heart (see Eph. 4:15). We must do this in the compassion, love, and grace of God. Our motivation must not be to pull them down but to lift them up by removing deception and restoring the bonds of unconditional love.

Pray this prayer with me:

Lord Jesus, I confess that I need help from my church family. They can see the blind spots in my life that I cannot see. They have the objectivity I need to find my way in difficult and confusing situations. Above all, their unconditional love and godly faith are indispensable to my growth in the kingdom. Finally, I know they need these things from me as well. Grant me the grace to serve them in humility and gentleness as we all grow up in You.

Take Your Seat and Put Your Feet Up

Today's Scripture Reading: Ephesians 1–2 *Key Verses:* Ephesians 1:22–23, 2:6

He put all things under His feet, and gave Him to be head over all things to the church, which is His body, the fullness of Him who fills all in all . . . and raised us up together, and made us sit together in the heavenly places in Christ Jesus.

The only way you can accomplish God's kingdom agenda is by obeying Him. Obedience places you on another level. As one "under authority," you are entrusted with authority as a representative of God!

This happens only when you obey God and are found "in Christ" (Rom. 8:1 NKJV). Only then can you activate and walk in the Father's promise to God the Son: "I will make Your enemy Your footstool" (see Ps. 110:1). Who is the enemy? There is only one enemy here, because there are only two forces in confrontation: the Spirit of the Lord and the spirit of darkness. We are to systematically put down everything that comes against the Spirit of the Lord.

Paul said in his letter to the Ephesians that we are seated with Christ Jesus in the heavenlies. This means we have the delegated authority and responsibility as His earthly representatives to put under our feet everything that comes against God's Spirit and anointing. Now put your feet up and rest for a while in Christ's authority. It is kingdom-building time.

Pray this prayer with me:

Lord Jesus, my chief aim in life is to love and obey You, follow You, and believe Your Word. That is all You require for me to enjoy full kingdom rights as a king and priest in Your kingdom. You gave Your all for me; I give my all to You. Now I am seated with You at the right hand of the Almighty, with Your enemies under Your feet.

July 6

I Am a God-Carrier

Today's Scripture Reading: Ephesians 6:10–18; Zechariah 4:6 *Key Verse:* Ephesians 6:12

We do not wrestle against flesh and blood, but against principalities, against powers, against the rulers of the darkness of this age, against spiritual hosts of wickedness in the heavenly places.

We are in a war. We are replacing man's flawed agenda with God's eternal kingdom agenda in the local church, in the community, and in our nation.

When you walk in your God-given authority, you can literally influence the spiritual climate wherever you go—even in the nation's capitol. You do not need to beg for anything. Simply go in, knowing who you are, and change the spiritual climate.

When the Spirit of the Lord dwells in you, your very presence can alter the atmosphere. After all, didn't the Lord say to Zerubbabel through Zechariah the prophet: "Not by might nor by power, *but by My Spirit*" (Zech. 4:6 NKJV, emphasis mine)? What spirit will you carry with you throughout the day?

Pray this prayer with me:

Lord, it is so easy to forget how battles are won. I keep thinking I am fighting against people or human institutions—I am not. Since I am enforcing Your kingdom rule in the heavenlies, I am fighting against spiritual adversaries, not people. Only Your Spirit can win this battle; my own might, power, or accumulated knowledge cannot. Today I march to war in the Spirit and not in the flesh. In Jesus' name I pray. Amen.

THE ONLY COMMAND IN THIS WAR IS "CHARGE!"

Today's Scripture Reading: John 18:36 *Key Verse:* John 18:36

Jesus answered, "My kingdom is not of this world. If My kingdom were of this world, My servants would fight, so that I should not be delivered to the Jews; but now My kingdom is not from here."

John 18:36 is probably one of the most misquoted Scriptures in the Bible, which may explain why most of us do not understand the kingdom. The first part of the verse, "My kingdom is not of this world," is not an excuse for the church to withdraw from the world and go into hiding. Our unlawful retreat has allowed the world's systems to have their way, and now they are paralyzing us!

Ironically, most of our casualties occur while we do our best to *avoid* confrontation with the world's systems. We hide in our comfortable religious bunkers and systematically retreat rather than advance because we do not think we have the authority or jurisdiction to take on the world's systems.

We serve a kingdom that is not of this world, but the King reclaimed the earth when He rose from the dead. Why would God give you a seat of authority with the privilege of resting your foot on your enemy's neck if there was no conflict? Souls are at stake, and a harvest is coming. Where do they come from? We snatch them out of the flames of hell and wrestle them from the fiery grip of the devil!

Jesus won the battle, but He expects us to handle the mop-up and occupation operations! Why do we gather in stadiums and churches to lick our wounds like a defeated army waiting for emergency evacuation? We seem to want somebody to preach something to make us feel good so we can go back home and continue to be oppressed, and brokenhearted until the next meeting. This sad victim cycle will continue until we stand up in Jesus' name and engage the kingdoms of this world in boldness and power!

Do not excuse yourself from military service any longer. The King has called and appointed you; now go out and aggressively engage the kingdoms of this world. You have the power, the authority, and the mind of Christ. Nothing and no one can stop you—except you.

Lord, today I accept my commission in Your invasion and occupation army. I will be gentle with people, but brutal with the enemy. I do it all in Jesus' name.

THE SPIRIT OF THE LORD IS UPON YOU

Today's Scripture Reading: Luke 4:18–19 *Key Verse:* Luke 4:18

The Spirit of the LORD is upon Me,
Because He has anointed Me
To preach the gospel to the poor;
He has sent Me to heal the brokenhearted,
To proclaim liberty to the captives
And recovery of sight to the blind,
To set a liberty those who are oppressed.

Whose Spirit is upon us? *The Lord's.*
To whom are we to preach the gospel? *The poor.*
To whom are we sent with healing power? *The brokenhearted.*
What are we to proclaim? *Liberty.*
To whom do we proclaim liberty? *The captives.*
To whom do we proclaim recovery of sight? *The blind.*
And whom are we sent to liberate? *The oppressed.*

This is the kingdom agenda. Notice that it begins with the destruction of the spirit of poverty. Everything Jesus said after that is connected to the leading spirit, the spirit of poverty. The kingdom agenda is not about money; it is about the kingdom in all its beauty and complexity. And all of it is based on obedience.

Another question: despite Jesus' command, to whom do we direct most of our ministry, money, resources, and attention? Answer: *to the well-off, the whole, the free, the redeemed, the ruling saints seated in comfortable, upholstered pews in expensive buildings in nice neighborhoods.* (I will leave the meaning of this to you . . .)

It is time for us, as the church, to return to our God-given plan for taking the enemy's territory.

Pray this prayer with me:

Lord Jesus, I receive Your calling as my own. I can presume to fulfill it only through Your strength, power, and authority, and not my own. Thank You for the privilege of taking the good news to those who are desperate for any news that brings them hope.

July 9

We Have the Solution—Do We Have the Resolution?

Today's Scripture Reading: Isaiah 58:5–12 *Key Verse:* Isaiah 58:11

The Lord will guide you continually,
And satisfy your soul in drought,
And strengthen your bones;
You shall be like a watered garden,
And like a spring of water, whose waters do not fail.

God made this promise to those who minister to the poor and the broken. It is part of Isaiah's "fast of the Lord" in Isaiah 58. It is the kind of practical fast that always pleases God. One of the most unique parts of this promise says, "Those from among you / Shall build the old waste places; / You shall *raise up the foundations of many generations;*/ And you shall be called the Repairer of the Breach, / The Restorer of Streets to Dwell In" (Isa. 58:12 NKJV, emphasis mine).

To raise up the fallen and cursed foundations of "many generations" takes more than one church service. This kind of transgenerational deliverance happens only when we prove ourselves worthy, ascend to the hill of the Lord, sit in our seat, and as God has ordained, bless those who have less.

It is then that God blesses us and says, "Now you can raise up generations that have fallen. You will have the ability to lift them up and repair the torn and divided places. You will have the power to restore entire cities to the kingdom in My name."

This one promise provides the solution to every problem we have in America (even without the assistance of the Senate or the House of Representatives)! We will never see such deliverance, however, until the church begins to understand and operate in kingdom principles. It all begins with you, me, and the other individual believers who comprise the body of Christ.

Pray this prayer with me:

Lord, You really have given us everything we need to succeed and establish Your kingdom in the earth. All I have to bring to the table is my will, my weakness, my total dependence on You, and my faith in Your promises. The rest is recorded at the end of the Book—we win. In Jesus' name, help me to fulfill Your will and my destiny in Your kingdom.

July 10

Restore the Covenant and Raise Up the Poor

Today's Scripture Reading: 1 Samuel 2:8; Isaiah 58:6–12 *Key Verse:* 1 Samuel 2:8a

He raises the poor from the dust / And lifts the beggar from the ash heap,
To set them among princes / And make them inherit the throne of glory.

Even as we sit in our seat of authority with Christ in the heavenlies, we have an urgent mandate to deal with the spirit of poverty according to Isaiah's landmark prophecy. We tend to ignore this spirit altogether, blame its victims for their own plight, or charge in headlong in our own strength and resources. All three choices are rooted in error and only make the problem worse.

The truth is that we will never be free from this spirit ourselves or extend biblical compassion to those in its shadow until we address poverty from a biblical point of view. The spirit of poverty derives directly from the breaking of covenant, from the disobedience of the church concerning the principles of God. We are not doing what God ordained—we have failed to care for the poor and left the job to the secular state. Our sin has created a void in the spirit realm. The adversary has been only too willing to fill that void with alternatives or consequences that have brought spiritual slavery to millions and enhanced his own dark kingdom.

Just as Adam's original sin brought a curse on all mankind, so have the church's sins of commission and omission over the centuries brought multiplied pain and misery to mankind. Now it is up to us to repent and follow in the footsteps of our Redeemer to bring restoration, healing, and redemption to society through the gospel.

Pray this prayer with me:

Lord, search my heart and reveal any wrongdoing in me. I repent of my neglect, blindness, and inaction concerning the poor and impoverished. I resist evil in the name of Jesus and command it to flee. I declare a "year of Jubilee" and a season of fresh beginnings for those who trust in Jesus' name. Amen.

July 11

Locate Your Dislocation

Today's Scripture Reading: Ephesians 4:15–16 *Key Verse:* Ephesians 4:16

The whole body, joined and knit together by what every joint supplies, according to the effective working by which every part does its share, causes growth of the body for the edifying of itself in love.

Have you ever dislocated a joint or experienced debilitating pain when something in your back seemed to slip out of place? Aside from the immediate discomfort of the situation, you usually feel tingling in the affected limb and perhaps even some dizziness and muscle weakness. You definitely do not feel like doing your work or moving around much!

Why is it that nine out of every ten churches in this country (according to my estimation) do not impact even the single block of property their building occupies? The answer is that they are out of joint. They are out of the *order* of God; therefore, the *power* of God is missing from the homes and lives of their people, individually and corporately. We can never have God's power unless we come into agreement with one another and into God's order at home and at church.

Health professionals agree that dislocated joints must be put back in place to restore proper function and full strength to human bodies. The Great Physician is hard at work on the partially paralyzed church body. At times He gently manipulates a misplaced bone until it voluntarily slips back into place. In the worst cases, He must forcibly move a bone from dislocation to proper placement to the accompaniment of loud howls and cries of pain.

He *will* conform us to the image of His Son, even if it hurts. It is the only way to restore full function, strength, and communication ("nerve function") to the disjointed body of Christ.

Examine your life. Is it in line with God's order, or is there a painful misalignment somewhere? If something is out of line, yield to the gentle touch of the Holy Spirit and voluntarily slip back into place. Life is much more joyful and productive when everything is in its proper place.

Pray this prayer with me:

Lord, I have put up with this "limp" for too long. The "ache in my shoulder" and the "catch in my back" have made me less than I am. Holy Spirit, show me where my life, my marriage, my home, or my ministry is out of order. Lord, help me to put things back in their proper place and order so I can serve You with all my strength. In Jesus' name I pray. Amen.

DISCARD YOUR "RIGHTEOUS LYNCH MOB" CREDENTIALS

Today's Scripture Reading: 1 Samuel 26 *Key Verse:* 1 Samuel 26:9

David said to Abishai, "Do not destroy him; for who can stretch out his hand against the Lord's anointed, and be guiltless?"

When sin shows up in a leader, the church tends to take on a lynch-mob mentality, much like a mob of revenge-crazed townspeople in an old Western movie. God does not work that way, however.

When Nathan the prophet went to confront King David about his sin with Bathsheba and the murder of her husband, Uriah the Hittite, he did not go to remove David from the throne. God sent him to remind David of his sins so he would repent (see 2 Sam. 12).

When Saul refused to fully repent for his disobedience, God took care of it, but He chose to handle the problem over a period of years instead of through the summary execution many of us would have favored.

If you were in David's place, would you have taken the opportunity to "strike a blow for justice" and kill the unjust King Saul when you had the chance? He did not. He said, "The LORD forbid that I should stretch out my hand against the LORD's anointed" (1 Sam. 26:11 NKJV).

It is our responsibility as the church in this nation to call people to repentance, to call them into the will of God. It is *not* our responsibility to interfere, meddle with, or hurry the process. Above all, we should never presume to condemn or punish God's anointed leaders apart from the biblical process He clearly describes in the New Testament.

Pray this prayer with me:

Lord Jesus, we give the church back to You today. It was always Yours, but for a while we thought it was ours and ran it that way. We release Your leaders too. You are big enough to clean up any messes they make, and You are wise and powerful enough to bring correction and rebuke when necessary—and You do. Thank You for using ordinary people to do extraordinary things in Your kingdom. In Jesus' name we pray. Amen.

JUDGMENT IS COMING TO YOUR HOUSE

Today's Scripture Reading: 1 Peter 4 *Key Verse:* 1 Peter 4:17, emphasis mine

The time has come for judgment to begin at the house of God; *and if it begins with us first, what will be the end of those who do not obey the gospel of God?*

The apostle Peter made this shocking statement nearly two thousand years ago, but somehow I sense God is saying this to us again. We have no idea how important our words and actions are in the plan of God, but we should. The world is watching.

The church should showcase the ideal. We should be standing proof that our invisible God is real and very much alive. Instead, our actions seem to say He is a liar or totally nonexistent. That is about to change.

In Saul's day a government gone wrong nearly destroyed its people. The same thing is happening today. When the house of God, the church, sets itself in order according to God's Word, it will operate in supernatural power, vision, and authority as never before.

The true church, the separated church, has every solution the world needs. We have the authority and supernatural wisdom needed to right society's wrongs and bring order wherever chaos reigns, but it all begins at the cross.

Pray this prayer with me:

Lord Jesus, today I return to the place where You first introduced me to the Father's true order—I return to the cross. Once again I confess my sin, as I have so often before. Although You have already saved me, I ask that You cleanse me anew today. Let my life be a visible proof that You live and love the people You created. May Your kingdom order be reestablished in my life today.

JULY 14

LEAD THEM, DO NOT "POLL" THEM

Today's Scripture Reading: 2 Timothy 4:1–5 *Key Verses:* 2 Timothy 4:3–4

The time will come when they will not endure sound doctrine,
but according to their own desires, because they have itching ears,
they will heap up for themselves teachers; and they will turn
their ears away from the truth, and be turned aside to fables.

Are you a leader in the church? Do not try to lead sheep by following sheep. You cannot do both. You either will lead them and do what God has ordained for you to do, or you will scratch their "itching ears" by following their every whim and wish and end up somewhere else.

Politicians try this ploy all the time, and with disastrous results for the electorate. They wake up in the morning and check the opinion polls to find out what their "firm opinions" will be that day! These so-called leaders are simply handing out sweets to win approval. This is not leadership; this is candy distributorship.

You do an injustice to the people who follow you if you do not lead them. God always gives His anointed leaders a "mantle" or special ability to do the job He assigns them. It may be tough sometimes, but to do anything less than lead is to rank the God who chose you as second-rate Himself! The same principle holds true in the home, on the job, and in the community. Are you leading or following those God placed under your authority?

Pray this prayer with me:

Lord, the only opinion I need to heed is Your opinion as revealed in Your Word, in prayer, and by direct revelation. I will listen to the opinions and wishes of others, but I will make my decisions on the solid bedrock of Your unchanging Word. In Jesus' name I pray. Amen.

JULY 15

IT IS THE HEART THAT MATTERS

Today's Scripture Reading: 2 Samuel 15; Hebrews 13:17 *Key Verse:* Hebrews 13:17

Obey those who rule over you, and be submissive, for they watch out for your souls, as those who must give account. Let them do so with joy and not with grief, for that would be unprofitable for you.

We need to understand something about God's divine order. Many people think that true Christianity is cultic and controlling. It is true that some leaders have abused their authority, but in God's viewpoint, it is the heart that matters.

As a pastor, I am the father of my church. Some people do not like that, and they give all sorts of excuses. But it is Bible truth. Paul said he ministered to people "as a father does his own children" (1 Thess. 2:11 NKJV). He also wrote, "You do not have many fathers; for in Christ Jesus I have begotten you through the gospel" (1 Cor. 4:15 NKJV).

Do not allow the Absalom spirit to have reign in your church. It delights in pitting young leadership against old leadership. What the younger ones do not understand is that they must attain the *heart* of the older spiritual leadership to even prosper.

Differences of opinion will always come, but sin enters when we discard God's anointed leader in the name of personal opinion. The anointing does not make anyone perfect, but it does provide a special ability to find God's way and lead in the midst of conflicting choices. What will happen if the senior leader makes a wrong decision—will God fall off of His throne? Will the kingdom come crashing down? Will the power of the Cross be made void? No.

Give God's leaders the freedom to make mistakes from time to time. Put every situation in the hands of God and pray often for your leaders. The Lord will make a course correction when necessary. If you have a different opinion, then make your case to a leader with respect as you would to a father (see 1 Tim. 5:1). Then give him the freedom to make a decision and stand by it. Give him the same grace and support you would want if you stood in his shoes.

Pray this prayer with me:

Heavenly Father, I choose to honor the spiritual leaders you have given and placed over me. Thank You for their leadership. Continue to guide and direct them, and give me grace to submit to their authority and to learn and receive from them with an open heart. In Jesus' name I pray. Amen.

ARE YOU AN ORPHAN?

Today's Scripture Reading: 1 Corinthians 4:14–17 *Key Verse:* 1 Corinthians 4:15

Though you might have ten thousand instructors in Christ, yet you do not have many fathers; for in Christ Jesus I have begotten you through the gospel.

Paul spoke forcefully about the existence and importance of spiritual fathers in his first letter to the Corinthians. A father is one whom God sovereignly chooses to pass on his heart and spiritual legacy to you as a divine inheritance for the future. A father shoots you into the future as an arrow of God's anointing, power, and purpose, bearing the accumulated obedience of many generations in your heart.

I am a firm believer in the priesthood of all believers and in the finished work of Jesus Christ on the cross. No man can save us, but it is God's choice that a man should *lead* us—and God does not ask our opinion about the man ahead of time.

That fact forces us to either live as if there really is a God in heaven who is well able to lead, guide, and correct His earthly leaders, or to openly rebel against His order and establish our own. Many churches construct elaborate "fences" consisting of committee after committee to "protect" the sheep from possible abuses by the shepherd. In the process, these churches also create a fear and distrust of leaders and strong leadership in their people. This overreaction toward past abuses is an abuse in itself, because it creates an entire generation of "fatherless" Christians who are deprived of their inheritance through truly biblical relationships with God-anointed leaders.

Godly leaders operate in the fear of God, knowing He will hold them personally responsible for the way they deal with His flock. Ungodly leaders face an uncertain future, not knowing whether the God they spurn will give them their next breath or cut them off. One thing is certain: God is the chief protector of His sheep, and He knows every detail about their well-being. That should set us free to enjoy the relationship and impartation God ordained for undershepherds and His sheep.

Do you have a spiritual father or mother? Are you "parenting" a young Christian in the faith or in the ministry as Paul did? Pray this prayer with me:

Heavenly Father, I acknowledge my need for a spiritual father or mother, just as Timothy and John Mark needed the "fathering" of Paul. I also have an obligation to "reproduce" in spiritual "children" the gifts and callings You placed in me. I trust You to lead me into those relationships You have ordained. In Jesus' name, amen.

HONOR THE FATHER'S GIFTS

Today's Scripture Reading: Ephesians 4:7–13; 1 Corinthians 12:18

Key Verses: Ephesians 4:11–12

He Himself gave some to be apostles, some prophets, some evangelists, and some pastors and teachers, for the equipping of the saints for the work of ministry, for the edifying of the body of Christ.

God wants us to honor His sovereignty and trust His ability to use ordinary flawed men and women as leaders (those are the only kind available to Him anyway). Most of us do not like the idea unless, of course, we happen to be the ones He has chosen. God's plan works because He knows all things, and because man's weaknesses, sins, and foolishness have never caught Him off guard.

Anointed human leaders are just that—they are very human people whom God has anointed for reasons only He knows. This means they go about their duties feeling all the same temptations and doubts that you do! God gives ordinary people His anointing to equip them for their assignment and to make up for their innate weaknesses and faults.

Church leaders should adopt a continual attitude of repentance, dependence, and gratitude. This explains why Jesus stressed servanthood so strongly when He prepared His disciples for leadership.

When God sends such leaders into a generation, He does not expect those leaders to accomplish His will when they are stuck with hundreds of lone rangers who each think he possesses a vision of equal importance to the leader's vision. Paul made it clear that we do not choose what body part we are to be in the church; it is God who sets us in place as it pleases Him (1 Cor. 12:18).

To submit to human leaders, when we know they are flawed just like we are, demands an even greater trust and faith in God. Yet in the end it all boils down to one question: is God really God, or is He not?

Pray this prayer with me:

Heavenly Father, even though I can see flaws and weaknesses in the leaders You put in my life, I can see Your hand and heart at work in them too. You placed a call upon my life also, and I know my own weaknesses all too well. I will honor the leaders You have given to me, and I will trust You to guide them even as I trust You to guide me each day. In Jesus' name I pray, amen.

YOU WILL REAP THE DISHONOR YOU SOW

Today's Scripture Reading: Romans 12, 13:7; 1 Timothy 5:17; Matthew 8:5–10

Key Verse: 1 Timothy 5:17

Let the elders who rule well be counted worthy of double honor, especially those who labor in the word and doctrine.

Do you realize that leaders in the secular realm get more respect than leaders in the spiritual realm? I can prove it to you.

When the president of the United States walks into the room, do you stand up? What happens when your pastor walks into the room?

If you do not stand up when the president walks in, you may get in a lot of trouble. Perhaps that is why we give more reverence to a man who represents a kingdom other than God's. It is clear that we underestimate the importance of honoring those in authority, and we pay a heavy price for it. When we model disrespect, rebellion, and the preeminence of self in front of our children, our employees, or our flock, then we can expect them to show the same things to us!

Do not complain when you think people reverence the pastor too much. If they are in error, it is better to err on the side of respect, honor, and humility in obedience to God than to err on the side of disrespect, dishonor, and pride. Tomorrow you may be on the phone asking that pastor for prayer and deliverance with that mentality staining your conscience.

Pray this prayer with me:

Lord Jesus, I know You have a plan for my life; and I know from Your Word that You placed me in my local church body. This means it is no accident that I am under the spiritual authority of the leaders in my church. Grant me the grace to give honor where honor is due and to do all things as if I was doing them specifically for You. As I honor and serve with the people You have chosen, I also become qualified to lead "as one under authority."

THE "PEOPLE'S CHOICE" CAN BE A DANGEROUS CHOICE

Today's Scripture Reading: 1 Samuel 8 *Key Verse:* 1 Samuel 8:7

The LORD said to Samuel, "Heed the voice of the people in all that they say to you; for they have not rejected you, but they have rejected Me, that I should not reign over them."

If you want to be anointed and move according to the Spirit of God, be very careful in how you respond to the people God places in your life. In His eyes, if you mistreat or misuse another Christian, then you have mistreated or misused Him! This applies especially to the way you respond (and talk about) those who are in authority over you.

Whether the authority is in the church or in the secular government, once you destroy that authority, the land becomes lawless. People in a lawless state refuse to respect the law or any other authority. This state of chaos has occurred repeatedly in human history during such upheavals as the French Revolution and in many European, Latin American, and African coups and civil wars over the past century.

Many times after rebel forces win control of a country, they decide to run everything by committee because it is the path of least resistance. Committees always try to do what is popular, but they often bypass the harder choices that are truly right.

The Israelites wanted to abandon God's government system using anointed priests, prophets, and judges, so God let them have exactly what they asked for. They wanted a human king, like the pagan nations around them had, so they got Saul. He looked good, he talked a smooth line, and he would do anything to please the people. He was even willing to disobey God and then lie about it. When God chose a replacement for him, Saul spent the rest of his life trying to kill God's anointed. It brought destruction to his family and division to his nation.

Do you really want a Saul ruling your life?

Pray this prayer with me:

Father, I refuse to exchange Your choice for "Saul, the people's choice." Even if I am unhappy with the decisions or actions of the leaders You have appointed, grant me the grace to love them and treat them with respect. They are Your servants, and You will bring wisdom and correction when necessary.

A Wrong Majority Does Not Make Right

Today's Scripture Reading: Numbers 13–14 *Key Verses:* Numbers 14:41–42, emphasis mine

Moses said, "Now why do you transgress the command of the LORD? For this will not succeed. Do not go up, lest you be defeated by your enemies, for the LORD is not among you."

God does nothing by chance or whim. He places people in leadership offices for very specific reasons, and how human and flawed the people may be does not matter. None of us would have chosen the twelve men Jesus chose as His disciples, yet He knew what He was doing.

Once we decide to voice our views, we sometimes like to force our opinion upon our leaders through weight of numbers. It does not work with God because our opinions have no power to change His plan and will, no matter how many of us line up to say our wrong opinion is right.

When the twelve spies issued their report on the promised land, the people refused to follow Moses' command to go up. Then, when they did decide to enter Canaan, it was too late. Moses told them not to go because God was not with them. Again, the Israelites chose to ignore and disobey their leader. They gathered their weapons and went to fight the Amalekites and Canaanites anyway.

The Israelites had such disrespect for their leadership that when leadership said go, they refused. Later on, when leadership said stay, they again refused and thus faced quick defeat. The majority of Israelites not killed in the futile battle died in the wilderness over the next forty years. To ignore or disobey the leaders God sets in place does not pay.

Do you have some attitudes that you need to change? Have you said some things you need to quickly retract and correct? If the Holy Spirit speaks to your heart as you read these words, do whatever He tells you to do, and do not delay. Your destiny may depend on it.

Pray this prayer with me:

Father, forgive me for the times I have harbored wrong or angry thoughts toward leaders in the church. Bless them, cover them, and lead them in Your wisdom and grace; and help me to receive and honor their leadership as gifts from Your hand. In Jesus' name I pray, amen.

July 21

God Is Enough

Today's Scripture Reading: Exodus 6:30–7:25 *Key Verse:* Exodus 6:30–7:2

Moses said before the Lord, "Behold, I am of uncircumcised lips,
and how shall Pharaoh heed me?"
So the Lord said to Moses: "See, I have made you as God to Pharaoh,
and Aaron your brother shall be your prophet.
You shall speak all that I command you."

Many years ago, God gave me this mandate: "God blessed them, and God said to them, 'Be fruitful and multiply; fill the earth and subdue it; have dominion over the fish of the sea, over the birds of the air, and over every living thing that moves on the earth'" (Gen. 1:28 NKJV).

So what gives me the right to say, "I am here to take over, not take sides"?

It does not come from my credentials, my training, or my personal accomplishments. My authority to say such a thing does not come from anything I have done or from any particular gift or ability that I possess. It comes from the Word of God and the destiny God sovereignly ordained for me. My authority comes from God's inexplicable decision to send me to the church and the nation with a message.

What has God called you to do? What has He said in His Word about it? You do not need anything or anyone else to give you authority. God is enough.

Lord God, Your Word and call are enough. You spoke to my heart and transformed my life. Now I owe my all to You. I am not called to take sides or mediate compromise. I am called to take over the enemy's territory for the kingdom of light, and I bless You in Jesus' name, amen.

July 22

Be Strong and Very Courageous

Today's Scripture Reading: Proverbs 29:25; Acts 9:26–29; Joshua 1:6–7 *Key Verse:* Proverbs 29:25

The fear of man brings a snare,
But whoever trusts in the Lord *shall be safe.*

Has God called you? Has He placed you before people? Then do not be afraid of them.

People do not scare me. When I go to a convention to preach, I go with the message God gives me. Sometimes preachers and host pastors get uptight when they see me coming because I do not necessarily say what they want to hear; I preach what God tells me to preach.

God will never place you before people to conform to their ways or ideas. He puts you there to transform them! You will confront demons that oppose your purpose for being there, but you have a kingdom agenda that must go forward.

The good news is that you do not have to walk in your own authority (you cannot anyway). God called, appointed, and anointed you to walk in His authority as His representative. Receive as your own the command God gave to Joshua just before he led Israel across the Jordan into the promised land: "Only be strong and very courageous, that you may observe to do according to all the law which Moses My servant commanded you; do not turn from it to the right hand or to the left, that you may prosper wherever you go" (Josh. 1:7 NKJV).

Now be bold and tackle great exploits in Jesus' name!

Pray this prayer with me:

Lord, I think I forgot about the need for courage in the Spirit-led life. You called me to do more than merely warm a pew. You called me to be a transformer, a courageous life-changer with the boldness to tell others the truth in love. Thank You for giving me Your strength, in Jesus name I pray, amen.

PRAY CONTINUALLY FOR THOSE IN YOUR CARE

Today's Scripture Reading: James 5:7–20 *Key Verse:* James 5:16

The effective, fervent prayer of a righteous man avails much.

If God delivered you and set you free, you are free indeed. You cannot help but be free when you know the truth. The Bible says Jesus came to destroy the work of the devil, and God wants you to know that it is finished.

The devil is not crazy, though. He knows that God has defeated him and sentenced him to the lake of fire (Rev. 20:10). Until the time comes when he will be bound and cast into that burning lake with death and Hades, the deceiver is doing his best to keep us from preaching this gospel of the kingdom. As long as the church remains clueless about God's plan for the kingdom, Jesus cannot come back. We have a job to do first, and we will not complete it until the church understands and fulfills its assignment.

The real reason the devil harasses you is to get at your Daddy. He cannot touch the Father, so he goes after His children. When you truly understand that you are a child of the King—if you ever get it in your heart and mind just how much God loves you—then you can tell Satan, "Devil, you have messed up. I am the child of the King. If you mess with me, you mess with Him; and He has decreed that no weapon formed against me shall prosper."

In the same way, you must understand that the devil will retarget his attack toward your children as you become kingdom-minded. When you become strong in the Word, he cannot bother you; so he will go after the people you love instead. For that reason, the more you grow in the Spirit, the more time you should spend on your knees praying for your children or other family members.

Pray this prayer with me:

Lord Jesus, thank You for setting me free indeed! Now I have a responsibility to pray continually for those You have placed in my care. Lord, I ask that You keep and protect my family in the power of Your name. Guide their steps and deliver them from every device of the evil one. May You be glorified in their lives. I commit them into Your hands, Lord. Thank You for all You have done, for all You shall do, and for who You are—the risen Lord, Messiah, and King of kings.

BUILD IT RIGHT SO YOU WILL NOT HAVE TO BUILD IT AGAIN

Today's Scripture Reading: Luke 6:46–49 *Key Verse:* Luke 6:46

Why do you call Me "Lord, Lord," and not do the things which I say?

These are strong words, but we are skilled at dismissing them with unspoken thoughts such as, He sure was tough with those disciples, wasn't He? (This implies that the Lord's question does not apply to modern-day disciples.)

The Bible is not "literature"; it is eternal truth. You cannot read it merely as something to evaluate, critique, catalog, and conveniently forget. The words of Jesus are as alive, vibrant, and penetrating today as they were two thousand years ago. They still have the supernatural power to cut to the heart and convict us of sin. The Master is still asking you and me that painful question: "Why do you call Me 'Lord' when you do not do the things I say?"

I do not want you to get bogged down in your recent sins of omission. He knows we are incapable of fulfilling all of His commands in our own strength and righteousness.

I want you instead to major on the majors, and the greatest theme Jesus preached throughout His ministry was the gospel of the kingdom. God is saying some vital kingdom things that we have not been doing. We have chosen to operate by a different set of rules and values, and they are killing us! Why? We cannot break God's laws; His laws break *us*. Jesus illustrated the importance of His question by comparing two men who built houses on different foundations: one on a rock and the other on shifting sands. We have tried to throw away the blueprints and building codes of the Father, and we are building our kingdom on sand with disastrous results.

There is no way that kingdom people can say, "Lord, Lord," and not do what He said to do. We have kingdom work to do. We must be about our Father's business, and we must go about it His way.

Pray this prayer with me:

Lord, You are the Builder. Today is the day I throw away my own plans and return to the master plan of Your kingdom. Forgive me for wandering from Your blueprints. From this day of new beginnings, I will build only upon the solid Rock of the kingdom, Jesus Christ, and every word that proceeds from Your mouth.

July 25

The Jesus in You Should Be Obvious!

Today's Scripture Reading: Acts 3–4 *Key Verses:* Acts 4:13–14

> *When they saw the boldness of Peter and John, and perceived that they were uneducated and untrained men, they marveled. And they realized that they had been with Jesus. And seeing the man who had been healed standing with them, they could say nothing against it.*

When you have genuine power and authority, you do not need to advertise or prove it. People who do that generally have an inferiority complex or some other self-esteem problem.

Peter and John did not brag about their Jesus Seminary degrees; they simply released the power of the kingdom into a crippled man's body and he was instantly set free. When the powers that be challenged the disciples' authority, they pointed to the King of kings and preached the gospel of the kingdom with unshakable confidence. It shook the Sanhedrin to the core.

One night I went to lift weights and saw a man who seemed to be nearly as wide in the shoulders as he was tall. The muscles of his chest were massive. He did not swagger, brag, or talk much, and he did not have to. He did not have to tell anyone in that place that he was strong; we could tell just by looking at him.

When you walk in the power of the kingdom gospel, you do not have to announce your authority or power. You do not have to prove it. Anytime you walk through a crowd of people, they can "see" it with a glance. Genuine kingdom people are called to take the message and power of the King into all the world with confidence and boldness.

I pray that more and more people will look at us and realize we have "been with Jesus"!

Lord Jesus, my job is simple. I go and do as You did. I speak Your Word, I do Your work, and I preach that Your kingdom is come. Grant me boldness to do more, dream more, dare more, and reap more for the kingdom, and to bring glory to Your name.

I KNOW YOU HAVE WORDS, BUT DO YOU HAVE POWER?

Today's Scripture Reading: Hebrews 12:1; 1 Corinthians 4:19–20

Key Verses: 1 Corinthians 4:19–20

I will come to you shortly, if the Lord wills, and I will know, not the word of those who are puffed up, but the power. For the kingdom of God is not in word but in power.

You have witnesses who testify to your authority.

When you walk into a room filled with friends, family, or coworkers and confront the very principalities of hell in their presence, they may ask you, "Who sent you?" Do not worry about who sent you. Jesus sent you, and when you speak all of heaven bears witness to what you say. Signs, wonders, and miracles will come because you spoke this gospel.

Is your marriage beginning to crumble? Speak this gospel. It does not matter what your spouse is like; it is God who honors the gospel. No demon or human being on earth or below can stand against the Word of God.

When you walk under the anointing, you can look your spouse in the eye and say, "You could have married somebody else, but you married me. Since you married me, you cannot help but be redeemed! Because you married me, you cannot help but treat me right; and you will never talk to me the way you did before. We are going to make this a good marriage, and God will affirm what I said because I said it!"

Pray this prayer with me:

Father, according to Your Word, an entire gallery of saints with the angelic hosts watches my progress in the kingdom from day to day. They wait and watch for the moment when I triumph in Your name. When I declare the gospel of the kingdom, I know signs and wonders will follow to confirm the Word and the authority You have given me. In Jesus' name I pray, amen.

PROCLAIM THE TRUTH BEYOND THE "FACTS"

Today's Scripture Reading: Daniel 3 *Key Verse:* Daniel 3:17

Our God whom we serve is able to deliver us from the burning fiery furnace, and He will deliver us from your hand, O king.

The three Hebrew men in Daniel's day put their trust in their unchanging God rather than in the ever-changing favor of men. We could learn something from their example. Nothing that happens in this nation or in the world can affect God's promises. Frankly, some of us need to stop watching so much television news programs. The national and international news networks may give us the raw data about the day's news, but they have no power to speak the truth. It is time for you to sit back and "tell your TV" the truth:

"Yes, employment is down, but God has a job for me."

"Yes, money is scarce, but my Father is rich in houses and land."

"Yes, I hear what you are saying, but I know what my God said: 'This Book of the Law shall not depart from your mouth, but you shall meditate in it day and night, that you may observe to do according to all that is written in it. For then you will make your way prosperous, and then you will have good success' [Josh. 1:8 NKJV]."

Speak with authority to those circumstances. God has given you His Word on it; you could not ask for anything more! He used the same method to speak the universe into existence where there was a void. How difficult can it be for your God to speak your blessings and provision into existence?

Pray this prayer with me:

All I need, Lord, is Your Word on my circumstances. You made a way for Noah, Abraham, Isaac, and Jacob. You met Joseph in the pit and promoted him to chief ruler under Pharaoh. You met Moses at the burning bush and used him in his old age to deliver a nation of slaves from the world's most powerful nation.

You touched the life of a humble shepherd and made him the greatest king in history, and you used a gentle maid to birth the salvation of mankind. Surely You are able to supply my few needs. I bless You and thank You for being Jehovah-Jireh, God my Provider, for all time. In Jesus' name I pray, amen.

July 28

My Job Description: Judge, King, Priest, and Light in Darkness

Today's Scripture Reading: 1 Corinthians 6:1–3 *Key Verse:* 1 Corinthians 6:3

Do you not know that we shall judge angels?
How much more, things that pertain to this life?

Paul said that the saints of God are destined to judge the world. We will judge even angels!

Unfortunately, we do not walk with that kind of authority right now. We are instruments of God's judgment on earth, but that judgment must be redemptive. That means our job is to remove the lies and distortions of the enemy so that people can see the truth of Christ and God's kingdom and respond to it.

We have waited and delayed long enough. Now it is time for us to stand on the truth of God's Word and step on Satan's neck! When things are wrong, we have a mandate to speak the truth in love and call it wrong regardless of what anybody else says.

We do not have God's permission to do this, however, with arrogance and condemnation. Our job, again, is to simply remove the obstacles so that people can see the truth. Our judging is not to condemn, but to liberate.

Pray this prayer with me:

Lord Jesus, my delight is to lift up Your name, Your Word, Your mighty deeds, and the gospel of Your kingdom to my generation. May my transformed life be Your light in the darkness, a beacon of hope for the hopeless. May it all be done through Your Spirit and to Your glory. Amen.

Make Disciples (Not Quickie Converts)

Today's Scripture Reading: Matthew 28:18–20 *Key Verses:* Matthew 28:18–19

Jesus came and spoke to them, saying, "All authority has been given to Me in heaven and on earth. Go therefore and make disciples of all the nations."

The final words of Jesus recorded in Matthew's gospel concern the source of Christ's authority and include His final command to us based on that authority. Jesus exercised only the authority that He received from His Father. In the same way, we must operate only within the authority we have received from Jesus Christ.

The Lord's final words to the church through the disciples constitute a dynamic, action-based, military-style commission or decree. After His resurrection from the dead, Jesus said, "*All authority* has been given to Me," and it applied to both realms—heaven and earth. Our assignment came next, and it was brief and to the point; it was our kingdom-building mandate: "Go therefore and make disciples."

Only a few of us have gone, and nearly none of us have made disciples. We prefer to take a shortcut and do the "onetime convert" thing. It takes time, commitment, and incredible patience to truly make disciples. You can build church attendance with quick converts, but to build the kingdom requires disciples. You can bequeath a denominational title or religious stereotype on a quickie convert, but only disciples can receive an impartation of *authority* based on relationship. Shortcut Christianity has to go; God wants nothing less than a kingdom of disciples, not a collection of skin-deep, name-only, greasy-grace converts.

Pray this prayer with me:

Lord Jesus, teach me how to reproduce in others what You did in my life. Show me how to share Your heart with the hurting and demonstrate Your love to the unloved. Help me make true disciples throughout my life for Your glory; in Jesus' name, amen.

FIND YOUR SPIRITUAL HOME AND STAY THERE

Today's Scripture Reading: 1 Corinthians 12:12–31 *Key Verse:* 1 Corinthians 12:18

God has set the members, each one of them, in the body just as He pleased.

Do not think it is so easy to leave and join a church. You should never join a church and submit to its "headship" or leadership unless God sends you there!

Where has God sent you? You need to find out where God wants you to go to church and then let Him plant you deep in the soil of that congregation so you can produce a fruitful harvest year after year.

Do not talk about visiting a church and trying to "catch the pastor's spirit and vision." As soon as you walk in the door, you will find it. It is like the deep calling unto the deep. Once you find that place called "home," your heart will leap and in your spirit you will sense a *yes* resonating through your being. That peace will not change even when you discover the inevitable faults and problems in your new home-church body. That means God sent you there to be part of the long-term solution instead of contributing to the problem.

Headship is a powerful authority in the kingdom. God ordained it to provide safety, security, spiritual nourishment, correction where necessary, and training for the work of the kingdom. For all these reasons and more, you should attend church only where God has called you.

Pray this prayer with me:

Father, I thank You for leading me to the pasture You have chosen and for placing me under the care of the undershepherd You selected for me. Bind us together in the bond of love, and empower me to receive and submit to my leaders for Your glory. In Jesus' name I pray, amen.

July 31

Do the First Things First

Today's Scripture Reading: Romans 10:1–13 *Key Verse:* Romans 10:3

They being ignorant of God's righteousness, and seeking to establish their own righteousness, have not submitted to the righteousness of God.

The body of Christ has a serious problem that endangers its ability to fulfill even the least of God's commands: there is no authority.

"Bishop Long, what do you mean, 'There is no authority'?" The problem arises because many of the folks we call "church people" are not really saved. True conversion and life transformation do not happen just because someone "joins the church." Only the Spirit of God can join a human spirit to Christ's spiritual body. A mere outward ceremony or a signature on a certificate means nothing to God or to the individual involved.

That automatically means that much of what pastors teach and preach from God's Word goes over people's heads. No matter how well educated they may be, they cannot understand Bible truth because they lack spiritual discernment.

This means that authority is lacking on three fronts. Since many of the people in the pews have not been reborn by the Spirit, they cannot recognize or receive the innate authority of God's Word. Nor can they recognize, receive, or benefit from the spiritual authority delegated to God's anointed church leaders. Third, the people themselves have no authority in their voices when they try to speak on behalf of God's kingdom because they are disconnected from the Light of the kingdom, the Vine, the Life who gives life to the church.

Authority in the church begins when Christ takes His throne in the human heart. There is no substitute or shortcut for the born-again, blood-washed experience of salvation through Christ Jesus. Do first things first, then move on to other things.

Pray this prayer with me whether this information is new to you or you have followed Christ most of your life:

Father, I confess with my mouth what is confirmed in my heart: that Jesus Christ is Your only begotten Son who came in the flesh, lived a perfect life among men, preached the kingdom on earth, laid down His life on Calvary to pay the price for my sin, and rose from the dead on the third day. He is my Salvation, my Redeemer, my Savior, and Messiah. I am born again through the shed blood of the Lamb, a new creation who will never again be the same. Thank You for new life in Jesus' name, amen.

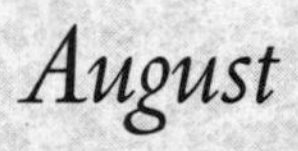

THE CHALLENGE OF TRADITION

DO NOT GRIEVE THE HOLY SPIRIT; YIELD TO HIM

Today's Scripture Reading: John 16:13–16; Ephesians 4:30 *Key Verse:* Ephesians 4:30

Do not grieve the Holy Spirit of God, by whom you were sealed for the day of redemption.

When the Spirit of the Lord is in the house, even babies cannot cry at the wrong time. Our problem is that too much of man's "stuff" is in the church.

All across this land, preachers dare to call their churches "houses of prayer" but refuse to let babies and children in the main sanctuary. How can this be? Didn't our Lord say, "Let the little children come to Me, and do not forbid them; for of such is the kingdom of heaven" (Matt. 19:14 NKJV)? How can preachers presume to tell people how to handle the devil if they cannot handle their own petty frustration when the noise of a hungry baby disturbs their stuffy sermons?

In the New Testament, all the believers met at the same time in the same place. Such an anointing rested on those who walked in the power of the Holy Ghost that even the children understood what the Spirit was saying.

The Lord wants the flesh stuff out so the Holy Spirit can come in. We grieve the Spirit with all our foolish traditions and man-made ways. God arrested me one day to say, "I do not have an unemployment agent for the Holy Spirit. You have been trying to do His work in His place, and that is why nothing is going on. Now let go and let Him operate and accomplish His work or I will close this place down, because He will not be unemployed."

God is reminding the whole church: "I had My Son die so that the Holy Ghost could come." Remember that Jesus filled you with the Spirit to give you power to be a witness. When you walk in this gospel, you do not have to announce your power. You do not have to mention that you are baptized in the Holy Ghost or advertise your religion. Just walk through the crowd and let His light shine through you. Tell people about the King and the kingdom and expect signs and wonders to follow you, confirming the Word of God.

Pray this prayer with me:

Father, please forgive me for all the times I have tried to do everything instead of seeking Your face for wisdom. The Holy Spirit is constantly waiting to lead me to all truth and direct my path, but I have tried to find my own way. No more. Come, Holy Spirit; fill me, direct me, teach me, change me into the image of the Beloved One. Use me to bring glory to His name.

ARE YOU STILL CARNAL?

Today's Scripture Reading: 1 Corinthians 3 *Key Verses:* 1 Corinthians 3:2–3

I fed you with milk and not with solid food; for until now you were not able to receive it, and even now you are still not able; for you are still carnal.

Too much of the preaching that pours from our pulpits is "too high for the pews." We preachers are always trying to discover new things to preach. It is no wonder that church services have become entertainment-driven. We come and enjoy the choir, hear something "new," and then go out and do nothing!

Digging up new stuff is useless when we do not even understand or do the old stuff.

I have some shocking news for you: *Church is not for you to enjoy;* it exists to change you! Its purpose is to help you hear and understand the voice of God—what He is speaking and how He is speaking it—so you can move in the dimension God has ordained. Jesus is more interested in doers than mere hearers of His Word. How would you classify yourself and your local church? Are you doers or hearers only?

Pray this prayer with me:

Lord Jesus, forgive me for lending only my ears to the kingdom. I have listened to words of life week after week, but I never let them sink in to change my thinking or ignite my heart to do Your Word. Change me and remake me, Lord. I choose to be a doer of Your Word, even if I can start with only one thing today.

IS YOUR CHURCH ALIVE AND FLOWING OR LIFELESS AND STAGNANT?

Today's Scripture Reading: Matthew 22:29; 23 *Key Verse:* Matthew 22:29

Jesus answered and said to them, "You are mistaken, not knowing the Scriptures nor the power of God."

Most churches are not scriptural; they are "boardural." That means boards run them like a business corporation. Many of them operate like something that has nothing to do with God! They do not know Scripture because they do not exercise or follow the patterns and precepts that Scripture prescribes.

Most of these churches are miserable and unbearably jealous of any church that is scriptural in its government and operations. Most of the jealousy arises because these other churches are birthing new things all the time.

Churches founded on the management mechanics and minds of men tend to be like the Sanhedrin of Jesus' day: having an outward appearance of stability while being lifeless and stagnant within. They usually have not seen anything new or lively in a long time, and they are quick to criticize anyone who experiences a genuine move of God.

While this sad saga goes on year after year, an entire nation of people watches and waits in the desperate hope that somebody somewhere will capture a view of the promise of God.

The harvest is ready, and God is waiting. This is the season to be like Joshua and Caleb. Carry a sample of "grapes" and a long list of all the goodness you have seen back to the thirsty people in the desert of tradition. Give them a faith-filled report and tell them it is time to get up and go where God ordained for them to go. Are you ready?

Pray this prayer with me:

Heavenly Father, I am ready to carry the good news to all who will hear. You bought my life with Yours; now I devote the rest of my earthly life to proclaiming eternal life in You. By Your grace, I will take the gospel of the kingdom to the very gates of hell to rescue the perishing in the power, love, and life of Your Son, Jesus Christ. Amen.

August 4

God Sent You to Bring in a New Order

Today's Scripture Reading: 2 Corinthians 6:14–18; Ephesians 4:22–24 *Key Verse:* 2 Corinthians 6:17

Come out from among them
And be separate, says the Lord.
Do not touch what is unclean,
And I will receive you.

From Genesis to Revelation, the Scriptures constantly command us in one way or another to "come out and be separate." It is amazing to see how strongly we resist this command! We prefer to represent the kingdom while continuing to play with hell! That is like playing for both the Atlanta Hawks and the Chicago Bulls—you simply switch sides at your convenience to stay on the winning team.

When you came to Christ, your heart was instantly saved, but your mind remained worldly. That is why the Word says, "Put off . . . the old man which grows corrupt according to the deceitful lusts, and be renewed in the spirit of your mind, and . . . put on the new man which was created according to God, in true righteousness and holiness" (Eph. 4:22–24 NKJV).

If you work in corporate America, perhaps you find yourself in constant conflict because you have to walk in two kingdoms while your spiritual life grows. At times you feel trapped in your mind and body, knowing that you represent something higher than the business "kingdom."

Remember that God placed you there to bring in a new order, not to conform to the old order. That knowledge will sustain you in your situation. Trust the Holy Ghost and do what He puts on your heart when He gives you leadership responsibilities in the workplace. If He says it is time to leave, then leave—even if you do not know where you are going. You have to be like Jesus, who knew when something was finished.

If God assigned you to a place just to do a certain thing, the time will come when you must leave that business and let those who think they are in authority discover that they are not in authority. (Make sure you do not do something like this until you know it is finished.)

Pray this prayer with me:

Dear Father, I have decided to follow Jesus and no other. At times I have tried to carry my cross with one hand and my bundle of favorite sins with the other. I repent for my compromise and ask for grace and power to carry the good news of the kingdom into the realm of darkness as the Spirit leads me. In Jesus' name I pray, amen.

AUGUST 5

PUT AN END TO THE HARVEST OF FOOLS

Today's Scripture Reading: Romans 1:18–25 *Key Verse:* Romans 1:22

Professing to be wise, they became fools.

Whichever way you look at it, this nation is in trouble. The passage in Romans 1 describes our problem: "Professing to be wise, they became fools." This nation professes great wisdom, but we have reaped the harvest of fools.

The root problem began in the church when Christians in essence claimed their independence from God and His Word. We let the flesh lead us, instead of the Spirit, and we came up with all kinds of schemes and plans that are contrary to the kingdom.

Some of us did not like the idea of anyone going to hell, so we came up with the "God is love (without righteousness)" scheme where everyone and anyone can enter the kingdom as is. (We may come as we are, but we must go through the door of repentance; we cannot leave His presence the way we came in!) Others did not like dealing with the poor, so they limited their gospel to "us four and no more just inside the door," while their cities fell into ruin.

Some people felt the Bible was archaic in its instructions about the discipline of children, so they labeled it "child abuse" and substituted Dr. So-and-So's doctrine of "kids will be kids" instead. One woman decided school prayer was ruining her son so she got the Supreme Court to declare it unconstitutional (but America's courts still have witnesses and presidents swear on a Bible before testifying or taking office). School has not been the same since, and our foolish harvest continues.

When certain preachers decided they did not want to get involved in politics or governmental decisions in the name of the fictitious "separation doctrine," kingdom influence disappeared from the ethical foundations of government with predictable results.

Our foolishness in the church is destroying our communities and our children. Ironically, we usually end up asking the government to fix things it has no way to understand. Virtually everything needs to be fixed in this nation, but the fix starts right in your house. This nation can never climb out of this pit until the redeemed of the Lord return to the kingdom and God's kingdom principles. It starts with you right now.

Pray this prayer with me:

Dear Father, I am coming back home to the kingdom in all my ways. My thoughts, dreams, and hopes are focused on Your eternal kingdom and nothing else.

UNPACK YOUR BAGS; WE HAVE SOME PREACHING TO DO

Today's Scripture Reading: Matthew 24:4–14 *Key Verse:* Matthew 24:14

This gospel of the kingdom will be preached in all the world as a witness to all the nations, and then the end will come.

Eschatology—the study of the end times—is a hot topic. Many of our perennial best-selling authors write seemingly unending numbers of end-time books. People are talking about Israel aligning with other nations, and Christians by the millions are consuming stacks of books claiming to explain every detail of the books of Revelation, Daniel, and Ezekiel. It seems as if everybody is getting scared.

Just unpack your bags. It is not time yet.

It is not time because this gospel is not being preached. We preach more than ever before, but we do not preach the gospel of the kingdom as revealed in the Bible. We must remember that God cannot and will not honor what is not His.

Anyone can tell you how to be a popular preacher: preach to people's pain. Pain is virtually inexhaustible in this world, so you will always find itching ears. Whatever you do, do not tell people to repent and be obedient to God's Word. Do not even hint about the inevitable consequences of sin. (I am sorry if I offended you with that distasteful three-letter word).

Sin is not a politically correct concept among present-day charismatics, so ensure success by referring to sin by less convicting and less accurate terms such as "indiscretion" and "little problem." (Do not mention that sin was such a big problem that God sent His Son, Jesus, to lay down His life to destroy its power over us.)

The problem is that the gospel is about repentance of sins. No amount of talking, explaining, justifying, or prevaricating can change that fact. Only after we start preaching the gospel of the kingdom again can we can talk about packing our bags for a homecoming.

Pray this prayer with me:

Father, I am unpacking my bags and blowing the dust off of the rest of my Bible. The things at the end happen after we do the things in the middle. Millions have not heard the good news of the kingdom. People in my own neighborhood, grocery store, and workplace have not seen the kingdom or met You. I have too much work to do for You to check out now. I ask You to anoint me to be a fearless witness for the King and the kingdom; in Jesus' name, amen.

AUGUST 7

HAVE YOU BEEN WAITING INSTEAD OF WORKING?

Today's Scripture Reading: John 16:26–27; Philippians 2:9–11

Key Verses: Philippians 2:9–11

God also has highly exalted Him and given Him the name which is above every name, that at the name of Jesus every knee should bow, of those in heaven, and of those on earth, and of those under the earth, and that every tongue should confess that Jesus Christ is Lord, to the glory of God the Father.

Do not listen to that weary, worn, and sad so-called gospel that says we must wait on Jesus' return to get power. Jesus brought all the power we are going to get when He came here two thousand years ago.

When Jesus comes again, the focus will not be upon us or our power; it will be upon Christ the King and His power. Adam and Eve worked in the middle of Paradise; and just for the record, we will work even after He sets up a new heaven! (Just because of that, some of you do not want Him to come.)

God gave us all the power and authority we need to fulfill kingdom purposes when He gave us the right to use the name of Jesus. Do not wait until "later" to tap in to the power of Jesus' name; we need it now.

Pray this prayer with me:

Holy Father, I confess that I have been waiting when I should have been working. I have been looking for the day when every knee would bow to Jesus' name, but they already bow under the authority of His name! Thank You for giving me the authority to speak that holy name in the pursuit of kingdom business—I have work to do for You. It is my privilege to bless You in Jesus' precious name, amen.

DO YOU HAVE A BIG BIBLE OR A LITTLE BIBLE?

Today's Scripture Reading: Psalm 119:97–104 *Key Verses:* Psalm 119:97–100

Oh, how I love Your law! / It is my meditation all the day. / You, through Your commandments, make me wiser than my enemies; / For they are ever with me. / I have more understanding than all my teachers, / For Your testimonies are my meditation. / I understand more than the ancients, / Because I keep Your precepts.

Do you believe that social problems derive from the schemes of multinational corporations, class warfare, capitalist exploitation, or rampant racism? Everybody else does. That explains the proliferation of all the summit meetings in vogue today.

I am sorry, but those things are not the cause of problems. We buy the lie because we think that the Bible talks only about the blood of Jesus, salvation, and freedom from sin. The kingdom encompasses far more than three basic truths. Without a doubt, these things are vitally important, but we must live by the whole counsel of God. Paul called these doctrines and a few others "the elementary principles" or ABCs of the faith, and he scolded the Hebrew believers because they would not move on to deeper things in Christ (see Heb. 6:1–2).

The Bible is eminently practical, but our tradition has limited it to a three-part box. This world is in a mess primarily because we broke our covenants with Almighty God. Every problem we face as the people of God and as representatives of the kingdom arises from a broken covenant.

We made things worse when we failed to promote the kingdom. Once we turn around and again lift up Jesus the King and His kingdom, then the world will see a way out of its seemingly impossible mess. Then, and only then, will poverty cease to be a problem.

Pray this prayer with me:

Father, I realize it is time to move on from the foundation to the upper levels of the faith and the kingdom. By Your grace, I will do it. I will allow Your Word to guide me into every earthly realm with kingdom vision and order in Jesus' name, amen.

AUGUST 9

DO NOT PULL THE PLUG ON GOD'S POWER!

Today's Scripture Reading: 2 Corinthians 1:20; Galatians 3:13–14; Hebrews 8:6–13

Key Verses: Galatians 3:13–14

Christ has redeemed us from the curse of the law . . . that the blessing of Abraham might come upon the Gentiles in Christ Jesus, that we might receive the promise of the Spirit through faith.

The church has a serious problem: the devil is beating up its members as if the supernatural event at the cross never took place! What is wrong with this picture? The problem is that the church has been taught another gospel that is based on man's wants instead of upon God's covenants. Ignorance of God's covenants sets you up for a rough time with the enemy.

When you do not know who you are, what you have in Christ and why, you tend to say, "The devil is doing it again . . . He got me down again." All the while, the devil says, "Go ahead and lift me up. Exalt me. Whatever you think I can do, I will do. Whatever evil tidings you allow yourself to receive, I will give to you. Go ahead and think that I have you bound. Go ahead and forget what Jesus came for. Forget that He said He had all power, and He will not—at least, in *your* life."

The truth is that we pull the plug on the power of Jesus Christ when we do not allow His power to reign in us. We run around like little pain-suckers searching for the most popular preacher. We want him to preach to our pain, grease us with oil, and send us away with the pronouncement that we are delivered. The sad part is that he does not tell you that if you feed your flesh and refuse to repent, then you cannot be delivered. That is why so many people run out of such meetings thinking they are delivered when they are not.

Do not be deceived. Remember what Jesus came for and put the devil under your feet where he belongs. It is part of your covenant with the Creator, the heavenly Father.

Pray this prayer with me:

Heavenly Father, I am plugging in to the promises I received through Jesus Your Son. I receive the promise of provision, protection, and Your abiding presence. I receive the call to be separate and set aside for You alone. I receive membership in Your kingdom and Your royal family, complete with its blessings and its responsibilities. Now I am seated with Christ, and His enemies are our footstool!

THIS IS NOT A SOCIAL CLUB; IT IS A WAR ROOM

Today's Scripture Reading: Matthew 24:3–14; Luke 9:23; Ephesians 6:12–13

Key Verses: Matthew 24:14, Luke 9:23

This gospel of the kingdom will be preached in all the world as a witness to all the nations, and then the end will come.

If anyone desires to come after Me, let him deny himself, and take up his cross daily, and follow Me.

We are called to preach the gospel of the King and His kingdom, but something is terribly wrong. The reason the devil is having such a field day with the church is because the church preaches "another gospel" that is different from the gospel of Jesus Christ.

We have a habit of mixing too many things together. Do you know that some pastors have trouble figuring out if their church members are even saved? One of my pastor friends told me, "Salvation has become so superficial today that [joining the kingdom] is like joining a social club."

The kingdom is not a social club; it is a warring army that is advancing against spiritual darkness and occupying new territory for its King, Jesus Christ! Eligibility requires complete commitment and great hunger for the things of God. Are you eligible?

Forget the social club. This is war! It is time to advance and preach the true gospel of the King and His kingdom!

Pray this prayer with me:

Heavenly Father, I thank You for the blessings of fellowship and relationships in my church, but I confess that at times I have placed these blessings ahead of my disciplined walk in Your Son. I have also been reluctant to proclaim the gospel of the kingdom to those You have placed in my life. Please forgive me, and grant me the grace and power to share Christ and His kingdom boldly today, in Jesus' name I pray, amen.

AUGUST 11

THE TRUE GOSPEL SAYS, "YOU REPENTED? PROVE IT."

Today's Scripture Reading: Acts 26:19–20; Matthew 3:8; 2 Corinthians 11:3–4

Key Verses: Acts 26:19–20, emphasis mine

King Agrippa, I was not disobedient to the heavenly vision, but declared first to those in Damascus and in Jerusalem, and throughout all the region of Judea, and then to the Gentiles, that they should repent, turn to God, and do works befitting repentance.

You probably know by now that the devil goes after those you love when he really wants to hurt you. Actually he is not interested in you either; he just wants to hurt the One he fears and hates more than any other—God Himself. Satan tries to do that by harming His children.

We have already examined this strategy of the enemy, but this is my point today: the devil actually likes for most of us to go to church! Why? He knows that most churches preach a tradition, a perverted and powerless gospel that blesses his dark kingdom and does harm to God's children.

How can you tell the difference between a perverted gospel and the real thing? You know you are hearing a perverted gospel if somebody preaches that you can "rub your Bible [metaphorically speaking] and get anything you want."

You are seeing a perverted gospel in action if the people in your church think they can live worldly lives, show up out of habit on Sunday, and still be blessed.

Finally, a perverted gospel teaches and encourages people that they can simply run to a prayer line or anointed preacher and enjoy instant deliverance from their clinging sin while they are still feeding their flesh.

The true gospel declares, "Bear fruits worthy of repentance" (Matt. 3:8 NKJV). John the Baptist said this to some Pharisees who wanted God's blessings without repenting of their sins or changing their sinful ways. Paul said the same thing to King Agrippa while explaining his heavenly vision of the gospel. God said no to sin then and He says no now.

The only genuine gospel is the gospel that Jesus ordained His disciples to preach in the New Testament. We must go back to the Rock and restart our journey the right way: God's way.

Pray this prayer with me:

Holy Father, I am not interested in shortcuts to holiness. I do not want to justify my sins; I want to be free of them. Cleanse me and make my life a living proof of Your power and of Your kingdom; in Jesus' name I pray, amen.

August 12

Preach the Kingdom, and He Will Confirm It!

Today's Scripture Reading: Matthew 24:3–51 *Key Verse:* Matthew 24:14

This gospel of the kingdom will be preached in all the world as a witness to all the nations, and then the end will come.

Jesus said the gospel must be preached before the end would come and before His return. This gospel will bear witness or provide evidence of the eternal kingdom to the temporary kingdoms and nations of the world.

We know from the prophetic and historic record of the New Testament that the gospel of the kingdom, wherever it was preached, bore witness to the validity of the kingdom message through miraculous signs and wonders. Jesus promised this would happen: "These signs will follow those who believe" (Mark 16:17 NKJV).

The New Testament records that it did happen after Jesus ascended to heaven: "They went out and preached everywhere, the Lord working with them and confirming the word through the accompanying signs" (Mark 16:20 NKJV).

Paul said he ministered "in word and deed, to make the Gentiles obedient—in mighty signs and wonders, by the power of the Spirit of God, so that from Jerusalem and round about to Illyricum I have fully preached the gospel of Christ" (Rom. 15:18–19 NKJV).

Today, most of our "signs and wonders" are artificially manufactured. God does not honor what we are saying because we are not declaring the gospel He told us to preach. Signs and wonders elude us because most of us are not living the way God said to live. Once we repent and begin to preach the true gospel of the kingdom, I have no doubt that signs and wonders will become an everyday occurrence in our lives. God delights in confirming His Word with power and authority—He just cannot find people with enough courage to preach the truth and live by it! How about you?

Pray this prayer with me:

Lord, here I am. Use me. I give You what I have and everything that I am. Now send me in Your power to proclaim the kingdom with signs and wonders following—even if it is on the job, in the mall, or in the church parking lot. In Jesus' name I pray, amen.

AUGUST 13

PAY THE PRICE AND PROCLAIM THE KINGDOM FROM THE HEART

Today's Scripture Reading: Matthew 13 *Key Verses:* Matthew 13:20–21

He who received the seed on stony places, this is he who hears the word and immediately receives it with joy; yet he has no root in himself, but endures only for a while. For when tribulation or persecution arises because of the word, immediately he stumbles.

It does not matter what you have heard, said, or read; everything that you receive from Jesus and the Holy Spirit will face testing. That is the only way you can absorb actual kingdom truths of God into your heart. Testing will stretch you, and you will feel like you have been through a life-and-death experience over that truth. You will even wonder whether or not God has forsaken you. He has not.

God will prove His Word true and He will meet you in the heart of that truth, but He probably will not come in the way you expected or at the time you had hoped. Of this much you can be certain: God will always show up right on time.

The costly process of moving God's Word from the vast storehouse of the mind into the intimate chambers of the heart is rare in the church today. We do not like sacrifice, pain, or discipline. However, the path of testing and trial is the only way to receive God's "seeds" of truth in the heart.

We have four choices when the seed of the Word is sown. First, we can let the enemy snatch it away. We can receive it on "shallow ground" and watch it wither and die under the heat of trials and persecutions. Third, we can let competing priorities choke it out.

The fourth way is God's way. Most people do not realize that the fourth example in Jesus' parable of the seed—the "good soil" that received the seed and yielded a harvest—also endured all the calamities described in the previous three examples! (See Matt. 13, especially verse 8.)

This "good soil" endured marauding birds (usually a picture of the enemy at work), scorching sun, and the dangers of encroaching weeds and thorns. In spite of these tests and trials, a harvest grew. Only a precious few are willing to pay any price to possess God's truth and become proven proclaimers of the kingdom.

Pray this prayer with me:

Heavenly Father, I want to receive Your Word the right way. Grant me the grace to stand and endure tests, trials, or hardship to receive Your Word in my heart. Then I will boldly proclaim the kingdom from the heart and not from the head. In Jesus' name I pray, amen.

AUGUST 14

GIVE ME THAT OLD-TIME REVELATION BY THE HOLY GHOST

Today's Scripture Reading: John 14:16–17, 15:26, 16:13; Romans 8 *Key Verse:* John 16:13

When He, the Spirit of truth, has come, He will guide you into all truth; for He will not speak on His own authority, but whatever He hears He will speak; and He will tell you things to come.

Why is it so important to be tested? The pressure of a test plants the seed of the kingdom gospel deep down inside of you. This is what the old saints had.

They did not have a radio program and they were not on TV. They did not even have a concordance or a commentary for the most part. All they had was the King James Version of the Bible and the Holy Ghost as their Teacher.

The King James Version features the English language as it existed in 1611 (five years before William Shakespeare died), complete with its "thou's" and "thee's" and "wist nots." Many modern saints avoid this translation as they would a minefield, but the old saints made it through all the "thou's" and "thee's" and "wist nots" just fine with the help of the Holy Ghost. Many of these saints had very little education and some of them had none, but they persevered and received God's seeds because the Holy Ghost was their Explainer and Expositor. They were hungry and willing to pay a price, so He brought them revelation knowledge.

I know we have all kinds of commentaries, teaching tapes, and videos available to us today—and I am thankful for them—but sometimes these tools become the toys of fools because we forget that they can never replace the work of the Holy Ghost.

Let me encourage you to close your Bible reference books, shut down your computer-based Bible search programs, turn off your audio- and videotape machines once in a while, and open up the Bible. Ask the Holy Spirit, "Teacher, teach me what the kingdom is about so I can get it in my heart." You will discover a whole new world awaiting you under the incomparable instruction of the Holy Spirit.

Holy Spirit of God, I ask You to teach me what I need to know about the kingdom. I look only to the Word of God and the heart of the Father as You show me these things. In Jesus' name I pray, amen.

AUGUST 15

DO YOU SEARCH THE SCRIPTURES DAILY TO SEE WHAT IS TRUE?

Today's Scripture Reading: Acts 17:11–12; 2 Timothy 3:16–17 *Key Verse:* Acts 17:11

These [Bereans] were more fair-minded than those in Thessalonica, in that they received the word with all readiness, and searched the Scriptures daily to find out whether these things were so.

Do not accept everything I say as "the gospel truth." Study these things for yourself, and remember that you have your own personal teacher, the Holy Spirit. Paul the apostle actually commended the saints at Berea because they refused to take his word at face value! He praised them because they "searched the Scriptures daily" to see if the things Paul said were true.

Do not put your Teacher "out of work." He is not interested in taking a permanent sabbatical; He is interested in teaching you how to do the will of God, establish the kingdom, and fulfill your destiny in Christ. Ask Him to illuminate the things you do not understand; ask Him to teach you and show you how to live, and He will.

Sometimes He may teach you through example and have you experience things as He teaches you about it. So do not be surprised if the Holy Ghost takes you on a field trip when you ask Him to show you something. (It will be the most exciting thing you have ever done!)

Pray this prayer with me if you dare:

Heavenly Father, thank You for the Holy Spirit, my Teacher and Guide. Holy Spirit, show me the Father's heart, and teach me how to honor and please Him. Instruct me in the ways of the kingdom and make my life fruitful for the King. In Jesus' name I pray, amen.

PROCLAIM THE KINGDOM WITH AUTHORITY

Today's Scripture Reading: Matthew 7 *Key Verses:* Matthew 7:28–29

When Jesus had ended these sayings, . . . the people were astonished at His teaching, for He taught them as one having authority, and not as the scribes.

Jesus communicated directly with the heavenly Father, and then He shared what He heard with others—and He did it with authority. It is just as important to speak by the Spirit as it is to see by the Spirit. Many people talk about what their pastor or some teacher says. This does not carry any spiritual authority because you just end up talking about that person instead of the revelatory truth from God and His Word. You must witness to what you learned from your inner being.

Too many people say, "Bishop Long said this," or "So-and-So said that," instead of "*I* see this." When you can receive something from the Lord yourself, and speak it out with inner conviction from the Holy Ghost, then you are giving God glory. It is far better to testify and witness out of your innermost being than to parrot what someone else said.

People in the world wonder if God really talks to people. We know that He does, but it is far better if we can prove it in our own lives on a daily basis. We have the privilege of living out what many people only dream about. We can have intimate communion with the Creator of the universe. He even directs our steps each day. It is our duty to share this kingdom privilege with others, but first we must walk in the Spirit and speak by the Spirit with authority.

Pray this prayer with me:

Heavenly Father, Jesus showed us that the key to speaking with authority in the earth is to seek Your face and listen to Your heart first. My opinion gains authority only as it conforms to Your will and purpose. I come before You today to listen more than to speak. Show me Your heart, Father, so I can do Your will today. I ask these things in Jesus' holy name, amen.

Keep Going and Do Not Stop to Tickle Any Ears

Today's Scripture Reading: Joshua 1 *Key Verse:* Joshua 1:9

Have I not commanded you? Be strong and of good courage; do not be afraid, nor be dismayed, for the LORD your God is with you wherever you go.

Joshua heard it all during the forty years he served Moses. The protests, excuses, justifications, and groaning seemed endless at times. You have heard them, too, if you have ever stretched beyond your comfort zone to speak the truth about God's will before a group of people:

"Why must I know this gospel?"

"Why do I have to be radical?"

"Why do I have to come against the paradigms of traditional religion?"

"Why do I have to endure criticism?"

Finally the day came when God gave Moses' assignment to Joshua, and he knew was about the face the challenge of his life. On that day, God bluntly reminded Joshua that he was a man with a mission from God, and He warned him in advance not to be afraid or dismayed.

The same thing will happen to you if you are serious about following Jesus. You may face these challenges on a drastically smaller scale, but they are still challenges. Remember that what other people say or do not say does not matter; you are filled with the Holy Ghost and dispatched on kingdom business. Whether people approve or not, you are ushering in the Spirit of God wherever you go.

People like to have their ears "tickled" with flattering words and flesh-pleasing messages that soothe the ego. The Word of God does not tickle people's ears; it simply declares divine realities that minister to the heart. Forget flattery—God's love is far better.

Just walk through your difficult times and keep your eyes on the Author of the covenant promises. Receive understanding and wisdom through this testing time and trust the King to bring you through it with more strength than when you began. Take comfort in this fact: the next time you speak about this subject, you will have an inner witness and a visible authority that others cannot deny or easily set aside.

Pray this prayer with me:

Father, please forgive me for asking, "Why?" more than I have said, "Yes, Lord." I know that You know what is best for me and for the kingdom—where You lead I will follow. By Your grace, neither the opinions of men nor the difficulty of my circumstances will turn me aside. In the end, I will testify of Your faithfulness with authority and power in Jesus' name.

AUGUST 18

I HAVE NO ROOM OR DESIRE FOR "ANOTHER GOSPEL"

Today's Scripture Reading: Galatians 1:6–9 *Key Verse:* Galatians 1:8

Even if we, or an angel from heaven, preach any other gospel to you than what we have preached to you, let him be accursed.

Did you know that there are a whole lot of accursed preachers in the world? The apostle Paul referred to these teachers and preachers in Galatians 1:8. The most dangerous perversions contain about 98 percent truth with a well-disguised 2 percent of deadly heresy woven in.

Paul and the apostles in Jerusalem had to deal with two kinds of false teachers: Jewish teachers who mixed legalism with the gospel, and Greek-speaking teachers who mixed in Greek philosophy with its hyperspiritualism and hatred of the flesh (known as the "Gnostic heresy"). Both groups gathered followers by "tickling their ears" and saying what they wanted to hear. Each group loved works and minimized or totally threw out the importance of the gospel of the cross and redemption by faith.

This is why you must study God's Word for yourself. The devil knows every word of the Bible, and he will try to baffle you with his knowledge of the Scripture if he can. (He even quoted a scripture to Jesus during the temptation in the wilderness in Matthew 4:6.) Remember how the devil completely twisted and reframed God's words when he tempted Eve in the Garden of Eden (Gen. 3:1–5)?

One of Satan's favorite tactics is to offer you "another gospel" that skillfully perverts what is of God to something totally different. This means that even preachers who use Bible references to support their ideas can be preaching a twisted gospel. Walk in the Spirit and know your Bible.

Pray this prayer with me:

Heavenly Father, You are my Rock and my Fortress. No matter how many untruths and flattering words come my way, I will not be swayed because I know Him who is the Way, the Truth, and the Life. Lift the blinders from my eyes so I can clearly see the deception of the enemy and walk holy in Your sight, Lord. In Jesus' name I pray, amen.

AUGUST 19

I Worship the God of the Scriptures, Not the Scriptures Themselves

Today's Scripture Reading: John 5:31–39 *Key Verse:* John 5:39

You search the Scriptures, for in them you think you have eternal life; and these are they which testify of Me.

Just knowing the Scriptures does not mean that you are preaching the kingdom gospel—or even that you are saved. The fact that you know Genesis from Revelation does not give you eternal life.

Have you ever noticed that some people can quote Scripture to you and you do not feel anything or sense any anointing? This is because those people think that knowledge about the Bible is the essence of eternal life.

Jesus told the same Jewish leaders who "searched the Scriptures" thinking their works gave them eternal life, "But you are not willing to come to Me that you may have life" (John 5:40 NKJV). Things have not changed much. Many churchgoers and church leaders would rather go to the letter of the law in the Scriptures than go to the living person of Christ. They have things backward. We must remember that the authority of the Scriptures comes from Him!

Pray this prayer with me:

Heavenly Father, I do not worship the Scriptures of God; I worship You alone, the God of the Scriptures. I find life in Your Spirit, not in the letters You sent us through Your Word. The Scriptures reveal You in part, but they cannot contain the fullness of Your boundless beauty, fathomless power, and eternal kingdom.

AUGUST 20

PULLING DOWN MOUNTAINS

Today's Scripture Reading: Isaiah 40:3–8 *Key Verse:* Isaiah 40:4

Every valley shall be exalted
And every mountain and hill brought low;
The crooked places shall be made straight
And the rough places smooth.

Isaiah had been preaching for a while, but he finally figured out what he was supposed to preach in the fortieth chapter. Mountains represent our proud opposition to the way of God. We the church oppose the way of God. In the midst of that, we exalt mountains of pride.

I will never forget when I handed out the constitution of our church and instructed the people to go through it, find what was not biblical, and take it out. Folks got mad. They started saying that I was trying to get too much control, that I was prideful. This challenged us all to get in the order of God because we had a high mountain.

God cannot come when we put ourselves first. His glory must confront our irrelevance. We have to bring down every high mountain.

Heavenly Father, forgive me for letting mountains stand between us. Right now I pull down that mountain, and I give You preeminence. In Jesus' name, amen.

August 21

We Also Seek the Lost Sheep in the Church

Today's Scripture Reading: Matthew 3:1–2, 10:6–7 *Key Verses:* Matthew 3:1–2

In those days John the Baptist came preaching in the wilderness of Judea, and saying, "Repent, for the kingdom of heaven is at hand!"

Why did God send John the Baptist? The Lord essentially was saying, "I do not have a problem with unsaved folk; they are doing what unsaved folk do. I have a problem with the supposedly saved folk. My children, the descendants of Abraham, are in trouble. If My children get right, I can handle the others." In other words, God looked at Israel as lost sheep needing a Shepherd.

Today, the church is in the same situation!

The Jewish people in John's day had the Law and the Prophets; they had the priestly traditions descended from Moses and the incredible history of God's faithfulness to His people—still they were like sheep without a shepherd.

It is even worse with us! We have the gospel of Jesus Christ with the miraculous virgin birth, the incredible miracles, the scourging, crucifixion, and resurrection of Christ from the dead—all in fulfillment of detailed prophecies. We have the Holy Spirit and all the gifts of the indwelling Spirit of God, yet large numbers of us are wandering outside the kingdom fold like sheep gone astray.

If you have believed and received the true gospel of Christ and the kingdom, then you also are called to expose the deceit that is in the body of Christ. Too many churches are dead and dry, and their people attend church only out of habit. Frankly, they do not know what else to do on Sunday.

John shook the unstable foundation of tradition that Israel's intensely religious society cherished when he considered them, in Jesus' words, "lost sheep" and spoke of God's kingdom. I do not know where you stand, but I think it is time for the same spirit of John the Baptist to invade our churches today and call another generation of religious "lost sheep" to repentance at the river. Is God speaking to your heart about repentance? Perhaps the Holy Spirit is calling you to proclaim the kingdom to lost sheep. If you hear God's voice, then do something about it right now.

Pray this prayer with me:

Holy Father, grant me the courage and faith to boldly proclaim Your kingdom and call the lost sheep around me back to the Shepherd. In Jesus' name I pray, amen.

AUGUST 22

TAKE THE PLUNGE, SINK DEEP, AND RISE AGAIN IN THE KINGDOM

Today's Scripture Reading: Mark 1:2–4 *Key Verse:* Mark 1:4

John came baptizing in the wilderness and preaching a baptism of repentance for the remission of sins.

All four gospel accounts describe John's baptism of Jesus in the river Jordan. Each writer used the same Greek verb, *baptizo,* to describe what John did. If we are anointed to call lost sheep to repentance in the spirit of John the Baptist, then we should know something about his prophetic purpose and ministry.

John was a forerunner whom God commissioned to proclaim a coming kingdom. He commanded his generation to prepare for the coming of the Lord through a baptism of repentance. John's baptism involved three processes: immersion (to plunge into liquid), submersion (to sink under the surface and cover over), and emergence (to rise from).

Our clearest picture of John's baptism of Jesus is of our Lord rising from the water just before the Holy Spirit settled upon Him like a dove (Matt. 3:16). All of this detail is important for this reason: John's baptism was no mere "dip" or sprinkle. It was a full-fledged plunging into and under the water because John's message did not call for partial or halfhearted repentance.

If judgment begins with the house of God (1 Peter 4:17), then we have no business telling the world to repent if we have not wholeheartedly turned from our own sins! God sent John the Baptist to confront the kingdoms of men with the kingdom of God. That divine confrontation demanded nothing less than a complete and radical change of heart.

Once again, the kingdom and a divine call for a radical change of heart and priorities must confront the church. You may not like confrontation, but if you carry God's passion for the kingdom in your heart, then you are anointed to confront lost sheep in love and grace. Once they turn from darkness, they must be plunged into the kingdom and covered over until they rise to a new life in the kingdom.

Pray this prayer with me:

Heavenly Father, let the proclamation transformation begin with me. Plunge me into Your kingdom until I am covered with Your passion and purpose. Hold me under until every unholy sin and desire in me dies, and release me to rise to new power and purpose in Your kingdom. Then empower me to proclaim the King and His kingdom the rest of my days; in Jesus' name, amen.

SEEK GOD AND PREACH THE REPENTANT GOSPEL

Today's Scripture Reading: Isaiah 40:3; Matthew 4:17 *Key Verse:* Isaiah 40:3

The voice of one crying in the wilderness:
"Prepare the way of the LORD;
Make straight in the desert
A highway for our God."

If you want personal peace, you must prepare the way for the King in your life. If you want to see Jesus return, then the church must turn away and repent of its sin and compromise. We have failed to preach a repentant gospel, so we have left unconfronted entire generations who live lifestyles apart from God and His kingdom. It is the gospel of the kingdom that commands the prodigals, "You must return to your Father's house."

I have news for you: you cannot confront anyone if the Spirit of the Lord does not dwell in you in His fullness. This will never happen if you are content to seek knowledge of the Scriptures instead of the God of the Scriptures.

You cannot "prepare the way" for anyone without growing in the Spirit. Has anyone told you recently, "You have really grown in the Spirit"? If not, this should be a convicting message for you. On the other hand, if your family grumbles and complains that you "do not fit with them anymore" (they may not say it outright), take it as a compliment! They are saying you have grown in the Spirit.

Pray this prayer with me:

Heavenly Father, I confess that at times I have found it easier to seek knowledge and the approval of men through my study of the Scriptures than to seek You. Now I realize that the Scriptures should always point me back toward You, but they can never take the place of our one-on-one relationship. It is good to be back in Your presence again.

Crack Tradition's Mold and Embrace the Newness of God

Today's Scripture Reading: Isaiah 43:16–21 *Key Verse:* Isaiah 43:19

Behold, I will do a new thing, / Now it shall spring forth; / Shall you not know it? / I will even make a road in the wilderness / And rivers in the desert.

Does the possibility of moving to a new level in God disturb you? Religious tradition is like concrete—once you wade in and stay for a while, it sets up and locks you in. Any change of position from that point on can be a painful proposition.

Perhaps you are too baptized in tradition and old church stuff to entertain change. The problem is that you serve a God who *moves* from glory to glory. He has His Holy Ghost jackhammer ready to free you from man's tradition, but you must *want* to be free to get free. He cannot help you if you would rather sit in a pew and keep God separated from your daily life.

I understand how pleasant it is to walk into a church foyer and receive nicely printed church bulletins, to listen to the announcements delivered like clockwork, and to hear a lively singing choir. It feels good to beat First Church to the restaurant after a punctual dismissal of the church service. We like to have everything in order because it makes us feel comfortable. The problem is that very little if any of that has anything to do with the kingdom.

God wants to move you out of religion and into relationship, but that demands change. Can you stand to be free with God? Would you have a problem if your pastor said, "God told me not to preach. We are all just to lie on our faces before Him at the front of the auditorium." You know you have a problem if you would mumble under your breath, "There better be some service. What are we paying him for?"

The answer is this: you are paying your pastor to be obedient to God. Jesus paid the price so you could be obedient to Him too. Is it not time to break out of tradition's mold and step into the "new" with Jesus Christ? Your King and the kingdom are waiting.

Pray this prayer with me:

Heavenly Father, I have been slow to release the comfortable things so I could embrace Your new things. Please forgive me and set me free from the traditions of man. Where You lead, I will follow—even if You are taking me into something so new and different that I have never seen it before. In Jesus' name, I will follow You.

GOD WILL DELIVER YOU FROM THE FACES OF MAN

Today's Scripture Reading: Jeremiah 1:7–8 *Key Verse:* Jeremiah 1:8

"Do not be afraid of their faces,
For I am with you to deliver you," says the LORD.

The church needs deliverance today! No, it does not need to be delivered from the enemy; it needs deliverance from people. Have you taken a friend to a church service where the Holy Spirit really spoke to your heart? When the preacher gave the invitation, did you choose not to walk to the altar because you wondered what the other person would think? Has God spoken to you about joining a certain church, but you have not obeyed because of the different things other people have told you about it?

What worries you the most: what people will say or what God will say? If you worry more about what other people will think of you, then you need deliverance from people.

God told Jeremiah of his assignment as "prophet to the nations," "Do not be afraid of their faces, / For I am with you to deliver you." My friend, people will watch you all the way to hell! They will watch your dreams be destroyed. They will watch your marriage crumble and they will watch your children get into drugs, but they have no power to deliver. God said you should not be afraid of their faces, so do not even try to justify yourself to somebody else.

You will never do anything in your life if you are looking fearfully at the faces of people. Why should you spend your days sitting in church trying to save face, when all the while you are dying in pain? Forget everyone around you. If you need help, then get help from the One who loved you so much that He gave His life to make you free!

Pray this prayer with me:

Holy Father, I confess that I have been afraid of disapproval, rejection, separation, and the ridicule of other people. All I really need is You—I need Your approval, Your acceptance, Your intimacy, and Your praise and blessing. Deliver me from the faces of men and draw me close to Your face. In Jesus' name I pray, amen.

AUGUST 26

SOMETIMES YOU HAVE TO FALL BEFORE YOU WALK RIGHT

Today's Scripture Reading: Hebrews 12 *Key Verse:* Hebrews 12:7

If you endure chastening, God deals with you as with sons; for what son is there whom a father does not chasten?

Worldly rules and job descriptions are confusing and entangling the body of Christ. We get so mixed up and tied up with this extrabiblical stuff that we fail to really minister the kingdom.

The world's agenda says that church should be the handout station for everyone, so we tell people, "You can come to the church when you need help." Then people get mad if we do not help them buy food because we know that they spent all their money on drugs or gambling. God may want His people to be compassionate, but He also expects them to be wise.

Many Christians think the church should give everything to people when they make foolish mistakes. This kind of blind benevolence nearly always cuts short the mercy and wisdom of God. When we intervene, we halt what God was trying to do in a person's life. If someone has a chronic problem with financial irresponsibility, God may want him to go through the indignity of having checks bounce to make an impression deep in his heart and mind: *This is serious . . .*

You will not hear this in most pulpits, but I will say it: sometimes people need to be evicted. Sometimes they need to get fired. Sometimes they need to hit rock bottom so the Teacher can finally get their attention and speak to them.

We nearly always get angry when the pastor will not heed our requests and rescue the troubled person on our doorstep. We burn up the phone line to get undiscerning congregation members to join our pity party. Pity parties have no place in the kingdom. Only evil results when we have flesh meetings instead of kingdom meetings.

Forget the world's rules and job descriptions of who is to do what in the church. Concentrate on the kingdom. We cannot afford to do anything else—we have a kingdom to establish and a harvest to bring in.

Pray this prayer with me:

Dear Father, I embrace Your correction and receive Your rebuke with joy. By Your grace, I will not cut short the work of Your hand in my life.

HAVE YOU COMPLETED YOUR REEDUCATION?

Today's Scripture Reading: Genesis 12:1–3 *Key Verse:* Genesis 12:1

The LORD had said to Abram:
"Get out of your country,
From your family
And from your father's house,
To a land that I will show you."

God always removes a man (or woman) from his original place of education and separates him from his support system and comfort zones before He qualifies him for leadership. It is the only way He can educate him according to the kingdom of God. If you look in the Bible, you will see this same pattern every time.

Consider Abram. God told him, "Get out of your country, / From your family / And from your father's house, / To a land that I will show you." The Lord was actually saying, "I am getting ready to reeducate you—not Uncle Bud and Aunt Sally—according to the standards of the kingdom. I have to separate you and educate you in the ways of the kingdom. Then, once you are revolutionized, you can turn and revolutionize them. Abram, you cannot set anyone else free if you have not been set free."

We have too many preachers in the pulpit who have not undergone revolution in their thinking about the kingdom of God. I foresee some rapid and radical reeducation going on in the near future.

Pray this prayer with me:

Holy Father, I want to go all the way. Transplant, transform, and transfuse me with Your Holy Spirit. Change me to the image of Your Son, Jesus, so I can glorify You and build Your kingdom. In Jesus' name I pray, amen.

LORD, I CHOOSE YOUR WAY

Today's Scripture Reading: Hebrews 3; Joshua 24:15 *Key Verse:* Joshua 24:15

If it seems evil to you to serve the LORD, choose for yourselves this day whom you will serve, whether the gods which your fathers served that were on the other side of the River, or the gods of the Amorites, in whose land you dwell. But as for me and my house, we will serve the LORD.

Egypt's most renowned wise men educated Moses as a prince of Egypt in Pharaoh's house, and he knew he had a divine call on his life. Yet he missed the mark because he was premature and tried to do things his own way. God had to move him out into the wilderness to deprogram him from the forty years he spent receiving the Egyptian mentality. It took God another forty years to implant a kingdom mentality in Moses!

God also led the children of Israel through the wilderness for forty years. He could have taken them the short way, but then they would not have been educated about the kingdom. God parted the sea, they went across on dry land, and then they saw their enemies drown. God led them by a pillar of fire by night and a pillar of cloud by day. He did everything to show them the kingdom, but they missed the mark because they were afraid, and they were too hardheaded and ignorant to receive kingdom or kingdom principles. In the end they got exactly what they asked for: they stayed in the wilderness, and God took their children in instead.

Now answer this question: Will you submit to the kingdom of God or will you continue to wander in the wilderness of your own way? You would never reject God or openly defy His commands, but there is that one area where you have not crossed the Jordan . . .

Keep the covenant of God and enjoy freedom, blessings, and the fulfillment of divine destiny in your life. Anything else is disobedience, and that brings only a curse. As you probably know by now, the choice is yours.

Pray this prayer with me:

Heavenly Father, I am tired of my own way. I submit to You. I give in, I give up, and I give everything to You. I want Your way or no way. Take me all the way into Your perfect will, into Your kingdom, and into Your presence. In Jesus' name I pray, amen.

CALLED AND "GRACED" BEFORE TIME BEGAN

Today's Scripture Reading: 2 Timothy 1:8–11 *Key Verses:* 2 Timothy 1:8–9

God . . . has saved us and called us with a holy calling,
not according to our works, but according to His own purpose
and grace which was given to us in Christ Jesus before time began.

Do you think God saved you just so you could be saved? It is not true. If God saved people just so they could be saved, I would be in a different business called "Long and Sons' Funeral Services." We would go on the road and conduct revivals with great altar calls. As soon as you got saved, my son Cody would be behind you with a casket and I would get my check from you. Then we would seal it up. You see, if God's only intention was to save you, then you would die as soon as He saved you.

God intends far more for you than salvation alone. He saved you with a holy purpose in mind. I do not care what people have said to you in the past. It does not even matter if your mama or daddy tried to put you down all your life. They did not make you, and you do not belong to them. The eternal God merely used them to deliver you into earth's realm. Most important, they did not leave a throne in heaven to die and take upon themselves all your sins.

God called you for a divine reason. Now that you know the truth, it is your responsibility to seek Him and to fulfill your kingdom destiny.

Pray this prayer with me:

Holy Father, it amazes me that You knew my name and reserved grace for me in Christ Jesus even before time began. No words of man or spirit matter except the words You speak concerning me. Lord, I seek to do Your will and build Your kingdom. In Jesus' name I pray, amen.

The Adoption Is Official: Now Get to Work!

Today's Scripture Reading: Ephesians 2:8–10; Matthew 5:16; Philippians 2

Key Verses: Ephesians 2:8–10 emphasis mine

> *By grace you have been saved through faith, and that not of yourselves; it is the gift of God, not of works, lest anyone should boast. For we are His workmanship, created in Christ Jesus for* good works, which God prepared beforehand that we should walk in them.

Many Christians think of salvation in Christ as "fire insurance" against the flames of hell. That is the excuse many among us give who do not live right, do not care, and do not work! All that most of us heard was, "Go to church and get saved." We even like to stand up and testify, "We are so glad that all our children are saved."

It is true that God's grace saves us, not our works, and it is also true that we have the bad habit of reading only the first part of a Scripture passage. Paul makes it clear in Ephesians 2:10 that we were created to work! The work starts after the adoption papers are signed and sealed in the Holy Ghost! This is the activity Paul was talking about in his letter to the Philippians when he wrote, "Work out your own salvation with fear and trembling" (Phil. 2:12 NKJV). God saves us, but He expects us to keep His commands and do the work of the ministry as responsible members of His kingdom family. The kingdom is a family affair, and every family member is a working member.

For all these reasons, I am not satisfied simply to know that my children are saved. I will be satisfied only when I know that my children are walking in the ways of God as true disciples, rightly dividing the Word of truth. I will be satisfied when my children clearly understand their destiny and follow in the multigenerational anointing God has placed in me.

Pray this prayer with me:

Heavenly Father, I thank You for Your grace—not only to be saved, but also to do the good works You ordained for me. I also pray for the next generation of folks, that they will embrace the work of the kingdom along with the gift of life. In Jesus' name I pray, amen.

AUGUST 31

THERE IS A CURE FOR SPIRITUAL ALZHEIMER'S

Today's Scripture Reading: James 1:23–24; Romans 10:17 *Key Verse:* Romans 10:17

Faith comes by hearing, and hearing by the word of God.

Our nation hears the Word of God in church services, on television, on the radio, and on the Internet, but the nation still has no faith. Why? It is not because its people do not hear the Word of God. It is because they hear it but do not heed it.

Secular groups often invite me into their meetings to pray, but then they continue to run things like heathens. They honor God to the point of letting Him come in and take a bow, but then they say, "Let us handle it from here."

More important than the secular, why do the *people of God* have no faith? It is because all they do is listen to the Word.

People who hear but do not do the Word develop a spiritual form of Alzheimer's, where they forget who they are and why they are here! I am not making this up. James the apostle put it this way: "If anyone is a hearer of the word and not a doer, he is like a man observing his natural face in a mirror; for he observes himself, goes away, and immediately forgets what kind of man he was" (James 1:23–24 NKJV).

Biblical faith demands that you do what you hear from God. When I hear the Lord and do what He says, then my faith increases. That is why the Bible says God's righteousness is revealed "from faith to faith" (Rom. 1:17 NKJV). When God calls you, He is calling you closer. If you do not move in faith, then you will never see God in a fresh and more intimate way. Pray with me:

Father, forgive me for hearing but not heeding, for listening but not obeying. Lord Jesus, from now on I will obey what You tell me so my faith will grow.

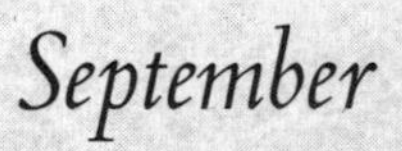

September

Blessed to Be a Blessing

SEPTEMBER 1

LIVE TO GIVE, NOT TO RECEIVE

Today's Scripture Reading: Matthew 5 *Key Verse:* Matthew 5:42

Give to him who asks you, and from him who wants to borrow from you do not turn away.

Some people think, since I try to financially bless everyone who walks with me, that I do it because I have a lot of extra resources. They did not know me in the lean years when I had next to nothing, but I tried to bless others then as well. You do not wait until you have something to give something!

People may say, "When I get something, I am going to take care of you." It is not about what you have; it is about what is already in you—it is your mind-set. If you are not prepared to give now, then you will not give when you get something. If someone promises you something in the future but will not give you half of the fifty cents he has now, forget it. He could get $500,000, but he would not give you five dollars because it is not in his heart to do it.

God is looking for people who say from the heart, "Even if I do not have anything, I will share." He will give you more because He knows that you know how to bless others. If you do not have any money, just bless people with a smile. Put your arms around them and hug them. Share the love of God with them.

It is the mind-set that counts, not the dollars. Pray with me:

Heavenly Father, I have been waiting for You to bless me before I can bless someone else. I see that is wrong. Forgive me for that selfish mind-set. Lord, I will bless and love others with what I already have. I know that You will bless me with more as I give out what I have. In Jesus' name I pray, amen.

SEPTEMBER 2

GOD WILL NOT OWE YOU FOR LONG

Today's Scripture Reading: 2 Corinthians 9:6–10; Galatians 6:7

Key Verse: 2 Corinthians 9:10

May He who supplies seed to the sower,
and bread for food, supply and multiply the seed you have
sown and increase the fruits of your righteousness.

God's law of sowing and reaping really works—you ought to try it.

I am determined to put God's laws to work in my life, so I bless as many people as I can. I give away suits that I have worn only twice; still, every time I go to my closet I feel halfway upset. I am an active preacher, pastor, and public speaker. My ministry requires me to travel extensively and speak before audiences many times each day in all kinds of settings. Suits are my equivalent of a mechanic's overalls. Nevertheless, I feel awkward sometimes because that closet of mine seems like it is bulging with suits. It makes me wonder if I am not giving enough, so I give away four or five more suits.

Do you know what happens when I do that? Somebody blesses me, or I discover a dramatic sale on suits, or something like that. When you give as a way of life, God teaches us a vital lesson about His laws of sowing and reaping. It really is simple at its heart: you cannot outgive God. It is a theological, empirical, and practical impossibility! (Nevertheless, He wants us to try . . .)

Whatever you have, give it away—even if it is a penny! Whatever you are doing, be faithful in it. If your job is to clean toilets, then clean them faithfully. God will give to you if you are faithful in spirit as well as in deed. Believe me, God will give back to you. He will give you your own rest room—with a whole house or business attached to it!

The only way to follow in the footsteps of Jesus is to give like Jesus—and He gave everything He had and was for you. In return, God the Father gave Him all power and a name above every name! Even God's Son could not outgive the Father. I dare you, I challenge you, I urge you as a brother in Christ: give. Give in faith and watch the glory of God unfold in your life.

Pray this prayer with me:

Heavenly Father, I used to think giving was just a "have to" part of life in the kingdom. Now I see that it is a "get to" privilege and a part of our covenant with You. By Your grace, I will live to give in Jesus' name, amen.

SEPTEMBER 3

DO NOT SELL IT—GIVE IT AWAY!

Today's Scripture Reading: Luke 6:30–38 *Key Verse:* Luke 6:38

Give, and it will be given to you: good measure, pressed down, shaken together, and running over will be put into your bosom. For with the same measure that you use, it will be measured back to you.

You need to get rid of the "selling" mentality.

God did not bless you so that you could sell your old stuff. As odd as it sounds, I want you to get that out of your head. Instead, find someone who needs what you have and bless him with it! Just call it God's Economics 101.

When my wife and I were married, I bought her a new car. She wanted to know how she should sell her old one, but I said, "Let's find someone in need and give it to him." We learned that one of the members of our church needed a car, so we gave him the keys and said, "Here, take it!"

You see, *I ride in my harvest*. I invested through giving, and then I reaped what I invested. It is not some complicated theological formula: I give stuff away!

Are you blessed? Then do not talk about how you are trying to sell things. I do not care if you think you are giving someone a "deal" on your stuff at half price. You did not deserve it in the first place. (None of us does.) God gave it to you as a favor, so do not talk about selling it. You will earn far more in God's marketplace of giving than you will from a sale. I dare you to call somebody up and give that stuff away. Then just watch and see what God does in your life!

I will give you a hint: He will start flooding you with so many blessings that you will find it hard to contain them. All that means is that it is time to give away more blessings!

Pray this prayer with me:

Heavenly Father, You have blessed me in countless ways; now it is my turn to become a blesser. Lead me to those in need so I can give and bless freely without conditions or strings attached and with no thought for gifts in return. I dare to believe Your Word, and everything I sow I plant by faith in Your faithfulness. In Jesus' name, amen.

SEPTEMBER 4

YOU ARE BLESSED TO BE A BLESSING

Today's Scripture Reading: Luke 4:18–19 *Key Verse:* Luke 4:18

The Spirit of the LORD is upon Me,
Because He has anointed Me
To preach the gospel to the poor;
He has sent Me to heal the brokenhearted,
To proclaim liberty to the captives
And recovery of sight to the blind,
To set at liberty those who are oppressed.

When Jesus said that the Spirit of the Lord was upon Him to preach the gospel, the first group He mentioned was the poor. There is only one kind of news the poor want to hear, and that is good news about their finances.

You have to concede that Jesus understood that; it was the first thing He brought up. You may say, "But Jesus also said that we would always have the poor among us."

Do you know why we will always have the poor among us? It is because we will always have people who refuse to acknowledge or honor the principles of God. For the same reason, there will always be people who will not tithe. They will not understand and walk in God's kingdom ways.

I hope none of these descriptions fits you, because God has blessed you to be a blessing to others. It is part of your calling in the kingdom of God. For this reason, listening to and learning God's principles on finance are vital. Remember: it is the first thing Jesus addressed in His adult ministry. Make it the first thing you address after you finish your devotions today.

Begin by praying this prayer with me:

Father, I acknowledge that Your Spirit is upon me today. Because I have received Jesus Christ as my Lord and Savior, You have passed His commission on to me and my brothers and sisters in the church. I will honor Your law of sowing and reaping through my tithes, offerings, and liberal giving to others. Your Word is true: I have been blessed to be a blessing, and I will obey in Jesus' name, amen.

"TEST ME AND HOLD ON!"

Today's Scripture Reading: Malachi 3:10–12 *Key Verse:* Malachi 3:10

"Bring all the tithes into the storehouse,
That there may be food in My house,
And try Me now in this," says the Lord of hosts,
"If I will not open for you the windows of heaven
And pour out for you such blessing
That there will not be room enough to receive it."

When you give a tithe, you are bringing it to God's earthly "storehouse," the local church. There God does not spend your money; His people spend it to provide for the facilities and tools they use to build up and serve His kingdom on earth. God does not need your money as much as you need to give it. God is looking for your faith, and anything related to giving away your money will take faith!

That is why He was saying in Malachi, in essence, "Try Me. Believe Me! If I can get you to exercise your faith through your money, then I will have you covered everywhere else. You will have plenty of faith to believe Me for anything else after that."

If you have given the firstfruits of your income and that has stretched your faith, God will give it back to you in a heartbeat. Tithing is not about the money. The most important aspect of faithful tithing is that it proves you can handle more blessings without the blessings handling you. It is practical proof that you put God above your money.

Once you have proven yourself faithful to give, God will tell you secret things and share fresh ideas that no one else will believe, and your faith will grow in giant leaps. He will share incredible insights with you because you have proven that you have enough faith to walk where few—if any—have gone before.

Pray this prayer with me:

Holy Father, I accept Your challenge and I dare to prove Your Word is true. I will tithe my firstfruits to You with joy and faith, knowing that You will honor Your Word and pour out a blessing to me so I can be a blessing to others. In Jesus' name, amen.

THE SIMPLE SOLUTION TO A CHRONIC CURSE

Today's Scripture Reading: Malachi 3:8–12 *Key Verse:* Malachi 3:8

Will a man rob God? Yet you have robbed Me!
But you say, "In what way have we robbed You?" In tithes and offerings.

Too many church members are selfish. Many of us go to church and suck the Word out of our pastor with a simple and sinful goal: we get ours for our family, then we go home. If you do that, then you do not understand God's divine perspective and the way His divine hand moves among men and nations. We commit the same sin Malachi exposed 2,500 years ago if we go to church under the eyes of God and still rob Him!

Many Christians celebrated "the year of Jubilee" for God's people just before the new millennium began (see Lev. 25:10). They received raises, houses, and all kinds of things. Let me ask you a blunt question: are you getting blessed while robbing God? Are you among the millions of Christians who have so embraced man's culture that they could care less what their pastor goes through in the ministry as long as they can go to church and take what they need and leave? Do you really care about God?

If my questions are making you angry, then I may be hitting too close to home. If you are nodding your head in agreement, and if you have been tithing faithfully and joyfully, then you have not been cursing yourself. Instead, you have qualified yourself for a runaway, uncontainable blessing from the Father of blessings.

I want you to prosper and be blessed so you can be a blessing. Malachi said that if you rob God in tithes and offerings, then you are cursed. I am willing to risk your approval of my ministry and this book if I can help you step out from under a curse and into a blessing. The solution is simple: give your tithes to your church, and pray for faith to move on into offerings over and above the tithe.

Make the tithe the first check you write every time you receive income of any kind. You will be surprised at how the rest just seems to stretch and grow effortlessly. Look at tithing as a "get to" faith opportunity producing immeasurable blessings in your life and finances.

Pray this prayer with me:

Heavenly Father, You give me the power to earn income, and You give me breath day by day. I count it a privilege to return 10 percent to Your storehouse, and I anticipate seeing Your faithfulness demonstrated in my life as I obey in my tithes and offerings. In Jesus' name, amen.

Consider, Repent, Give, and Be Blessed

Today's Scripture Reading: Haggai 1:1–7 *Key Verse:* Haggai 1:7

Thus says the Lord of hosts: "Consider your ways!"

You have sown much but bring in little. You eat but you do not have enough. You drink but you are not filled. You clothe yourself but you are not warm. You receive a raise, but somehow it does not even put a dent in the bills. Something is terribly wrong, and the Lord says, "Consider your ways."

If you have a job and you do not tithe, you are cursed. You will miss the season of God's favor and get caught in the error of nonrepentance. You cannot move in the favor of God while showing such disrespect for Him!

Only a small percentage of America's church members tithe regularly. This means that only a small percentage of people in the kingdom understand that tithing is part of being a true worshiper—one who worships God in spirit and in truth.

If all you do is go to church and sing and pray to God without tithing, then all you are doing is giving Him lip service. God is no fool, and You cannot deceive Him. Jesus said, "Where your treasure is, there your heart will be also" (Luke 12:34 NKJV) in the context of giving to the poor. It applies equally well to this first priority of giving: the tithe. Pray with me:

Heavenly Father, forgive me for not tithing. I have been trying to hold on to money, and it has been slipping through my fingers. I have considered my ways, and I see that I have been robbing You. Forgive me. From now on I determine to give You a minimum of 10 percent of all my increase—and more as I have faith. In Jesus' name and power I embrace this change, amen.

STRETCH YOUR FAITH AND GIVE—SO YOU CAN GIVE EVEN MORE

Today's Scripture Reading: Matthew 13:23; Deuteronomy 8:18; Ezekiel 44:30 *Key Verse:* Ezekiel 44:30

The best of all firstfruits of any kind, and every sacrifice of any kind from all your sacrifices, shall be the priest's; also you shall give to the priest the first of your ground meal, to cause a blessing to rest on your house.

God offers us an opportunity for blessing if we will bring our firstfruit offerings into His storehouse, the church. Normally the only way you can bring Him a firstfruit offering is to have a crop.

A place of even greater faith and blessing begins with the firstfruit offering. Do you want to stretch out in faith and press beyond the thirty- and sixtyfold return to the hundredfold return Matthew 13:23 described? In that passage, Jesus explained the meaning of the parable of the sower to the disciples, and He said that the lives of those who hear His Word and practice it will produce those enormous returns.

If you dare to believe God's promises and want to test the truth that you cannot outgive God, then you can plant financial seeds into the church, your pastor and his family, the brethren, and the poor over and above the tithe (we call them freewill offerings). This is the heavenly equivalent of a high-yield investment requiring a much higher level of faith.

I challenge you to do more than tithe and give an additional firstfruits offering on the harvest you have already received. If you have the faith, begin to increase the percentage of your tithe and offering to 11 percent, then 12 percent, then 15 percent, and so on. In effect, you are tithing a portion of what you *expect* to harvest through God's blessing.

Remember that none of these returns are just for yourself or because of your deeds. You are blessed to be a blessing, and all of it comes from God.

Heavenly Father, thank You for Your faithful provision of all my needs. But I want to honor You by stretching my faith in Your faithfulness. You have given me giving ideas that require more than a thirty- or sixtyfold return, so I accept Your challenge in Jesus' name. I will go beyond the tithe and even beyond the normal offering to plant seeds for tomorrow's harvest, though that harvest is yet unseen. You know my heart, and I am learning to follow Yours. Thank You for the privilege of living to live and give in Jesus' footsteps. Amen.

WILL YOU PUT YOUR MONEY ON THE STATE OR ON GOD?

Today's Scripture Reading: Leviticus 23:9–11 *Key Verse:* Leviticus 23:10

Speak to the children of Israel, and say to them: "When you come into the land which I give to you, and reap its harvest, then you shall bring a sheaf of the firstfruits of your harvest to the priest."

God wants you to move beyond seeing what you get before you give. That is tithing, and you should already be doing that. God says, "I want to see how much faith you have for what you want to be done in your life this year." Bring Him something from your very first income of the year, something that represents what you believe you will receive from Him the rest of the year! Sow this firstfruits offering into God and see if He does not bless you totally beyond your expectations.

Why does God urge us to do this? Solomon wrote: "Honor the LORD with your possessions, / And with the firstfruits of all your increase; / So your barns will be filled with plenty, / And your vats will overflow with new wine" (Prov. 3:9–10 NKJV). God is saying, "Not only will I bless you materially, but I also will so fill you with new joy and a new spirit that they will be running over in your life!"

Here is the problem: Millions of Christians ignore these promises while planting "seed" in lotteries around the country week after week. The unspoken message this sends to God is that they have greater faith in the odds of winning the lottery than in the likelihood that God will keep His Word!

God offers you a far better deal: Sow into His "giving contest," and He *guarantees* that you will win more material blessings than you can contain and joy unspeakable as well! I do not know about you, but I do not want the kind of money that keeps me awake at night with worry.

God is offering you a deal that lets you sleep in peace night after night and get up every morning with a supernatural joy that is contagious! On top of that, your "winnings" can go right back into the kingdom through Spirit-led giving for even more material blessings and eternal rewards. This is God's offer; the choice is yours. Will you put your money on the state or on God? There is no better time to pray than right now:

Heavenly Father, Your offer is almost beyond belief, but I do believe You. I will invest my money, my life, and my future in Your kingdom bank for a maximum return on my investment. In Jesus' name, I am banking on Your Word, and it never returns to You without accomplishing its purpose! Amen.

ARE YOU AN ARMANI DRESSER BUT A BARGAIN-BASEMENT GIVER?

Today's Scripture Reading: 2 Corinthians 9:5–11 *Key Verse:* 2 Corinthians 9:6

This I say: He who sows sparingly will also reap sparingly, and he who sows bountifully will also reap bountifully.

It is easy to discern whom you really love. All you have to do is look at where you put your money and time. (You are right—this devotional might get a little rough for a while.)

Think about it: do you spend more money on your clothes than you give to God? Do you dress with Armani style but give to God bargain-basement style? If you do, then you love yourself more than you love God. In reality, you are your own Jehovah-Jireh ("the God who provides"). We may not like it, but we cannot hide the truth. It is plain for everyone to see.

It gets worse when we teach our children to grow up the same way. Despite our best efforts, our children—the next generation—will copy what we *do* more than what we say. If we live extravagantly but save poorly, our children will tend to take things one step further in their adult years. They will ultimately ditch the giving part altogether and bring a greater curse upon themselves and later generations.

God has a plan to make men and nations operate more effectively and efficiently. It is rooted in the law of sowing and reaping. It requires us to see beyond the now and anticipate what must be done for the generations to come. This is the very heart of kingdom living.

God planned for His Son to invade our world and lay down His life even before He created the earth—He made provision for us before we ever existed. What are you passing on to your children and your children's children? Are you teaching them how to be blessed so they can be a blessing, or are you teaching them how to live and acquire goods to live selfishly in this life, while making no provision for the generations to come? Consider your ways and make provision for tomorrow's generation in the kingdom.

Pray this prayer with me:

Holy Father, I repent for my nearsighted ways in the area of giving and sowing seeds for tomorrow. In Jesus' name, I will be a bountiful and joyful giver. In Your grace, I will teach my children by example how to give bountifully and reap joyfully while sowing precious seed into Your kingdom. Amen.

GOD GIVES HIS BLESSINGS (WITH NO SORROW ADDED)

Today's Scripture Reading: 2 Corinthians 9:6–15; Proverbs 10:21–22 *Key Verses:* 2 Corinthians 9:7–8

Let each one give as he purposes in his heart, not grudgingly or of necessity; for God loves a cheerful giver. And God is able to make all grace abound toward you, that you, always having all sufficiency in all things, may have an abundance for every good work.

God wants to bless you. He wants to pay your bills and correct your domestic situation. Why? He does not want you to be distracted from His kingdom purpose.

Let me give you some advice (once again, I am going to get personal here): do not get into any more debt. Do not get a new credit card—even if you receive ten attractive invitations in the mail tomorrow (and you probably will). If you cannot afford something, then do not touch it.

"But God promised me this!" If that is true, then you can surely wait until He brings it within your price range. Stores have sales, and God's favor always involves the miraculous. Keep checking the price until God brings it to you. Do not get impatient! God's Word says, "The blessing of the LORD makes one rich, / And *He adds no sorrow with it*" (Prov. 10:22 NKJV, emphasis mine). Above all, do not fall for what the Word calls "the snare of man"—do not spend money to impress people you do not even like!

If you will remain faithful in these little things, God will bless you with more. Pray this prayer with me:

Dear Father, from this day forward I will give cheerfully to You, to Your church, and to those in need. I am confident that You will supply everything I need plus an abundance of more so I can accomplish every good work You assign to me! And no sorrow will come with Your provision. In Jesus' name I praise You, amen.

September 12

Learn to Be Content

Today's Scripture Reading: Proverbs 10:21; Philippians 4:12–13

Key Verses: Philippians 4:12–13

I know how to be abased, and I know how to abound. Everywhere and in all things I have learned both to be full and to be hungry, both to abound and to suffer need. I can do all things through Christ who strengthens me.

Are you harboring a well-hidden grudge against God? Perhaps you live in a nice home but you are upset with God because you want a bigger house. You know that God will give you everything you need, but you are still secretly upset with Him because He has not supplied you with a bigger house. You feel that He has failed you, so you constantly battle thoughts of resentment bordering on bitterness.

Tell me this: how many houses can you live in at one time? Paul summed up the kingdom attitude about wealth and possessions when he said, "I have learned in whatever state I am, to be content" (Phil. 4:11 NKJV).

Too many of us have yielded to the driving compulsion of the world to reach for far more than we need and to lust for what we seemingly cannot have. Satan makes sure that no matter how much money, fame, or stuff we accumulate, it will never, ever be enough! We need deliverance from this consuming mentality.

God wants to multiply your wealth and bless you so you can be a blessing to others. Settle this in your spirit and remember that God's kingdom has no room for selfishness. As long as we act and live like a people constantly consumed, God will not entrust us with great riches or power in the earthly realm. He knows we will just spend it on ourselves or use it for our own gain. God does not want us to live in poverty; however, it is even worse to live in bondage to the love of money! The book of Proverbs says, "Better is a little with the fear of the LORD, / Than great treasure with trouble" (Prov. 15:16 NKJV).

Pray this prayer with me:

Heavenly Father, deliver me from the lust of the world for more stuff. I repent of my consumer mentality. Holy Spirit, teach me how to be content in whatever state I find myself so I can be blessed to be a blessing; in Jesus' name, amen.

AVOID THE PAIN: DO NOT COMPLAIN

Today's Scripture Reading: Matthew 6:33; Numbers 11:1–2 *Key Verse:* Numbers 11:1

When the people complained, it displeased the LORD; for the LORD heard it, and His anger was aroused. So the fire of the LORD burned among them, and consumed some in the outskirts of the camp.

Make sure you maintain a right attitude of thankfulness and gratitude to God.

The children of Israel turned their faith to things after God delivered them from the bondage of Egypt and led them into the wilderness. They complained because they did not have meat. They complained because of their clothes. They complained about water. They complained because they did not have some of the vegetables and herbs they had in Egypt. They complained about their leaders, and ultimately, they complained about God. In the end, it cost them their promise and their very lives. Is that a price any of us can afford to pay?

Are you upset with God for any reason right now? I know you would not want to admit it in public, but this is between you and God. Perhaps you are angry with Him because you have been believing for a car and you still have to take the bus. Does the bus get you to work and then back home? Maybe you need to realize that you drive a car by yourself, but on a bus you have a whole harvest field just waiting to be picked for the kingdom. Are you bought with a price? Are you not a kingdom representative on assignment? Then what are you upset about?

Keep your faith in God, not in things. Jesus said, "Seek first the kingdom of God and His righteousness, and all these things [which the Gentiles seek] shall be added to you" (Matt. 6:33 NKJV).

Pray this prayer with me:

Holy Father, I am sorry for all the times I have complained about how I am treated or about the things I have not received. Thank You for loving and saving me through Your Son, Jesus. Forgive me, I ask, and I will seek first Your kingdom and trust You for the rest. In Jesus' name, amen.

September 14

Honor the Lord with Your Firstfruits and Prosper

Today's Scripture Reading: Proverbs 3:9–10; James 1:18 *Key Verses:* Proverbs 3:9–10

Honor the LORD with your possessions,
And with the firstfruits of all your increase;
So your barns will be filled with plenty,
And your vats will overflow with new wine.

Why do we give the firstfruits? In a nutshell, God says that if we bring Him a part of what we think we will harvest and offer it to Him with joy, then He will cover, sanctify, and make holy everything that we are supposed to receive that year.

This means nothing can take away what He has ordained for you. Nothing can hinder or hold it back. You will receive everything God intended to give you as a blessing because He has sealed it and the devil cannot touch it. God puts it under the blood of Christ so you can walk in all of it and be what He has ordained.

Do not worry about it if you were faithful to say, "I know You will bless me, so I am going to give You a good piece of it even before I see it." This is the heart of faith and trust, and God will not overlook such an offering.

Pray this prayer with me:

Heavenly Father, You are My Source of abundant supply. I offer You the firstfruits, the best of what I have received, believing in faith for what will come by Your grace in the months ahead. I do it all in the name of Jesus, amen.

THE MORE YOU BLESS, THE MORE YOU WILL BE BLESSED

Today's Scripture Reading: Matthew 13:11–17 *Key Verse:* Matthew 13:12

Whoever has, to him more will be given, and he will have abundance; but whoever does not have, even what he has will be taken away from him.

God will give more to anyone who already has something, and He will take away from anyone who has nothing. It sounds like foolishness, does it not? It sounds like a reverse—Robin Hood scheme where you take away from the poor and give to the rich. Nevertheless, that is what God said.

What does it mean? God is saying, "I will give more to the person who is a good steward over what I have given him. I will bless the one who is obedient in the principles that I have given him. I will do it by taking away what I have given to people who are poor stewards and disobedient servants." It is important to notice that God is not talking about heathens. He is talking about church folks.

You were happy when you got that large tax refund check, but then all those unexpected problems cropped up. *Zip*—the stove went out. *Bam*—your transmission broke down. If these kinds of calamities are happening to you on a level that you cannot attribute to coincidence, then you should check your stewardship. God may be taking from you and giving to somebody else to help you step back into alignment with His way of doing things. This may not be the case, but you would be wise to carefully consider your ways.

Just think about it. The next time God gives you new furniture, do not sell your old furniture at a yard sale. Go find somebody who needs it and give it to him! Bless somebody. The more you bless, the more you will be blessed. This is not rocket science; it is simply the divine law of sowing and reaping in action.

Pray this prayer with me:

Heavenly Father, the blessings You have given me seem to be slipping through my fingers. A wave of problems suddenly came to siphon away my resources. Holy Spirit, search my heart and show me if there is any unrepented-of sin or ungodly way in my life. I ask for forgiveness and restoration in Jesus' name. I commit all that I have and all that I long for to You. Make my life acceptable to You, Lord. I ask You to once again grant me Your grace, mercy, favor, and abundant provision so I can be a blessing.

YOU WILL BLESS EVERYONE AROUND YOU FROM YOUR OVERFLOW!

Today's Scripture Reading: Malachi 3:10; Matthew 25:14–30

Key Verse: Matthew 25:21

His lord said to him, "Well done, good and faithful servant; you were faithful over a few things, I will make you ruler over many things. Enter into the joy of your lord."

In the book of Matthew, Jesus revealed the kingdom principle that God will bless the faithful with more and remove whatever He had placed in the care of the unfaithful.

If all you have is a one-room house with an outhouse, God will give you more if you are a good steward over that possession. Faithfulness is the great leveler in the kingdom. God is essentially saying, "If you understand that whatever you have is to be used for the kingdom, then I will bless you and give you even more. But if you do not understand that, or if you choose to keep things for yourself anyway, then what you have I will take away and give to someone else who is faithful."

God declared in Malachi, "'Bring all the tithes into the storehouse, / That there may be food in My house, / And try Me now in this,' / Says the LORD of hosts, / 'If I will not open for you the windows of heaven /And pour out for you such blessing / That *there will not be room enough to receive it*.'"(Mal. 3:10 NKJV, emphasis mine).

Why would God waste His blessings by pouring out so much that we cannot hold it? He is not a wasteful God. When Jesus fed the five thousand in Matthew 14:20–21, He had the disciples collect the remaining bread in twelve baskets. Another time He fed four thousand, and the disciples gathered up seven baskets of food (see Matt. 15:37–38).

What He is saying through the prophet Malachi is this: "I am going to bless you so much that everybody around you gets to be blessed." If you are faithful with what you have, God will bless you so much that you will bless people with your overflow! Now that is kingdom economics in action.

It is time to change. It is time to take up His cross, *deny yourself*, and follow Him. It makes all the difference.

Pray this prayer with me:

Father, I believe Your Word and trust Your promises. In Your grace, I will be faithful to carefully steward and multiply those things You entrust to me. Make me a blessing to those around me in Jesus' name, amen.

SEPTEMBER 17

YOUR FAMILY IS ALSO BLESSED TO BE A BLESSING

Today's Scripture Reading: Genesis 26:1–5 *Key Verses:* Genesis 26:3–4

Dwell in this land, and I will be with you and bless you; for to you and your descendants I give all these lands, and I will perform the oath which I swore to Abraham your father. And I will make your descendants multiply as the stars of heaven; I will give to your descendants all these lands; and in your seed all the nations of the earth shall be blessed.

Millions of families are in crisis today. Divorce, abuse, poverty, abandonment—all hell has broken out against the family. Why?

Satan has an agenda for the family's demise because he knows that wealth and power begin to multiply through the generations. He knows that incredible riches in the physical and spiritual realms can come through the diligence and stewardship of a family. He is out to destroy the family so he can nullify the threat of their accumulated wealth, power, and wisdom from generation to generation. He will do almost anything to keep a family from fulfilling its destiny

Have you noticed that whenever families have focused their resources across generational lines, they have begun to dominate their occupation or field of enterprise?

There are a few family names, such as Rothschild, Rockefeller, Dupont, Kennedy, Hearst, Ford, and Getty, that are recognized around the world. These families come from different ethnic, economic, and religious backgrounds, but they have certain things in common. While some of the powerful families in world history allegedly resorted to immoral or unscrupulous methods to build their fortunes and power, most conserved their wealth and passed their wisdom and leadership abilities from generation to generation to create economic and political dynasties on earth.

We have a greater kingdom on our minds, but it is still composed of families.

Our families should be blessing other families, communities, and even nations. Your family has a truckload of blessings just waiting in heaven. All you need to do is believe God and pull it down and distribute throughout the earth in Jesus' name. Pray with me:

Heavenly Father, I am beginning to see the bigger picture. You want me to think transgenerationally. You want me to work in the kingdom and plan with my children and my children's children in mind. You want to bless me—and my children and their children—so we can become a blessing for generations to come. So be it. I will believe Your Word and receive Your blessings in Jesus' name, amen.

Sow in Faith and Reverse the Curse

Today's Scripture Reading: Matthew 13:3–23; Mark 4:3–20 *Key Verse:* Mark 4:13

He said to them, "Do you not understand this parable? How then will you understand all the parables?"

Jesus said that if you do not understand the parable of the sower, then you will not understand any of His parables. This is like saying you will not understand the Bible because God has framed all of His Word in the context of sowing and reaping.

Paul wrote, "Do not be deceived, God is not mocked; for whatever a man sows, that he will also reap" (Gal. 6:7 NKJV). The very thoughts you cling to and take in, the things you meditate and chew on, will multiply in your life.

Perhaps we have lived on the edge of "not enough" so much because we really do not understand the law of sowing and reaping. If you are expecting a harvest but have not been tithing, then you can forget it according to God's Word!

Do not wait until you are out of debt to start giving tithes and offerings. The kingdom does not work that way. When you withhold the tithe and hold back the offerings and from giving, you are literally sowing yourself in debt. The law of sowing and reaping applies to everything, and it cannot be broken. That is why so many Christians are broke.

Reverse the curse immediately by sowing a different seed. Instead of sowing doubt and unbelief with your lips, speak the Word of God in faith and praise Him for His many blessings. Instead of sowing a curse by holding back the tithe and offerings, sow them in the soil of the kingdom with joy. You will begin to harvest a totally different kind of crop that will bring gladness and abundance to your life. Pray with me:

Heavenly Father, I am taking You at Your Word and I am planting new seeds of money, faith, and the confession of Your Word today. I thank You in advance for a harvest of blessings that I cannot contain so I can finally become a blessing to others. I repent for the times I have withheld my tithe, and today I reverse the curse through obedience and joyful giving. In Jesus' name I pray, amen.

RESTORE THE COVENANT AND RENEW THE POWER TO GET WEALTH

Today's Scripture Reading: Deuteronomy 8:11–20 *Key Verse:* Deuteronomy 8:18

You shall remember the Lord your God, for it is He who gives you power to get wealth, that He may establish His covenant which He swore to your fathers, as it is this day.

Why don't Christians generate wealth in large numbers? The answer is in Deuteronomy. We have broken our covenant with God—we broke our promise and severed our agreement. The Lord will not help us when we are out of covenant, so we lose the power to get wealth!

We must reestablish our covenant with Him through repentance and true obedience to His Word. God clearly explained that the "power to get wealth" is crucial to His kingdom so that "He may establish His covenant." God wants unsaved people around you to notice how He blesses you *and* how much you bless others with those blessings!

The world says you become wealthy by focusing exclusively on the accumulation of money while ignoring everything else. We do things differently in God's kingdom. He says we accumulate wealth by focusing upon Him and His kingdom; and rather than hoard and reinvest our earnings, we are to give them away as fast as we can! The growth of our assets does not depend so much upon compounding interest or profit margins as it does upon the faithfulness of God.

It is time to remember God and to remind ourselves who it is who gives us power to get wealth. When we do this, He will bless us so we can establish His covenant in the earth and build His kingdom.

Pray this prayer with me:

Holy Father, I am bringing everything to a halt right now. I repent for forgetting You in all my frantic works and struggle to get ahead. In this moment I arrest every thought, still my heart, and focus my eyes upon You alone. You are the Source of my strength and ability; You give me my creative ideas and the power to succeed. My life is Yours, and You are my Hope and Song. I know You will bless me so I can demonstrate the power of Your kingdom covenant right in the middle of my world. In Jesus' name I praise You, amen.

OBEY TO AVOID THE AUTOMATIC CURSE OF POVERTY

Today's Scripture Reading: Deuteronomy 28:15–68 *Key Verse:* Deuteronomy 28:15

It shall come to pass, if you do not obey the voice of the Lord your God, to observe carefully all His commandments and His statutes which I command you today, that all these curses will come upon you and overtake you.

No study of God's Word is complete and honest if the studier avoids or minimizes the consequences of disobedience. For our own protection, we must understand that a curse automatically falls upon anyone who willfully disobeys God's commands and kingdom principles.

What is the curse? It is poverty.

You will notice something alarming if you read Deuteronomy 28:15–68—you will get a clear picture of this nation! America has developed a spirit of poverty primarily because of its willful disobedience to the covenant with God. Overall, we are nation of truce breakers, and yes, I am speaking of the body of Christ too. The body of Christ has committed treason by abandoning kingdom principles in favor of the traditions of men.

Only one path back into the blessings of God exists: we must return to kingdom principles. No matter how stubborn we are, and no matter how many people transgress God's laws and principles, we are powerless to break or undo God's laws. The opposite happens: God's laws will break us.

The refreshing side to all this is that simple obedience allows us to bypass all these curses and difficulties. When we observe God's covenant and honor Him, He showers us with blessings without sorrow.

Pray this prayer with me:

Holy Father, I choose to obey Your voice and heed Your Word. I will remember You and praise You as my Redeemer and Rock. By Your grace, I will keep Your commands and statutes with joy. I command poverty to flee and prosperity to flow; in Jesus' name, amen.

September 21

Welcome to the Upside-Down Kingdom of Blessing!

Today's Scripture Reading: Matthew 6:9–13 *Key Verses:* Matthew 6:9–13, emphasis mine

In this manner, therefore, pray:
Our Father in heaven,
Hallowed be Your name.
Your kingdom come.
Your will be done
On earth as it is in heaven.
Give us this day our daily bread.
And forgive us our debts,
As we forgive our debtors.
And do not lead us into temptation,
But deliver us from the evil one.
For Yours is the kingdom and the power and the glory forever. Amen.

How does God's kingdom "come"? It comes when we displace the kingdom of darkness.

If we really do not have anything, it is possible that we do not totally understand the kingdom of God. If we really understood how the kingdom works, we would give away more riches and earn more.

Remember that everything is upside-down in the kingdom by the world's standards. To receive, you must give. The only way to receive wealth God's way is to give away wealth!

When we give, we declare to the spirit of poverty that it has no hold over us. We just give more and break its grip! You will never find a better way to live, because this is God's plan and will for you. These are the basic building blocks of kingdom living. Are you ready to really start living God's way? Then get ready to give.

Pray this prayer with me:

Heavenly Father, I thank You for bringing me into Your kingdom through Jesus Christ. I am convinced that Your upside-down kingdom is right-side-up, and the kingdoms of this world are wrong-side-out. It is a privilege to give, to sow, to believe, and then to receive from Your hand. I am blessed to be a blessing, and that is what I will be. Amen.

YOU ARE A WALKING "KINGDOM EMPOWERMENT ZONE"

Today's Scripture Reading: Matthew 25:31–46 *Key Verse:* Matthew 25:40

The King will answer and say to them, "Assuredly, I say to you, inasmuch as you did it to one of the least of these My brethren, you did it to Me."

Have you heard the buzz term *empowerment zone?*

People everywhere are trying to get in on the world system's kingdom of the empowerment zones. The federal government created these zones to correct problems in our society, but I guarantee you that years from now, everyone will discover that they still missed it.

"Empowerment" is not new to God. He ordained before the earth began that His people of faith would empower others through their blessings and the power God gave them.

God did not command you to bless those who are already blessed; He wants you to find those who are less blessed so you can bless them. He wants you to raise them up to a new standard. The only thing He asks about those you bless is this: "Find the 'least of the brethren' and give to them."

In most churches, you see the blessed blessing the blessed. That is not God's best. We need to find those who do not have much and elevate them to new levels of understanding and discipleship so they can walk on their own. That is one reason Jesus said, "Go therefore and make disciples of all the nations" (Matt. 28:19 NKJV).

Someone had to meet you somewhere and sweat and pray over you so you could reach the place where you are today. Don't you think you have an obligation to go back and find someone who is just like you were—weary, worn, sad, crazy, and going to hell—and turn his life around?

Heavenly Father, You sent Your Son to save me and transform my life. Help me to do the same for someone else. Guide my steps and lead me to the person You want me to serve. Give me boldness to share the gospel of the kingdom, and then to stay with him in prayer, fellowship, training, and support until he can disciple others. In Jesus' name I pray, amen.

WHAT ARE YOU DOING TO MEET NEEDS IN THE CHURCH?

Today's Scripture Reading: 1 Corinthians 12:20–26; James 1:27 *Key Verse:* James 1:27

Pure and undefiled religion before God and the Father is this: to visit orphans and widows in their trouble, and to keep oneself unspotted from the world.

Look closely at the people sitting in your church service next time you attend. Are any single mothers struggling to raise children on one income with limited time and resources? Do any widows need help? Are there elderly people who cannot drive or have difficulty getting around? Do you see teenagers without fathers or mothers who need someone older to talk to? What are you doing to bless them?

I challenge you to do more than bless those who are already blessed. Seek out the people who need help. Teach them, work with them, serve them, and educate them about God's kingdom principles. Bring them to a new level of faith and show them how to sustain themselves in the Lord.

Cover these people in prayer and practical service and support the way God says we should cover the body. Share the way God said to share. When you do, He will be there whenever you cry out to Him.

Pray this prayer with me:

Holy Father, I repent of focusing my attention, approval, and blessings on the blessed and especially gifted members of my church. Now I want to see with Your eyes and reach out with Your heart to bless those in need. Give me discernment and compassion to touch their lives, bring blessing, and restore hope in Jesus' name, amen.

I WILL BLESS THE FAMILIES OF THE EARTH THROUGH YOU

Today's Scripture Reading: Galatians 3:26–29; Genesis 12:1–7 *Key Verses:* Genesis 12:1–3

Get out of your country, From your family And from your father's house,
To a land that I will show you. I will make you a great nation;
I will bless you And make your name great; And you shall be a blessing.
I will bless those who bless you, And I will curse him who curses you;
And in you all the families of the earth shall be blessed.

Abraham was more than a man whom God greatly blessed. He also was a blessing to others because of God's promise: "I will make you a great nation; / I will bless you / And make your name great; / And you shall be a blessing." What did God do to Abraham in this verse? He identified the call and purpose of Abram with His call and purpose according to His own schedule and agenda. It would not happen because Abram wanted it to happen; it came to pass God's way.

God still wants to bless all the families of the earth through His kingdom. For that reason, He has to remove us from the familiar to prepare us for the unthinkable and the miraculous.

Most of us in the church are disjointed from the corporate move of God. The truth is that if your vision does not identify with God's overall plan, then it is a "wish-ion." Many are still stuck in the rut of Genesis 12:1—they have not left the "home" of the familiar and the comfortable, and they refuse to separate from the trappings of the past.Others are stuck in Genesis 12:2; they constantly remind us how God is blessing them long before we see any fruit in their lives. Very few reach the heart of the matter in Genesis 12:3, where they understand that everything happens because God has an overall plan for the salvation of the world—and He wants to demonstrate it through our physical and spiritual families.

Think about it in perspective: you are the beginning of a divine plan and eternal kingdom that does not stop at your grave! It flows through your physical and spiritual bloodline on an eternal journey of glory and wonder.

What an awesome privilege we have in Jesus Christ! Pray this prayer with me:

Holy Father, thank You for including me in the inheritance of the kingdom through Jesus Christ. Now I can pass along the anointing, blessing, and destiny of the call to my children and my children's children. Thank You, Father. Amen.

I HAVE THE KINGDOM ON MY MIND

Today's Scripture Reading: Matthew 6 *Key Verse:* Matthew 6:33

Seek first the kingdom of God and His righteousness.

God wants us to seek and think about His kingdom in virtually everything we do. Since He always looks at the motives of the heart, He knows whether or not you are thinking primarily about yourself when you pray, "God, give me that promotion," or "God, give me a car."

Remember that God blesses you so you can be a blessing to others, and He knows whether or not this principle is rooted in your heart and life. Understand that He gives you all His blessings so you can give them away in many ways. Some things you are to pass down to your children and their children after them. Other things you are to give away to others. God has given you everything you have and everything you are so you can bring others into the kingdom.

When you have the kingdom in your heart and on your mind, you can pray, "Father, give me a new car," or "God, give me that promotion," with proper motives and great effect. Why? You know that you can use those blessings as tools to share the gospel of your risen Savior with those who are under your authority or who work with you. They can create a platform and an open door for you to activate kingdom principles and lead someone into the kingdom through those blessings.

Once you understand that everything God gives you essentially belongs to someone else, He will start giving you more! Those blessings belong to Him, and He invests them in you so you can bless someone else. If He gives you a whole house full of new furniture, do not sell the old at a yard sale and do not call people to ask if they want to buy it. Give away the old furniture and do it in Jesus' name! Tell them God told you to bless them because He blessed you! Then you will enjoy good reaping seasons for the kingdom.

My Father in heaven, my life is not my own; my children and my spouse are not my own; and none of my possessions, abilities, or gifts belongs to me. Everything comes from and belongs to You, and that is the way it should be. Use me to glorify Your name, and show me where to sow my seed for a great harvest of giving, healing, salvation, restoration, grace, and mercy in the lives of others! In Jesus' name I will give, believe, and build the kingdom. Amen.

IT IS TIME FOR THE CHURCH TO SHINE

Today's Scripture Reading: Matthew 5:14–16; Acts 1:8 *Key Verse:* Matthew 5:16

Let your light so shine before men, that they may see your good works and glorify your Father in heaven.

The divine principle that we are blessed to be a blessing applies to far more than individuals in the church or God's kingdom. God is calling local church congregations to bless those who live on the block where the church meets. He requires entire congregations to work together to bless their neighborhoods or their entire cities. This amounts to a revolution in our ministry thinking.

God wants suburban churches to stretch themselves by faith at His direction to sow buildings, land, resources, and *people* in inner-city neighborhoods in Jesus' name. He wants big city churches to expand their vision and plant churches in rural areas where God's Word is hard to find. God wants to tear down every fence we have labored to build in the flesh over the last two centuries in America.

This may be a tall order, but when has God called us to do something we could easily accomplish in our own strength? *Never.*

Pray this prayer with me:

Heavenly Father, I pray for my local church family. Open our eyes so we can see the depth and breadth of Your vision. Anoint us and guide us to reach those who do not know You, those who live near our place of worship. Then direct our steps so we can bring Your light and power to our entire city and region in the mighty name of Jesus, amen.

SEPTEMBER 27

LORD, DELIVER US FROM SELF

Today's Scripture Reading: Romans 11:36–12:3; 1 Corinthians 6:19–20

Key Verses: 1 Corinthians 6:19–20

Do you not know that your body is the temple of the Holy Spirit who is in you, whom you have from God, and you are not your own? For you were bought at a price; therefore glorify God in your body and in your spirit, which are God's.

The problems that seem most dangerous to the church are those we create ourselves over a long period of time. This happens with subtle heresies that begin in truth and gradually move into apostasy; with cultural acceptance that transforms slowly to spiritual compromise.

One of our most serious problems is that we have trained congregations in the body of Christ to be spiritually selfish. We come to church services with the primary goal of enjoying ourselves and being blessed. It is good to be blessed, but God has a higher purpose and priority for our lives than that we be blessing-seekers all our days. Our inward focus on personal blessings for "us four and no more" has caused us to miss what God is doing in the earth today. We are fond of publicly praying to the Lord, "Your will be done." But we are really saying, "*My* will be done, and with as little trouble as possible, please, Lord." We do not understand that the only reason God blesses us is so that we can be a blessing!

I will say it again: it is time for a change. Pray this prayer with me:

Father, thank You for confronting us with our selfishness and self-absorbed religious attitudes. As we keep our eyes on You, expand our vision to see the needy and hurting who live around us and among us. I pray, "Your will be done on earth as it is in heaven"—and begin with me. In Jesus' name, amen.

SEPTEMBER 28

GOD DID NOT SAY, "BLESSED ARE THE PERPETUAL SPIRITUAL BABIES"

Today's Scripture Reading: Hebrews 5:12; Matthew 10:7–8

Key Verses: Matthew 10:7–8, emphasis mine

As you go, preach, saying, "The kingdom of heaven is at hand." Heal the sick, cleanse the lepers, raise the dead, cast out demons. Freely you have received, freely give.

Invariably, it is the well fed who fear missing a meal most. Paul was frustrated with well-fed Jewish believers in the first century because they kept taking in the Word of God but refused to give out or teach it to others. He told them, "Though by this time you ought to be teachers, you need someone to teach you again the first principles of the oracles of God; and you have come to need milk and not solid food" (Heb. 5:12 NKJV). We face the identical problem today in our churches.

God is saying to the church today, "I have already given you enough bread. I have given you enough Word in the previous years to sustain you in total supply and victory for several more years! I have given you enough of My revelation and authority to set you free from every bondage, difficulty, and obstacle entangling you and those around you. I have given you enough of My wisdom and power to cancel every debt, heal every sickness, restore every broken home and marriage, and fully establish and equip the body of Christ for the next generation."

God has fed us very well, but we have been sitting and doing nothing. It is time to rest in the revelation and supply that God has already given us. It is time to reach out and bless others with God's abundant supply of blessings.

Pray this prayer with me:

Heavenly Father, forgive me for avoiding the growth pains that come with maturity in the faith. You have placed a call upon my life, and it is time for me to answer the call to greater responsibility, service, and risk in Your name. In Your power and anointing, I will accomplish the task You set before me. I will reach out to others and bless them with the abundance of resources, teaching, and training You have given to me. In Jesus' name I pray, amen.

FORGIVE US OUR DEBTS AS WE FORGIVE OUR DEBTORS . . .

Today's Scripture Reading: Leviticus 25; Matthew 6:9–15 *Key Verse:* Leviticus 25:10

You shall consecrate the fiftieth year, and proclaim liberty throughout all the land to all its inhabitants. It shall be a Jubilee for you; and each of you shall return to his possession, and each of you shall return to his family.

If you still do not believe that being blessed to be a blessing is God's idea, then you should look closely at the God-ordained year of Jubilee in the Bible. It was a time in the Israelite cycle of years when people, land, and finances returned to their original places. As believers redeemed by the blood of the Lamb, we enjoy an unbroken state of grace in Jesus. As in the Jubilee in days of old, not only are we released and restored, but we are also required to release and restore others!

The Jubilee was a time to restore property lost through debts or tragedy. It was a time to put back together all the families separated through slavery or economic hardship. It was a season for family members to help less fortunate family members get back on their feet again. It marked the time when all debts were canceled. We live in that season permanently through the finished work of Jesus Christ. The Lord even talked about forgiving debtors when He taught His disciples how to pray! (See Matt. 6:12.)

When God challenged me on this requirement that I forgive my debtors, it was a hard pill to swallow. I did it anyway—to the tune of $86,000. People owed me the money, but I knew I had heard the Lord, so I canceled their debts.

When I challenged my congregation to do the same, they responded in an incredible way. When we forgave those debts, God released such a spirit of Jubilee among us that everything broke loose. We became even greater blessing to those around us!

Let me challenge you to step into a higher level of receiving and being a blessing. Begin by canceling the debts others owe you. It will release a whole new level of freedom, blessing, and anointing in your life because God takes notice when we step out by faith to obey Him and put His Word into practice. Pray with me right now:

Holy Father, I thank You for sending Jesus to be our eternal Jubilee. I want to walk in total freedom in my life, my worship, and my ministry to others. As a first step, by faith I forgive, cancel, and release all the debts owed to me by others. As I release them, I celebrate my release into new levels of blessing and being a blessing. In Jesus' name I pray, amen.

September 30

Are You Laboring in Love to Preach the Gospel?

Today's Scripture Reading: 1 Thessalonians 2:8–12 *Key Verses:* 1 Thessalonians 2:8–9

Affectionately longing for you, we were well pleased to impart to you not only the gospel of God, but also our own lives, because you had become dear to us. For you remember, brethren, our labor and toil; for laboring night and day, that we might not be a burden to any of you, we preached to you the gospel of God.

What does Jubilee mean to us today? How does it apply to everyday life in the body of Christ? None of us in America endures the bonds of slavery any longer, but slavery of the heart and mind is rampant, and it takes many forms. We are well acquainted with the problem of debts as well as the crushing weight of sickness and disease. The Lord of Jubilee can bring bondage-breaking power and anointing to every one of these situations.

The fact is that only a minority of the people in God's congregation need to be set free in Jubilee—most of us already rejoice in God's abundant blessings and live in a good measure of freedom and power. The majority of us in the kingdom are to take the benefits of Jubilee to those in bondage and lack. We are to embody Jubilee to those around us. Above all, we are to take the unconditional love of Jesus everywhere we go.

We are to bless others with the very blessings that God has given us. Are you blessed? Are you a blessing?

Pray this prayer with me:

Dear Father, help me not to be "weary in well doing." I want to be a blessing every day of my life to as many people as possible. Use me as an extension of Your hand and heart on the earth. Touch the hurting, the wounded, the broken, and the lost through me, Lord. And may You be glorified and honored above all. In Jesus' name I pray, amen.

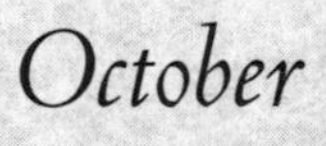

October

Covenant Community

GET RIGHT AND FORGIVE SO GOD CAN FORGIVE YOU!

Today's Scripture Reading: Mark 11:22–26 *Key Verses:* Mark 11:25–26

Whenever you stand praying, if you have anything against anyone, forgive him, that your Father in heaven may also forgive you your trespasses. But if you do not forgive, neither will your Father in heaven forgive your trespasses.

Do you have spiritual common sense? So many saints are so "deep" that they miss the blessings of God. They are so blind to the common-sense things of God that they actually hinder the move of the Holy Spirit.

Forgiveness is one of those common-sense things that some of the "deep" folks just pass over, but according to God forgiveness is not a suggestion. It is an absolute requirement. It is so important to the kingdom that God says you had better not be angry or unforgiving toward anyone when you pray or He simply will not hear you. You can forget about receiving forgiveness if you are not willing to forgive others.

When I read through Mark 11, I notice that God did not put a "Yeah, but" in those verses. It does not seem fair if your daddy molested you or your mama abused you physically and mentally, but forgiveness is not about fairness. This divine requirement is about your health and well-being, and it is about the well-being of God's family.

God wants you to forgive others so *you* can get off the hook, not those who harmed, misused, abused, or offended you. As long as you harbor unforgiveness, you are, in essence, handing your tormentor the end of the chain that is wrapped around your heart. When you forgive, you snap every link that gives that person (and the memories of what happened) the power to harm you. It also releases God's forgiveness to flood through your own life.

Finally, unforgiveness is one of the most deadly doorways for the devil. It provides a legal foothold in your life for Satan and his imps to harass and oppress you (see Eph. 4:26–27; Heb. 12:15; James 5:9). Unforgiveness will shorten your life and rob you of untold blessings. The person who hurt you probably will not even lose one night's sleep, so who is really being hurt by your unforgiveness?

The cost is too high for you to cling to your grudge even one more day! Get right and forgive so that God can forgive you! Now that sounds like spiritual common sense. Pray with me:

Heavenly Father, I choose to forgive and release each person who has hurt, harmed, or threatened me. I release them to You, and I ask You to release me from my sins and failures today, in Jesus' name. Amen.

October 2

Release Your Enemies to God's Mercy and Be Free

Today's Scripture Reading: Romans 12:19–21; Ephesians 4:31–32; Acts 8:23

Key Verses: Romans 12:19–21

"Vengeance is Mine, I will repay," says the Lord. Therefore
"If your enemy is hungry, feed him;
If he is thirsty, give him a drink;
For in so doing you will heap coals of fire on his head."
Do not be overcome by evil, but overcome evil with good.

What goes through your mind when I say, "Forgiveness is not an option"? Are you sitting there with this book in your hands thinking, *I am not going to forgive that person—no way?*

Your unforgiveness is actually doing a favor for the person who wronged you. When you choose not to forgive someone, you stand in the way of God doing what He needs to do to straighten him out. You have taken God's place with your unforgiveness, but you cannot touch that person the way God can.

Say that someone really did you a wrong turn, and ever since you have waited for and anticipated the day he would take a fall. Instead you had to hear him brag about his new car and the promotion he received (instead of you). Every time you turn around, that person is getting blessed! Why? It is because you are angry with him and refuse to forgive him.

God will not execute His mercy and justice in that person's life as long as you stand in the way. In essence, you have held God back from doing what He needs to do to straighten him out. And all you got out of the deal is a crook in your neck and the growing cancer on your soul called bitterness. Now that does *not* make spiritual sense.

Pray this prayer with me:

Holy Father, I repent of my unforgiving attitude toward others. Today I start afresh by forgiving those who have harmed me with their words, their deeds, and their attitudes toward me. I release them to Your mercy and grace, and go on in Your blessings. Thank You for forgiving me and for giving me my life back. Thank You for taking off the heavy weights of unforgiveness, anger, and bitterness, and for replacing them with joy unspeakable. In Jesus' name, amen.

Your Enemies May Not Know Better—Pray for Them

Today's Scripture Reading: Matthew 5:38–48 *Key Verses:* Matthew 5:44–45

I say to you, love your enemies, bless those who curse you, do good to those who hate you, and pray for those who spitefully use you and persecute you, that you may be sons of your Father in heaven.

Each time you refuse to forgive, you are actually being selfish. Have you noticed that the people who hurt and offend others the most are usually hurt themselves? They are so wounded inside that they lash out against you and everyone else as a form of protection. When you cling to an offense, you are focusing on yourself and not on the offender.

My three brothers and I rarely talked with my father because of the resentment we felt toward him. My daddy was a strict disciplinarian, and we thought he did not love us. When Daddy suffered a stroke, I finally got up enough nerve to talk to him at the hospital. I was in my early thirties by then, but it still took a lot of courage for me to ask him this question while he was lying in bed: "Daddy, why did you treat us the way you did?"

Daddy looked up at me with tears in his eyes, and he began to describe his childhood. I did not know that my father had left home when he was only fourteen years old. Nor did I know that he had had to raise all of his eight brothers and sisters by himself. He told me that his daddy stole his car, threw him out into the street, and took his money. I had no idea that my dad's father never hugged him.

My father cried as he told me what had happened to him, and immediately the Holy Ghost said, "Here is a seventy-year-old man who has been locked up for seventy years, not knowing any better and doing the best he can."

In that brief moment I received an instant release, and I began to feel sorry for my dad. He had gone through life not knowing how to love my brothers and me, even though he wanted to. He did not know how to touch me. He wanted to, but he could not.

Some of the people who hurt you may be jealous or afraid of you. That is why God commands us to pray for our enemies—they are hurt. That releases Him to step into their lives with supernatural power and straighten out their pain and rearrange their minds. Pray this prayer with me:

Holy Father, I forgive my debtors and those who have harmed me in any way. Bless them, restore them, heal them, and redeem them. In Jesus' name I pray, amen.

Got That Old Vigilante Christianity?

Today's Scripture Reading: Ephesians 4:31–32;
1 Corinthians 13

Key Verses: Ephesians 4:31–32

Let all bitterness, wrath, anger, clamor, and evil speaking be put away from you, with all malice. And be kind to one another, tenderhearted, forgiving one another, just as God in Christ forgave you.

There are too many "head-rolling" saints loose in the church. At the slightest offense, they want to take the law into their own hands and execute their own brand of justice on their offenders in the name of God. That is "vigilante Christianity," and Jesus will have nothing to do with it! (After all, it was that kind of "justice" that put Him on the cross in spite of His sinless life!)

Listen, if someone hurts you that badly, just forgive him quickly. Pray, "Lord, come on in and do whatever You have to do. I am stepping out of the way through the door of forgiveness. Now I release You to deal with this person in Your own way."

We actually think we have the right to pay someone back when he hurts or offends us. Virtually everyone has someone he has not forgiven—especially people from the distant past. How about you? Have you forgiven your mama? How about your daddy? Did you forgive the pastor from your former church?

Here is the acid test: *Is unforgiveness motivating you?* Do you catch yourself saying, "I am going to show him. I have a right!"

God says, "No, you do not have a right." If you cannot forgive, then do not even bother to pray. Just go about your business and remain powerless. God says, "Pass on your mercy, pass on your love, pass on your kindness." Get rid of that spirit of unforgiveness and allow the healing Spirit of God to flood your life!

Father, forgive them, for they know not what they do. I know You have heard those words before, Father. I forgive those who wounded me, and I release them into Your hands for healing and restoration. As for justice, none of us could survive our just sentence; so I ask that Your grace would cover them just as it has covered me. In Jesus' name I pray, amen.

October 5

Cut Away the Unwanted Baggage

Today's Scripture Reading: Hebrews 12:14–15; Matthew 18:21–22 *Key Verses:* Hebrews 12:14–15

Pursue peace with all people, and holiness, without which no one will see the Lord: looking carefully lest anyone fall short of the grace of God; lest any root of bitterness springing up cause trouble, and by this many become defiled.

Forgiveness allows us to process the good out of a difficult situation while discarding the potentially dangerous by-products of bitterness, malice, and chronic anger. When we refuse to forgive, it is as if we can no longer eliminate the dangerous wastes in our spirit. The poisons can accumulate and threaten our very existence if we allow the blockage to continue.

The equivalent of this function in the human body takes place in the colon, a large tube at the very end of the large intestine. (This devotional may be a bit graphic, but I guarantee that you will never forget the essence of its message!)

When a patient experiences chronic blockage in the colon, it can be so serious that surgery must be performed to preserve the patient's life. In a colonoscopy, surgeons remove all or a significant portion of the patient's diseased colon. He must be fitted with a specially designed plastic bag worn under his clothing that is attached to a tube extruding from his body. That tube allows the patient to excrete body wastes into the bag, and he will always have to carry around that bag and whatever it may contain.

In the realm of the heart, you undergo a spiritual colonoscopy when you choose to carry around a grudge instead of eliminating it through the normal channels of forgiveness and reconciliation. You are doomed to carry around that unsightly bag with its noxious wastes of unforgiveness, bitterness, strife, and anger twenty-four hours a day.

I have good news for you: this is totally unnecessary! You can be healed, restored, and freed of that nasty bag in a matter of seconds! All it takes is a genuine decision to forgive. Your healing is only a decision and a prayer away.

Heavenly Father, I refuse to have any "blockage" in my heart or spirit that will threaten my life in You and the kingdom. I freely forgive others so that I, too, may be freely forgiven. Release the life-giving flow of the Holy Ghost in my life, Lord, so that I may boldly declare and demonstrate the gospel of the kingdom and bring healing and restoration in Jesus' name. Amen.

DO NOT DIG UP OLD SIN— YOURS OR ANYONE ELSE'S

Today's Scripture Reading: John 1:29; Romans 4:7–8, 6:11–14

Key Verses: John 1:29

The next day John saw Jesus coming toward him, and said, "Behold! The Lamb of God who takes away the sin of the world!"

Blessed are those whose lawless deeds are forgiven,
And whose sins are covered;
Blessed is the man to whom the LORD shall not impute sin.

Do you ever wonder why we do not walk in the fullness of God's power? It may have something to do with our fondness for gossip, slander, lying, and backbiting. (I know I may step on some toes here, but some things just have to be said.)

Believers always seem eager to remind other believers about all the sins for which God has forgiven them. Are you still talking about other folks' sin? Do you go out of your way to remind them about something God has long forgotten? Why?

Jesus Christ went to the site of their sin and cleaned it up with His own blood, the shed blood of the sacrificed Lamb of God. Jesus wiped away their fingerprints with His garments of righteousness, and using His nail-scarred hands, He removed every piece of evidence proving that they were there. So, when you talk today about the original crime, you return to the crime scene and leave your own fingerprints there. Now you have become guilty of what they were forgiven for long ago.

Some people do not actively commit sin, but they still suffer the penalty of sin because they keep reminding people about their sins of the past, the ones God forgave and forgot long ago. These self-appointed "conviction agents" need to ask forgiveness for themselves!

Have you been gossiping, lying, and backbiting? You need to fall down on your knees and ask God to forgive you for messing up your life by talking about someone else.

Holy Father, please forgive me for the times I have reminded others of their sins instead of reminding them about Your faithfulness, mercy, and grace. You anointed my tongue to exhort and encourage, not to gossip and slander the brethren. I also forgive those who have tried to remind me of my past sins and failures, and I ask that You forgive them as well. In Jesus' name I pray, amen.

THE BLESSING OF DIVINE FORGETFULNESS

Today's Scripture Reading: Psalm 103:12; Hebrews 10:17 *Key Verse:* Hebrews 10:17

Their sins and their lawless deeds I will remember no more.

Are you going through the motions, feeling like you are still unforgiven? Let me ask you a question: Did you ask for forgiveness for that sin? Yes? Then forget it, because God did.

In Hebrews 10:17, God says that when you ask Him for forgiveness, not only does He forgive you, He also forgets it! He tosses that sin in the bottomless sea of divine forgetfulness that is filled with the blood of the Lamb. Once a sin sinks below those crimson waves, it will surface no more for all eternity.

If you asked Him to forgive you this morning, He forgave your sin and promptly forgot it. If you go back this afternoon and try to say something else about it, God will not know what you are talking about. You are reminding Him of something for which He has no point of reference. You see, unlike mankind, when God says something, He means it. God said you are forgiven. God said He will remember your sin no more. What does that mean? It means it is gone forever. God does not do things the way we do.

Pray this prayer with me:

Heavenly Father, thank You for sending Your Son to take away my sins forever. Now I realize that when You forgave me for my sins and failures, You also forgot them forever. Thank You for setting me free to serve You and help build Your kingdom. In Jesus' name I pray, amen.

We Will Be in One Accord Once We All Die

Today's Scripture Reading: Acts 2:1–4 *Key Verse:* Acts 2:1

When the Day of Pentecost had fully come,
they were all with one accord in one place.

There is something fascinating about the New Testament passage that describes the group of about 120 believers who were waiting in the upper room on the day of pentecost. Jesus had already risen from the dead and returned to His place of glory in heaven. The Bible says the people "were all with one accord," or in divine order.

This is more than just nice. It is miraculous. Remember that there were 120 people in that place. Just how do you get 120 people in one accord? You do it the same way you get twenty thousand in one accord! Everyone must die to self. The 120 were in agreement because they had no agenda—all that mattered to them at that point was obeying the Word of God.

The church must come to the point where it drops all its own agendas. If someone in the church sins, can the people set aside all personal feelings and say, "What does the Word of God say about it?" Can they deal with that sin according to what God reveals in the Bible?

God is looking for individuals who will rise up in every situation and say, "I do not have an opinion. I do not have a personal grudge. I do not have a personal agenda. I am not seeking to acquire any power or status. I just want to determine what the Word of God says and then do it." You have "one accord" when everyone agrees with God without asserting personal opinions. Are you prepared to die today? (And tomorrow . . . and the day after that?)

Pray with me:

Dear Father, You are my God, my only God, and my source of all wisdom, power, and guidance. Your Word is a lamp unto my feet, and I know I will not stumble as long as I obey Your commands. Lord Jesus, in obedience to Your Word, I take up my cross again today. I deny myself and die to self, and I will faithfully follow You step-by-step in unity with my brothers and sisters in the kingdom. Amen.

SHARE EVERY COMFORT YOU RECEIVE WITH ANOTHER IN NEED

Today's Scripture Reading: 2 Corinthians 1:3–4 *Key Verses:* 2 Corinthians 1:3a, 4

Blessed be the God and Father of our Lord Jesus Christ . . . who comforts us in all our tribulation, that we may be able to comfort those who are in any trouble, with the comfort with which we ourselves are comforted by God.

When the Lord walked through the valley of the shadow of death with you, when He stood by you during a faith-stretching health crisis or financial meltdown, He did it with more on His mind than just your welfare. He cares for you, but He also likes to see a profitable return on every investment He makes.

According to the apostle Paul, God is saying to us, "The same comfort that I gave you, I expect you to give others." He did not give you that grace just so you could have a secret "grace release" party. He expects you to give the same grace to somebody else in need.

Maybe you should have gone to jail. Maybe you should have been dead, or bankrupt, or sick—but God's mercy covered you. You are still alive by the grace and mercy of God. Therefore, God says, "I dare you to turn your nose up at anybody after what you have been through. In My mercy I kept you when you should have been caught. I preserved you when you should have been dead. I lifted you up when you should have gone bankrupt. *Now it is your turn . . .*"

Never ask God to give you "justice," because you are not prepared to handle what He would give you if you got what you really deserve! We are all standing solely upon the grace and mercies of God. Every time you mess up, get back on your knees. The only reason you can rise again is because God, in His great mercy, has been forgiving you and covering you by His grace. (And always remember to give Him thanksgiving, praise, and worship for the wonderful things He has done.)

Pray with me:

Heavenly Father, I thank You for every breath You have given me. Thank You for Your tender mercies and Your covering grace day by day. I do not ask You for justice; I ask You for mercy and grace in Jesus Christ. Holy Spirit, teach me how to extend to others the same compassion, mercy, and grace I have received from You. In Jesus' name I pray, amen.

October 10

Look for the Character of Christ in Those Who Lead You

Today's Scripture Reading: 2 Corinthians 11:13–15; 1 John 4:1–8; Galatians 5:19–6:3 *Key Verses:* 2 Corinthians 11:14–15

Satan himself transforms himself into an angel of light. Therefore it is no great thing if his ministers also transform themselves into ministers of righteousness.

Get ready. After God touched your life, you changed your associations and cleaned up your mess. Now you are looking for people to speak into your life and show you how to be wise. This is a good and natural part of finding your place in the covenant community called the church.

Be careful. I assure you that God is sending someone specifically chosen to disciple and train you in the ways of the kingdom. The devil, however, is getting ready to slip in a counterfeit. The devil may not know all things like God does, but he knows how to watch us and learn our ways. He knows how you talk and think. He has even kept his own version of "records." He will send someone your way who knows exactly what to say to catch your attention.

If you walk in the flesh, you may be taken in. If you walk in the Spirit, something will trigger a warning flag in your spirit, and you will perceive the device of the enemy.

Watch out for folks who feed your depression or pessimism about the ways of God. You do not need "friends" like that. God's representatives will immediately identify with the way you feel, but they will not get down and wallow in it with you. They will gently but firmly pull you higher and deeper into God's Word and the eternal things of the kingdom. In a hundred different ways, great and small, they will point you back to God's faithfulness from generation to generation. They do not have to be preachy; they will just be "salty" with God's truth.

By all means, seek godly companions, counselors, and teachers in the faith. But do it wisely and look for the character of Christ in their lives. You will know when you find them. The Holy Spirit will softly tug at your heart as if to say, "This is the one I sent to you."

Pray this prayer with me:

Heavenly Father, Your Word says that we have many instructors but not many fathers. You alone are my heavenly Father, but I sense a need for a guide, a seasoned saint who can do more than provide information. Lead me to someone who can teach me by example how to follow You and become more like Jesus. I thank You in advance for leading me every step of the way. In Jesus' name, amen.

YOU DO NOT HAVE TIME FOR FOOLS

Today's Scripture Reading: Ephesians 5:15–16 *Key Verses:* Ephesians 5:15–16

See then that you walk circumspectly, not as fools but as wise, redeeming the time, because the days are evil.

Your eternity is tied up in time, and time is moving quickly.

God did not bring you this far to allow some fool to mess up your life. He brought you through the fires of hell to purify you and purge the poison out of you. That is why He stripped away certain things that you used to cling to. He permitted certain events to occur so you would become a pure seed that He could plant with confidence. You are an investment of God.

Right now, God says, "I expect you to walk with wise people." Listen, you do not have time to spend your days with just anybody. God orders every step you take, so make sure no godless fool or undisciplined churchgoer pulls you off of that holy path!

I like to go to basketball games, but I have to go with someone who is wise. That pretty much leaves out "just anybody." My life is not my own; my steps are ordered of the Lord.

I know that I am *not* going to the basketball game just to watch the basketball. Someone I do not know bought a ticket for the seat on my right. That means that since God directed my steps to that seat, then He must have something for me to tell that person while I am there. Pray with me:

Heavenly Father, You are ordering my steps. I redeem the time and will be wise. I will spend my time with the wise. I know that You are guiding my every step. Lord Jesus, I am listening for Your direction.

October 12

Choose Your Friends Carefully; You Will Become Just Like Them

Today's Scripture Reading: Proverbs 12:26, 13:20; Philippians 2:19–23 *Key Verses:* Philippians 2:19–22

I trust in the Lord Jesus to send Timothy to you shortly . . . For I have no one like-minded, who will sincerely care for your state. For all seek their own, not the things which are of Christ Jesus. But you know his proven character, that as a son with his father he served with me in the gospel.

God's Word says it is important for you to carefully choose the people with whom you associate. Why? Invariably you will become like them!

Jesse Curney is associate pastor at my church. People are amazed at the way he walks and preaches like me. He did not even realize it until I pointed it out one day. Over the years he has unwittingly transformed his style to become more like mine.

That is why your associations are so important to your future! If you do not bother to separate yourself from fools, you will not even know you are changing. Then one day you will wake up and realize you are a fool with nothing but wasted potential to show for your life.

If you are careful to invest your time and effort in relationships with the wise, you will wake up one day and realize that you, too, have become wise and have been entrusted with many young sons and daughters in the faith. It all depends on the caliber of those with whom you spend your time.

Pray this prayer with me:

Holy Father, every breath and every day You give me I must invest wisely. Lead me to godly friends and wise counselors who hear Your voice and do Your will. As these friends lead me higher in Your will, show me those whom I can lift up and guide in Your way. I ask these things in Jesus' name, amen.

Who Is in Your Corner?

Today's Scripture Reading: Psalm 1; Proverbs 12:26 *Key Verse:* Proverbs 12:26

The righteous should choose his friends carefully,
For the way of the wicked leads them astray.

What kind of people do you need in your corner in the battle of faith? You need to associate with people who build up your faith and increase your confidence and dependence on God. I am not talking about "nice guys" or "nice girls." I am talking about the kind of people who will make a conscious effort to encourage you. If your friends and associates do not make a conscious effort to build you up, then they will end up wearing you down.

Picture yourself as a prizefighter about to enter the ring and fight with the devil to get the Word of God out. When you go back to your corner, who is waiting with towel in hand, ready to give you water?

As the battle for the Word wears on, you will need associates in your corner who will rub your shoulders and boost you to victory. "You are the man God chose! Keep going—you can do it. You prepared for this day, and no man or devil can stop you from fulfilling God's will. Come on, get up again and go get him. Make him wish he had never tried to hinder this work of God. You were born for such a day as this, so do not hold back. Go for the knockout!"

Everyone needs the support and counsel of trusted friends and associates. It is your God-given protection from the enemy and even from yourself!

Good friends will tell you the truth, not just what you want to hear. Nathan was one of David's truest friends, and he told David the truth even though David was a king and a feared warrior. Do you have a Nathan, a Paul, a Barnabas, or a John in your corner? Ask God for godly friends and counselors and He will answer your prayer. It is in perfect alignment with His will for your life. Pray with me:

Heavenly Father, my heart burns to fulfill Your will and do great exploits in Your name. Send me godly counselors and trusted friends who will speak the truth in love and share my vision for Your kingdom. Forge us into a team unified in faith, vision, hope, and the fire of the Holy Ghost; a team that is fully yielded to Your will. Thank You for these things. In Jesus' name I pray, amen.

OCTOBER 14

WHAT THEOLOGY SHOWS UP IN YOUR CD COLLECTION?

Today's Scripture Reading: Proverbs 13:20; 1 Corinthians 15:33 *Key Verse:* Proverbs 13:20

He who walks with wise men will be wise,
But the companion of fools will be destroyed.

I have this conversation far too often:

"But, Bishop, they make me laugh."

"They are fools. God is saying that a fool will mess you up. I am telling you, stop hanging around with fools."

Paul wrote, "Do not be deceived: 'Evil company corrupts good habits'" (1 Cor. 15:33 NKJV). God said, "Do not be a fool." Whether you call them your friends or associates does not matter. The Bible is plain and true: "*Evil company corrupts good habits.*"

"Evil company" can be defined many different ways. We "keep company" with music artists on CDs, with authors in books and celebrities in magazines; and with a whole universe full of "stars" on television. In recent years, we have begun to spend more and more time keeping company with strangers on the Internet.

In others words, you may not even know the people you keep company with, but they exert their influence nonetheless! What kind of music do you pump into your ears during the day? You may not know the singer, but if he serves anyone or anything other than God, then he has invaded your mind and messed it up.

I realize that I am meddling now, but ask yourself if you listen more to that music than to your Father in heaven. If you listen to the singer more, then that singer is corrupting you! He or she has already pulled you away from your first love.

Hour by hour, you take in the theology and values of the singers, songwriters, and musicians you listen to. Survey your CD and cassette selection for the morals and beliefs they promote. You listen to those things for hours and then go to church on Sunday. Do you really think your pastor is going to straighten out so many hours of indoctrination in just one hour? If you do, then you may qualify as a fool who is keeping evil company. Is it time to make some changes? Pray this prayer with me:

Father, I have been keeping some bad company lately. Thank You for warning me about the danger I am in. Give me the wisdom and courage to change my life and my close associations. It may be difficult, but I will see it through because I love You more than anything and anyone else. In Jesus' name I pray, amen.

IS SOMEONE SUCKING THE LIFE OUT OF YOU?

Today's Scripture Reading: 1 Corinthians 15:33; Acts 8:23 *Key Verse:* 1 Corinthians 15:33

Do not be deceived: "Evil company corrupts good habits."

Bad relationships and friendships have destroyed the potential and ability of millions of people. Whoever cannot increase you will eventually decrease you. If they are not taking you higher, then they are dragging you lower. Examine the people occupying time in your life and start separating yourself from the spiritual leeches.

Jesus allowed only two kinds of people in His life: those who ministered to Him and those who received His ministry. Have you noticed that He did not spend time with the Pharisees? They did not minister to Him or listen to Him because they were too religious.

Do you feel worn-out, spiritually dead, and lonely? Who is around you? Is someone sucking the life out of you like a vampire or a tick? Are you walking with someone with whom you cannot even talk? If you cannot share your deepest inner feelings, dreams, and fears with him in safety, then there is a problem. You are locked up and dying on the inside, and this kind of friend will not even know it. He will just keep on grinning.

Jesus did not hang around that kind of person. You will not receive any life-giving ministry as long as you have a bunch of "zeros" around you. They cannot help you, but they can usually manage to keep anyone else from helping you! They cannot take you anywhere, but with all their bad baggage cluttering your life, they will keep anyone else from even trying to take you to a new place.

You need to move those zeros out of the way! Stop wasting your time with non-productive relationships, and do not feel guilty about making changes. All of them have the same opportunity you did—they can choose Christ and pursue His purposes with all their hearts or they can keep their "zero growth, zero effort, zero results" game plan. The problem is theirs, not yours. You chose Christ, and that means you must follow Him with everything you have.

Heavenly Father, thank You for sending Your Son to rescue me from darkness and translate me into the kingdom. Now it is time to report to "basic training." Guide me and strengthen me as I trim away the unproductive or openly evil relationships in my life. Help me to be a powerful witness for You and the kingdom throughout this change of environment. In Jesus' name I pray, amen.

October 16

Grant Me the Grace to Embrace My Divine Irritants

Today's Scripture Reading: Proverbs 27:17; Mark 3:14–19 *Key Verse:* Proverbs 27:17

As iron sharpens iron,
So a man sharpens the countenance of his friend.

Have you ever noticed how God brings people into your life who always seem to push you to the limits of your patience? The American mind-set at this writing seems to favor running with people who will not take you anywhere personally, spiritually, or professionally, but I am not talking about them. I am referring to those God-ordained irritants who push us to the edge.

Jesus would not spend much time with people who did not take Him anywhere. But He allowed Judas into His company. Why? It was because He knew Judas would play a crucial role in catapulting Him into His divine destiny on Calvary.

He also put up with a loudmouthed and impetuous fisherman named Peter who seemed to have virtually no theological training at all. He also had to deal with the ambitious plotting and wrangling of James and John, the proud sons of Zebedee (also known as the "Sons of Thunder"). They were constantly arguing over who would ultimately occupy the highest place of honor in heaven.

So do not worry if God sends people into your life who do not even seem to like you. If God sent them, then their annoying qualities will not drag you down; they will help catapult you to your finest hour in the Lord. Those divine irritants may not put you on a cross, but they will keep you on your knees. That, my friend, is what God is looking for.

Pray this prayer with me:

Holy Father, long ago I accepted the fact that Your ways are not my ways. I want to ask why You chose to send such irritating people into my life, but I already know at least part of the answer. Please forgive me for my sins and give me the grace to embrace my "divine irritants" in love and learn the lessons You want to teach me. In Jesus' name I pray, amen.

October 17

Beware of the Blessing-Stealers

Today's Scripture Reading: Joshua 1:1–9; Zechariah 4:6–7 *Key Verse:* Joshua 1:7

Be strong and very courageous, that you may observe to do according to all the law which Moses My servant commanded you; do not turn from it to the right hand or to the left, that you may prosper wherever you go.

There is another class of people you should watch out for: the people who will try to talk you out of your blessing. They will actually try to shrink your faith in the name of religion or "common sense."

Small-minded people have a particularly bad habit of looking at you like you are crazy because *they* did not hear that particular thing from God. (I suppose they think God would never do something without clearing it through them!)

Very often, blessing-stealers are Christians with a very small vision of God. They are doing all they can to believe God just to pay their rent. Go higher. Associate with people who are believing God to help them buy a house, debt free!

You serve a God who is bigger than a rent-paying God. Get to know Him as the all-powerful Jehovah-Jireh. He declares, "I will pay it off, and not simply in your children's lifetime, but right now. I am God your Provider."

People who struggle to believe God just for rent will rarely be able to believe what God is saying to you. Family members also have a unique ability to steal a blessing by persuading you that you did not hear God. They find it hard to believe that God could use you—after all, they remember you in diapers. Even Jesus had to deal with this problem.

Be prepared when people try to talk you out of your mission and promise. If they cannot persuade you, they may begin to criticize and ostracize you. Do not turn aside; be bold and courageous. Look neither to the right nor to the left, and be sure to do all that the Lord placed in your heart!

Pray this prayer with me:

Heavenly Father, I know I heard Your voice, and I know You gave me divine assignments and holy promises. It is You who is at work in me both to will and to do Your perfect will, and I will obey. I place my faith in You, and I will not be moved. By Your Spirit, I will possess the promise You gave me. In Jesus' name I pray, amen.

OCTOBER 18

WATCH WHERE YOU SIT!

Today's Scripture Reading: Psalm 1 *Key Verse:* Psalm 1:1

Blessed is the man
Who walks not in the counsel of the ungodly,
Nor stands in the path of sinners,
Nor sits in the seat of the scornful.

When God says we should not walk or talk with certain people, He really is referring you to Psalm 1. The first verse describes the progression of damnation. First you walk in the counsel of the ungodly. Then you find yourself standing in the path of the sinner, and finally you end up sitting in the seat of the scornful.

You begin by seeking and following ungodly advice, then you begin to associate with rebellious sinners known for their sinful ways and thinking. Finally you take your seat as a leader among the jeering, scornful crowd of hecklers who openly ridicule anyone who dares to attempt something new for God. It is a deadly path that leads to destruction.

When God speaks to you and gives you a task or promise from His heart, do not share it with this kind of people. Jesus put it this way, "Do not give what is holy to the dogs; nor cast your pearls before swine, lest they trample them under their feet, and turn and tear you in pieces" (Matt. 7:6 NKJV).

Make sure you associate with people who speak and follow godly counsel. If you do not, then you will get some doubt and unbelief mixed in with the advice you receive from others. People who gather their advice from the gossip columns, soap operas, talk shows, and tabloids will quickly contaminate what God told you.

Let me give you a test for your friends. If you try to wallow in a pity party, what do your friends say? Will they join you, or will they remind you who you are and what God has done in your life? Will they say, "Do not quit now. It is too late to turn around and go back to the past now. Keep going and trust God. This pity party only gives the devil credit for his efforts to steal your vision and blessing!"

Who is sitting with you right now?

Holy Father, Your plan for my life is too important and valuable for me to squander it by following foolish advice and ungodly counsel. Give me wisdom and discernment to know what is in the hearts of those who would be my friends. Lead me to godly friends and counselors who will do all they can to direct me toward the goals You have set for me in the kingdom. In Jesus' name I pray, amen.

Words Can Carry More Than Meaning—They Carry a Spirit

Today's Scripture Reading: Matthew 12:33–37; Proverbs 16:24, 18:4–8; Isaiah 11:1–3

Key Verse: Matthew 12:35

A good man out of the good treasure of his heart brings forth good things, and an evil man out of the evil treasure brings forth evil things.

Words do not just carry a meaning. They carry a spirit. Jesus said our words come out of the treasure we have hidden in our hearts. Isaiah prophesied of Jesus that He would have "the Spirit of counsel and might" (Isa. 11:2 NKJV, emphasis mine).

Do you remember waking up on a Monday morning in a great mood? You were happy, singing, and feeling good! Then you arrived at the office, plant, or grocery store and the first person you saw was the very person you did not want to see! Then he opened his mouth and said something that seemed to carry a dark spirit; it weighed you down and robbed you of your joy.

When sin or unclean spiritual influences contaminate a person, God has to go into the computer of his mind and soul to remove the sin virus. The person has unresolved sin issues in his heart, even though he may not talk about it. According to Jesus, whatever he speaks proceeds directly from the "evil treasure" in his heart. That means that what he says involves more than just words; those words also carry a spirit with them.

This is yet another reason you must watch who you associate with. Pray this prayer with me:

Holy Father, Your Word commands me to be holy, even as You are holy. That means that I cannot afford to take the advice of or associate with people who have no respect for Your holiness. Lead me to godly people who have the Spirit of counsel and might—saints who will give me words of wisdom and faith in crucial moments. I trust You totally, for You direct my steps and guide my way for Your glory. In Jesus' name I pray, amen.

GOD ESTABLISHES HIS KINGDOM USING COVENANT FAMILIES

Today's Scripture Reading: Genesis 12:2; Revelation 1:4–6; Galatians 3:29

Key Verse: Genesis 12:2

I will make you a great nation; I will bless you
And make your name great; And you shall be a blessing.

God's ways are higher than our ways, and His thoughts are higher than our thoughts (Isa. 55:8–9). Perhaps that is why He chose to evangelize the world through His covenant families instead of an angelic military organization or all-powerful human apostles.

It delighted Him to work miracles through normal, ordinary, everyday family people. The difference between the people God uses and those He does not use is *covenant.* He made mighty promises to those who would love Him and obey His Word. He sent His Son, Jesus Christ, to pay the price for our freedom; then Jesus turned over His mission to the ordinary people in His new family, the church. The world has never been the same since.

It is that simple. God intends to redeem this world through His covenant with His people, through the family. He promised that through Abraham's seed all the nations would be blessed, and He kept His word. Jesus Christ, the divine Seed descended from Abraham and David through Mary, blessed the whole earth through His life, His willing sacrifice, and resurrection from the dead.

Through Jesus all believers share in Abraham's inheritance by faith. The only thing God asks us to do is stay true to the covenant. We are to operate with the kingdom in mind, see and perceive with kingdom eyes, and judge all things as kings and priests in His eternal kingdom. If we believe and obey, it is only a matter of time before He will reach the world through us and fill the earth with His glory.

It all starts with the covenant family in your home. Then it moves on into your local church, the nation, and around the world. Pray with me:

Dear Father, I want to see things Your way, not my way. Sometimes I cannot understand why You would want to establish Your kingdom using the same people who eat cereal across the table from me morning after morning. All I know is that You have chosen me and my family. You extended Your covenant to us and gave us a mandate to preach the gospel of the kingdom everywhere we go in this life. Be glorified and honored in this family, Lord. In Jesus' name I pray, amen.

October 21

Take Control and Restore Kingdom Order to Your Home

Today's Scripture Reading: Colossians 3:18–21; Genesis 18:18–19

Key Verse: Genesis 18:19

I have known him, in order that he may command his children and his household after him, that they keep the way of the Lord, to do righteousness and justice, that the Lord may bring to Abraham what He has spoken to him.

Have you noticed that Satan seems always to direct his main offensive thrust against the family? We should not be surprised. It goes all the way back to the book of Genesis. Adam was here a long time before God made Eve, and the devil did not even try to bother him—until he got married! Then he managed to get to Adam through his wife. By the time you reach Genesis 4, Adam's children are already killing each other.

This should give us a clue about why there is such an uproar in our homes today. It should explain why spouses seem so hard to get along with, and why our homes are filled with endless arguments and discontent. There is a reason why children rebel against their parents and why parents lash out and commit atrocities against their own children.

The devil is having a wonderful time destroying the family, and we are not doing anything about it! He knows that if he can distort, distress, or destroy the family, then he has hindered or aborted God's plan. That is because the way we train, guide, and order our families directly affects the way God delivers the benefits of His covenant.

In the end, there is only one answer for the family: the same God who created the family. We are the covenant people of God. Your victim days are over; your ruling days are here. It is time to take over and throw the devil out of your home and family situation.

Put Christ at the head of your home today. Confess your sins together, rebuke the enemy, and invite the Holy Spirit to envelop your home in the peace, joy, and love of Jesus. Once you restore kingdom order to your home, you are free to pursue your destiny in the footsteps of the King. Pray with me:

Heavenly Father, forgive me for relinquishing the leadership of my home to the enemy. In Jesus' name, I take authority over every unclean influence and attack against my family. I dedicate my home and family members to You, Lord. Holy Spirit, permeate our home with the life and light of God, and make us a beacon of hope to others in Jesus' name, amen.

OCTOBER 22

YOUR KINGDOM COME—AND THE KINGDOM OF DARKNESS MUST GO

Today's Scripture Reading: Matthew 13, 6:9–10 *Key Verses:* Matthew 6:9–10

Our Father in heaven, / Hallowed be Your name.
Your kingdom come. / Your will be done / On earth as it is in heaven.

You are in an occupation war between the kingdom of this world and the kingdom of God. Satan is a defeated foe, but for now he remains free, pending execution of his sentence. He is using his remaining time to wreak havoc in one last desperate dash against God's supreme authority.

The only visible difference between the kingdom of God and the kingdom of darkness is how it relates to family. I am sorry to break the news, but the government cannot do the things God ordained us to do; nor can it do the things only God can do.

When we relinquish our families to government entities and programs, we are actually turning them over to the kingdom of this world—and we are destroying them in the process. Man's antipoverty programs do not produce economic independence; they actually discourage the poor from seeking jobs and generate even greater dependence on public handouts.

Our government agencies "protect the family" by spending millions of dollars to encourage so-called "safe sex" (translation: the freedom to commit fornication or adultery with anybody one chooses without personal accountability, responsibility, or lifelong commitment in marriage).

The nation's public schools aggressively teach evolution as a fact while labeling biblical creation as a narrow-minded myth. Evidently our wise educators feel it is in our best interest for America's children to grow up thinking they are merely nameless, purposeless, and totally accidental "slimeballs" rather than unique individuals whom God created for a divine purpose. Perhaps that is why our children are growing up to believe that there is no such thing as right and wrong; everything is relative when God is absent from the equation.

No, God has a better way—the kingdom way. It is time to stand up and take back the reins of authority over the earth.

Heavenly Father, I have heard the truth. Enough is enough; it is time to establish the kingdom of truth, light, and joy in the earth. It is time for the kingdom of darkness to go. Guide me and show me what You want me to do today to advance Your kingdom in my household, in my church, and in my community. In Jesus' name I pray, amen.

OCTOBER 23

BROKEN COVENANTS PRODUCE NOTHING BUT TROUBLE

Today's Scripture Reading: Exodus 19:3–6; Leviticus 26:14–20 *Key Verse:* Exodus 19:5

If you will indeed obey My voice and keep My covenant, then you shall be a special treasure to Me above all people; for all the earth is Mine.

Why do we have so much trouble in the family? The answer is deceptively simple: we break covenant with God and one another more often in the family than anywhere else!

We shoot ourselves in the foot when we continually break covenant with God and one another. For example, covenant breaking robs us of the ability to generate and sustain the wealth and riches God ordained for us.

We break our covenant responsibilities as mothers, fathers, and spouses by shirking our duties to provide for the family. Instead of accepting and fulfilling our responsibilities through hard work and faith in God, we say "Amen" to the social gospel preachers who say the government "owes us" everything we need. My Bible says, "The government will be upon *His shoulder*" (Isa. 9:6 NKJV, emphasis mine). It also says, "*My God*"—not "my government"—"shall supply all your needs" (Phil. 4:19 NKJV, emphasis mine).

As soon as we accept responsibility for where we are and move back into covenant with God, the family will begin to mend. The church will begin to grow and flourish. The city will begin to rise from the ashes of ruin. The nation will rise up in new righteousness, blessing, and prosperity.

First we must stop using worldly rules and principles to accomplish heavenly tasks. There is only one way to govern your house and raise your children, and that is God's way. The kingdom of God covers your house too. Pray this prayer with me:

Holy Father, please forgive me for all the times and ways I have broken covenant in my home. I am returning to the basics of kingdom life; Your Word replaces the advice and patterns of men in my finances, marriage, personal conduct, and the way I raise my children. In Jesus' name, we will honor our covenant with You, Father, and with one another.

It Is Time to Clean House—Begin With Me, Lord

Today's Scripture Reading: Hebrews 10:31; Galatians 6:7 *Key Verse:* Galatians 6:7

Do not be deceived, God is not mocked;
for whatever a man sows, that he will also reap.

I do not care how wonderful your church's service or prayer meeting is—it means nothing if the risen King of glory does not rule in your home.

Across the land, millions of nicely dressed people file into church buildings for a time of organized worship. Then they march back to their cars and return to hell at home where husbands beat their wives behind closed doors, where parents do unspeakable things to their children or browbeat them until their personalities are permanently warped.

One week later, the bruised are healed or concealed, the tears are dried, and the children firmly warned to keep their mouths shut before the fractured families of the kingdom make their way to repeat their religious facade. Is something wrong with this picture?

Fair or not, God gave the male the greatest responsibility for keeping His covenant and preserving the covenant of the family. Yet some of the men of the kingdom, individuals God appointed to provide for and protect the family, have become their family's most feared predator and abuser! God's Word says: "Do not be deceived, God is not mocked; for whatever a man sows, that he will also reap."

Nothing justifies abuse of any kind against God's chosen ones. Mister, the woman you battered last night belonged to God before she ever met you, and she will belong to God long after you breathe your last breath. He remembers every blow and evil word you speak against His daughter. Vengeance belongs to God, and you can never escape His hand. Seek the help you need, but do not give any excuses. Just repent and change your ways before God shortens your days.

The same warning goes to any parent who dares to touch God's children. The Bible literally says, "Take heed that you do not despise one of these little ones, for I say to you that in heaven their angels always see the face of My Father who is in heaven" (Matt. 18:10 NKJV). Believe it and live. Repent and sin no more.

Heavenly Father, forgive me, for I have sinned against You and those I love. Cleanse me and set me free to be the person you ordained me to be. Preserve my family in Jesus' name, amen.

REPAIRING THE HOUSE DIVIDED

Today's Scripture Reading: Matthew 12:25; John 13:34–35 *Key Verse:* Matthew 12:25b

Every city or house divided against itself will not stand.

Japan has one of the most dynamic and productive economies in the modern world. Its remarkable growth over the past fifty years can be attributed in part to the stability of the family unit in that society. The Japanese have succeeded where others have failed because they understand that wealth and riches are generated through the family and passed on to future generations. They go into covenant with one another, and they honor those covenants. God's laws work for anyone who follows them—even if they are not Christians.

The American economy is generally considered the strongest and largest in the world, but serious cracks show in our foundation. The most serious is the disintegration of the American family unit. The family is the nurturing place for tomorrow's generation; it determines in large part the health, productivity, and creativity of tomorrow's leaders and pioneers. By all indications, America's tomorrow does not look very promising unless changes take place.

Our economy shows the effects of the chaos and instability in our homes. We have husbands who do not want to accept responsibility or assume proper leadership roles, and we have wives who refuse to submit to anyone—especially to their husbands. Our homes resemble raging battlefields more than places of refuge because family members constantly struggle for first place, the final word, or the domination of others.

I have painted a gloomy picture, but it does not reflect my vision for America. God has a better plan, and it must begin with the families in His kingdom. Can you imagine what life would be like if our families were intact and fully functioning as beacons of hope and power in our cities? I think God would bless us with so much peace, and productivity that we would all be amazed! Do you want that in your home? Pray this prayer with me:

Heavenly Father, I am tired of the strife, chaos, and confusion in my home. I repent for taking this long to come to my senses. Today I restore the order of God in my home, no matter what the cost. Life is too short for us to live our days in strife and conflict. In Jesus' name, I release the peace of God, the order of God, the power of God, and the fear of God into my home in Jesus' name, amen.

OCTOBER 26

COVER EVEN WHAT IS NOT YOURS

Today's Scripture Reading: James 1:27; Leviticus 25:35 *Key Verse:* Leviticus 25:35

If one of your brethren becomes poor, and falls into poverty among you, then you shall help him, like a stranger or a sojourner, that he may live with you.

The kingdom of this world says, "Get all you can, and can all you get." God's kingdom says, "Get all you can, and stretch it, share it, and take responsibility even if you did not conceive it. Just make sure everyone is covered."

God commanded us to visit the fatherless and the widows for specific reasons (see James 1:27). First, God has taken the place of the departed father and husband in these fractured homes. He is personally voicing their needs and ensuring that they are met. Second, the main cause of biblical poverty is the destruction of the family unit, God's primary "productivity engine" for generating capital. That is why broken families have no hope if the body of Christ does not stretch itself and extend its resources to say, "You have everything you need—the body will see to it in Jesus' name."

Many of society's problems come about when the church relinquishes its authority or responsibilities in an area. When the church shifted the burden of ministering to the poor to the federal government, the massive welfare state came into being. It became a self-perpetuating poverty machine as it locked millions of people into the rut of the welfare rolls while penalizing those who dared to get jobs.

When the church backed out of the broadcast field, the world system swooped in with its own brand of prime-time entertainment. When the church withdrew from politics, the world system moved in with a vengeance and tried to totally exclude the church from the process. Enough is enough. It is time to reclaim our birthright in Christ Jesus! Pray this prayer with me:

Heavenly Father, I make this declaration in the name of Jesus on behalf of the church: We are the redeemed of the Lord. We have an abundance to share with the hurting and divine wisdom to give to the confused. We have healing for the sick and wholeness for the broken and weary. We have a heavenly kingdom to plant in the earth and a kingdom gospel that will set the world free. Now is the day of salvation—lead us where You will, Lord, and we will follow!

Drop the Spiritual Platitudes; Just Jump in and Help!

Today's Scripture Reading: James 1:26–27; Leviticus 25:35 *Key Verse:* James 1:27

Pure and undefiled religion before God and the Father is this: to visit orphans and widows in their trouble, and to keep oneself unspotted from the world.

Why do we have this spirit of poverty? We cannot really understand the kingdom until we understand God's mandate to the body of Christ.

He calls us to minister to the poor, and we must begin that ministry by extending a "relational covering" to broken families. Women suffer a catastrophic loss when their husbands die. In one blow, a woman loses her best friend, her lover, her covenant partner, and her principal source of income and economic security. Suddenly she is left to face an uncertain future alone.

Children who lose a father often wonder if they can trust anything in life. Fear and lack often mark their lives. In one tragic moment, they may have lost all hope of a college education, economic security, and physical safety—in addition to the immeasurable loss of a father's loving touch, wise counsel, caring ear, and approving smile.

We have an obligation under God to step in and fill these voids with our hearts, our hands, our money, and our time. The inconvenience does not matter. In God's eyes, these people are family, and we always take care of family. If we fail to cover the exposed hurts, wounds, and hearts of our widows and orphans, then the devil will use their pain and deprivation to keep us from breaking the spirit of poverty.

Empty spiritual platitudes do not satisfy God's mandate. Do not tell a weary woman who is raising children without a husband in the house, "Oh, but you have a Man! His name is Jesus." She might shout back, "Yes, I do have Jesus, but I need a man in this house right now to help discipline my children when they disobey! I need someone to help comfort them when they wake up crying in the middle of the night! I need somebody—anybody—to help."

Sometimes we get so spiritual that we are no earthly good. When we duck our God-given responsibility to widows and orphans, there is no way we can presume to put our feet on the devil's neck in the authority of Christ. It is time to do what God told us to do.

Dear Father, I have been content to live my own life in bliss while ignoring the desperate needs of the widows and the fatherless in my own church. Forgive me for my selfishness and show me practical ways to cover and uplift these precious ones. In Jesus' name, amen.

Do His Commands, Then Receive His Promise

Today's Scripture Reading: Isaiah 58:5–8 Key Verses: Isaiah 58:6–8

Is this not the fast that I have chosen: To loose the bonds of wickedness,
To undo the heavy burdens, To let the oppressed go free,
And that you break every yoke? Is it not to share your bread with the hungry,
And that you bring to your house the poor who are cast out;
When you see the naked, that you cover him, And not hide yourself from
your own flesh? Then your light shall break forth like the morning,
Your healing shall spring forth speedily, And your righteousness shall go before you;
The glory of the Lord shall be your rear guard.

Isaiah the prophet revealed the heart of God's kingdom agenda in verse 6 when he launched an offensive strike against the powers of this world. You can never break a spirit of poverty until you go after the wickedness in society, yet the church is conspicuously silent about the wickedness in the world. Why? Perhaps this is because many of its most prominent members are obsessed with the question, "When am I going to get mine?"

The next verse tells us to "share [our] bread with the hungry." Most of us think that we do not have enough time for the hungry. At most, we will give them some money and hurry on our way, hoping the money will not finance another bottle of cheap wine. It would be far better to take a few moments and sit down and eat with them! That way you can share the bread of fellowship and the Bread of Life with them in one sitting. (That is what Jesus did.)

God starts meddling in verse 7 when He told us to bring the homeless poor into our own homes. Are you praying for that big house because you are planning to bring in the homeless? The Lord keeps up the pressure when He commands us to cover the naked. (Most of our churches have a hard time just collecting toothpaste, deodorant, combs, and brushes!)

In the eighth verse, the Lord says, "Then your light shall break forth like the morning, / Your healing shall spring forth speedily." The promises of God come only after we obey the commands of God. Pray with me:

Heavenly Father, You make it clear that we have a lot of work to do. Do a work in my heart and mind so that prejudices, presumptions, and preconceived ideas will not hinder the establishment of Your kingdom. In Your strength, I will reach out to the poor, the homeless, and the downtrodden. Guide my steps and anoint my life to bring hope to the hopeless through the gospel of the kingdom. In Jesus' name I pray, amen.

OCTOBER 29

REPAIR THE GOSPEL NET WITH FORGIVENESS AND THE BOND OF LOVE

Today's Scripture Reading: Leviticus 25:9–17 *Key Verse:* Leviticus 25:9

You shall cause the trumpet of the Jubilee to sound on the tenth day of the seventh month; on the Day of Atonement you shall make the trumpet to sound throughout all your land.

We cannot celebrate Jubilee—a time of release and freedom—if we have not made a conscious effort to forgive our enemies (not to mention our kinfolk).

We cannot sit in the congregation of the Lord and nurture a bad attitude toward someone else. We have no business carrying grudges, angry memories, unforgiveness, and bitterness from years gone by, and then putting on a party hat and expecting God to bless our mess! God tells the church to raise its standards to match His holiness. Nothing happens in the kingdom until we observe and honor atonement, until we forgive and are forgiven under the unifying blood of the Lamb of God.

If that means you need to forgive a debt, then do it. If that means you need to repent for causing offense, then do it. If it means you must forgive a presumptuous friend for the seventy-seventh time, then do it. Extend the freedom of Jubilee forgiveness to someone else, and then experience it in your own life! This is the season to repair the "nets" of our covenant community, the body of Christ. We have been made fishers of men, and a great kingdom harvest looms ahead.

Holy Father, I choose to forgive others just as You chose to forgive me. Reveal Yourself to those in desperate need of healing, forgiveness, and hope. Be glorified in our love one for another and for the lost. In Jesus' name I pray, amen.

October 30

Do the Right Thing and I Will Answer Your Call

Today's Scripture Reading: Isaiah 58:8–10 *Key Verses:* Isaiah 58:9–10

You shall call, and the LORD will answer;
You shall cry, and He will say, "Here I am."
If you take away the yoke from your midst,
The pointing of the finger, and speaking wickedness . . .
. . . Then your light shall dawn in the darkness.

Why do the saints run around feeling so empty and shallow? It is because we are selfish. We keep asking God, "When will I get my joy back?" God patiently tells us, "You will get your joy when you clothe the naked, break the burden, and do the other things that I ordained you to do. Then your light will break forth like the morning!"

What else? "Your healing shall spring forth speedily, / And your righteousness shall go before you; / The glory of the LORD shall be your rear guard" (Isa. 58:8 NKJV). This means you do not have to worry about anybody coming up from behind because the glory of God has you covered.

Do your prayers seem to just bounce off the heavens without getting through? God promised, "You shall call, and the LORD will answer; / You shall cry, and He will say, 'Here I am.' / *If* you take away the yoke from your midst, the pointing of the finger, and speaking wickedness" (emphasis mine). If you extend your soul to the hungry and satisfy their afflicted souls, then your light shall dawn in the darkness and your darkness shall be as high noon.

You do not have to go to a convention or a preacher's "money line" to get this kind of deliverance. Just be a good steward with the little you have, and God will show up when you call!

Heavenly Father, all You are asking is for us to do the right thing. You want us to treat people the way we like to be treated. In return, You have promised to answer my call and cause my light to dawn in the darkness. Thank You for planting me in Your kingdom and in Your body. In Jesus' name I pray, amen.

Love Is the *Only* Way

Today's Scripture Reading: Galatians 3:26–28; James 2:8–9 *Key Verse:* Galatians 3:28

There is neither Jew nor Greek, there is neither slave nor free,
there is neither male nor female; for you are all one in Christ Jesus.

We are God's covenant community; we cannot afford to be judgmental, prejudiced, and bigoted. Do you realize that I call a white man my spiritual father? I am an African-American pastor and bishop, but a white man named Dr. Mark Hanby has been a true spiritual father to me and has often helped me in the ministry.

We all need to stop being judgmental. It is time to lay down our preconceived prejudices based on skin color, economic status, denominational background, education, and personal preferences. We need to acknowledge our debts to one another and rejoice in God's ability to bring unity in the midst of diversity.

It is the way of Christ and His kingdom, and it is the only way. Pray this prayer with me:

Holy Father, I repent for judging others on the basis of their differences from me or those within my circle of friends. You made every person, and You did it without apology to or consultation from any of us. By Your grace, I will embrace all men, women, and children as Your children. In Jesus' name I pray, amen.

November

It Is Showdown Time!

November 1

The Fruit Is Ready: Will You Pay the Price for the Harvest?

Today's Scripture Reading: Numbers 13:23–27 *Key Verses:* Numbers 13:23, 27

They came to the Valley of Eshcol, and there cut down a branch with one cluster of grapes; they carried it between two of them on a pole. They also brought some of the pomegranates and figs . . . Then they told him, and said: "We went to the land where you sent us. It truly flows with milk and honey, and this is its fruit."

When Moses sent spies into the promised land, they found grapes so large that two men had to carry a single bunch suspended on a pole! They called the valley Eshcol ("cluster") because of the cluster of grapes they carried to Moses.

It was harvesttime in the land of promise, and the spies had the fruit to prove it. The grapes were ripe for the picking as they hung from the vine in Eshcol. Unfortunately, that generation turned away in doubt and unbelief, dooming itself to live on wilderness rations. Everyone more than forty years old died outside of the promise. They never tasted the fruit of harvest because they feared the unknown.

God has promised us a great harvest of souls for the kingdom, and the fruit is ripe for the picking. Souls are waiting, dangling from the tangled vines of the enemy, and it is harvesttime. Drug dealers, prostitutes, adulterers, con artists, high school dropouts, alcoholics, and drug addicts are waiting to be plucked from Satan's grip.

They are waiting for you to snatch them from the kingdom of darkness and carry them into the kingdom of marvelous light. They do not want to hear you talking about your Cadillac and Mercedes, or your nice house in the suburbs. They want to know this: *Can you really hear Him? Is there a word from the Lord? Tell me about this Jesus you have been talking about.*

This is the catch: we have the same problem the Israelites had in Moses' day. The harvest is not going to cross the river and walk into the church. The church must leave the comforts within its four walls to cross the river of commitment and faith to bring in the harvest and possess the promise. It all starts with two words: *Yes, Lord.*

Pray this prayer with me:

Heavenly Father, I do not want to pull back in fear. The kingdom harvest is near and we must cross over the river of hesitation. Lord, I want to enjoy the fruit of the kingdom; if that means I have to join the battle to pick the fruit, then count me in. In Jesus' name I pray, amen.

November 2

Are You Ready to Show the Devil a Thing or Two?

Today's Scripture Reading: Matthew 8:28–32 *Key Verse:* Matthew 8:29, emphasis mine

Suddenly [the demons] cried out, saying,
"What have we to do with You, Jesus, You Son of God?
Have You come here to torment us before the time?"

Can you describe the devil's primary strategy? It is very simple. All he can do is stall for time until Jesus returns! He does that by keeping us from understanding and walking in the kingdom.

In Matthew 8:28–32, Jesus cast out a large number of demons from two men. Just before they left their victims, the demons cried out in a loud voice, "What have we to do with You, Jesus, You Son of God? Have You come here to torment us before the time?"

The devil and his cohorts know they are damned to hell and the eternal torment of the lake of fire (see Matt. 25:41 and Rev. 20:10). The demons in Matthew's account thought that their torment would begin at the end of time, but they were wrong. The devil's torment began the moment Jesus—and those who followed Him—began to preach the gospel of the kingdom!

Jesus did not wait until the end to torment the devil and his so-called kingdom. The Bible says He came to "destroy the works of the devil" (1 John 3:8 NKJV). So why are *you* waiting? Have you not been given power over unclean spirits in Jesus' name?

Are you ready to show the devil a thing or two? Let us walk in a pure gospel; let us walk in the kingdom and demonstrate the power of God right here and right now. It is awesome and powerful!

Pray this prayer with me:

Holy Father, thank You for sending Your Son to set us free and destroy the works of the devil. Now I accept Your mandate to pick up the cross and name of Your Son and continue His work in the earth. By Your command I, too, am sent to destroy the works of the devil without mercy or hesitation. May Your kingdom come and Your will be done on earth as it is in heaven. In Jesus' name I pray, amen.

NOVEMBER 3

IF YOU SAY IT, I WILL OBEY IT

Today's Scripture Reading: Numbers 14:39–43 *Key Verse:* Numbers 14:42

Do not go up, lest you be defeated by your enemies,
for the LORD is not among you.

Did you know that you can reach a point where even your repentance will not matter?

It is true. Let me say it again: you can reach a point where your repentance will not matter. God did not invest everything in you just so you could settle into a contented state of procrastination, wondering whether or not God is speaking. I am not making this up, and I am not proposing some strange new doctrine. Let me give you two quick examples, one from the Old Testament and another from the New Testament.

When God brought the children of Israel across the wilderness from Egypt's border to the river Jordan, He commanded them to cross the river and possess the land. Instead, the people chose to believe the evil report of the ten fearful spies and pulled back from God's commands and His promise.

It was only after He closed the door that they realized their foolishness and agreed to enter the promised land. By that time the sin was done, the door was closed, and their destiny was sealed. They were ready to go at last, but it was too late. God told them not to go, but once again they tried it their own way, and people died.

"Well, that was the Old Testament," you say. Yes it was, and this is the New Testament version involving the church at Ephesus: "I have this against you, that you have left your first love. Remember therefore from where you have fallen; repent and do the first works, or else *I will come to you quickly and remove your lampstand* from its place—unless you repent" (Rev. 2:4–5 NKJV, emphasis mine).

Do not wait. It is showdown time now! It is time to move. If you fail to act on God's Word, if you continually hesitate, procrastinate, and rebel, He may say, "I will just start all over with someone new."

Pray this prayer with me:

Heavenly Father, have mercy on me for my hesitation and procrastination concerning Your vision and command in my life. I hear Your voice, and I am ready to cross the river of fear if You will lead me and go with me. No more procrastination for me, Lord. If You say it, I will obey it. In Jesus' name I pray, amen.

NOVEMBER 4

MAKE UP YOUR MIND AND COMMIT EVERYTHING FOR VICTORY

Today's Scripture Reading: Luke 14:26–35 *Key Verse:* Luke 14:33

Whoever of you does not forsake all that he has cannot be My disciple.

Have you ever watched television documentaries about how the United States entered World War II after the bombing of Pearl Harbor? By the end of the war, we had assembled the largest and most powerful fighting force in the history of man; but we did not begin that way.

Our "air force" consisted of a handful of World War I vintage double-wing aircraft with open cockpits, very few instruments, and the speed of snails compared to the state-of-the-art fighters and bombers Japanese and German pilots flew. Our skimpy tank divisions also dated from World War I, complete with rust and missing parts. We had a very small and poorly prepared standing army.

The problem was that until the fateful morning of December 7, we did not have the will or determination to fight. Once we made up our mind, the entire nation changed its priorities virtually overnight!

We rationed crucial resources such as rubber, petroleum products, and steel, and we quickly converted entire auto production plants and shipyards into military equipment plants. Millions of men left their homes, jobs, and families to joint the fight, and everyone at home did his part as well. The Axis powers greatly underestimated what we Americans could do, and it cost them everything.

Another enemy has underestimated the power of the church. God's kingdom is about to rise suddenly and accelerate the time schedule of this cleanup and occupation operation. All we have to do is *make up our mind*. The weak-willed and undisciplined church we have today barely resembles the glorious church of power, light, and holiness pictured in the Bible. Something has to change, and God says it must change *now*. Judgment and mercy begin in the house of God, then they move outward to the unredeemed world. God is removing the old to bring in the new. It is showdown time for the church first, then the world. Are you ready for change?

Heavenly Father, You do not have to wait on me any longer. I have made up mind, and I am with You in this thing to the end—no matter what it costs. I am ready to advance Your kingdom now.

AS FOR ME AND MY HOUSE—WE WILL POSSESS THE PROMISE

Today's Scripture Reading: Joshua 1, 24:13–18 *Key Verse:* Joshua 24:15

If it seems evil to you to serve the LORD, choose for yourselves this day whom you will serve . . .
But as for me and my house, we will serve the LORD.

It is time to step out and take what God promised you!

Why? A separation is coming. There will be a separation between those who are content to be "just saved" and those who dare to follow God deeper and walk in their kingdom privileges. The lazy folk will get what they wanted: they will be "just saved," and they will be hurting. Those who are willing to stretch out by faith to possess the promise will walk right in and take it!

The Israelites faced this choice thousands of years ago at the river Jordan. One generation of folk made the mistake of passing up their opportunity to go in and possess the promise. They quit fighting and laid down their weapons just short of the goal because they figured they did not have to study war anymore. They settled for a new identity with God without the promise and lived out their days in a wilderness while subsisting on survival rations.

Now it is your turn. Your promise awaits you just across the river of fear and hesitation. You have to cross the river to enter the promise. Make the right choice. Dare to follow God into the unknown and you will literally begin to live in the promise itself, reaping the harvest of obedience and abundance while taking possession of all the enemy's strongholds. Victory is sweet when you sit at Jesus' feet. Pray with me:

Heavenly Father, I am going in. With everything You promised on the line, I refuse to settle for second best. I do not care about the floodwater, the giants, the walls, the enemy, or the critics who outnumber them all. The promise is mine because You said it is. All I have to do is cross the river and claim it for the kingdom in Your name. Lead me, and I will follow You in Jesus' name.

PULL YOURSELF TOGETHER AND TAKE OVER

Today's Scripture Reading: 2 Timothy 2:3–4; Romans 13:12–14 *Key Verses:* 2 Timothy 2:3–4

You therefore must endure hardship as a good soldier of Jesus Christ. No one engaged in warfare entangles himself with the affairs of this life, that he may please him who enlisted him as a soldier.

All right, you know your mandate in the kingdom. So why is sin overtaking you instead of you taking over the world?

"You do not understand. I have problems."

Is that your reply? I have to tell you that most of us have a far bigger problem than "those" problems! Our problem is that we have a head commitment to Jesus Christ, but our hearts and bodies have not caught up yet. We do not really understand God's purpose for the church.

It is time to get ourselves in order so we can take our place in God's plan and start living.

God has given us everything we need to succeed and live a life for Jesus. No excuse will do when we stand before Him. Besides that, the world cannot wait much longer. It is showdown time!

Pray this prayer with me:

Holy Father, I confess that I do not have things together yet. In my mind, I know that I have a job to do and that You have given me every tool and weapon I need to win. I just cannot get past the entangling fear and hesitation in my heart and the uncontrolled urges in my body.

Holy Spirit, flood my being with Your power. Touch the Word of God I have buried in my heart and make it alive in me. Ignite the fire of God in my heart and help me bring my body under control in Jesus' name, amen.

November 7

It Takes Only One Generation

Today's Scripture Reading: Colossians 3:5–17 *Key Verses:* Colossians 3:8–10, emphasis mine

Now you yourselves are to put off all these: anger, wrath, malice, blasphemy, filthy language out of your mouth. Do not lie to one another, since you have put off the old man with his deeds, and have put on the new man who is renewed in knowledge according to the image of Him who created him.

Are you mastering your enemy, or is your enemy mastering you? Sometimes I think Christians go overboard with their "do-it-yourself" attempts to be humble and passive. The big problem is that Jesus did not ask us to be passive. He asked for all-out commitment and total obedience to His commands, and there is not a hint of passivity in those demands.

Do not sit there and think, *Well, this affliction exists just to keep me humble.* That is a lie out of the pit of hell. Paul talked about a "thorn" God permitted in his life, but that did not come his way because he was sitting at home whimpering. He was battering the gates of hell with every ounce of strength he had, and he only increased his efforts when the affliction came.

God's plan called for the Israelites to invade and conquer the promised land *quickly*. Their hesitation, doubt, and unbelief brought their progress to a halt in the first generation. As for people of the second generation, they hit the ground running and took the land within one generation! They were so bold that their reputation went before them. Their enemies were shaking in their boots long before the Israelites ever showed up to knock on their door.

The time has come for you to master what has mastered you for so long. And God says, "Do it quickly!"

Holy Father, I will do it. I am ready to pull off the old and put on the new. I will not let up and I will not stop until I am clean and free to do Your will.

ARE YOU READY FOR THE FIRE?

Today's Scripture Reading: 1 Kings 18:19–40 *Key Verse:* 1 Kings 18:39

When all the people saw [the fire of the Lord], they fell on their faces; and they said, "The LORD, He is God! The LORD, He is God!"

It is time for a showdown, and it is God's turn to make His statement. Now He will not be talking to the world; He will direct this statement to His people.

Do you remember the confrontation Elijah the prophet had with the 450 prophets of Baal in 1 Kings 18? God sent fire down from heaven and consumed a water-soaked sacrifice right in front of those pagan prophets and the assembled people of Israel!

It is time for a radical change of thinking. I want you to stop thinking of Elijah's confrontation as "a nice historical story." It is not, and it never was just a story. It is even more than a true historical event because it is a prophetic picture of the church and our nation today!

Judgment is coming, and it is coming to the house of God first. Then it will go to the nation. Ask yourself this crucial question, and answer it in total honesty: *Am I ready for the fire of God to fall?*

Holy Father, I make no excuses; I am not ready for judgment. I have lived under Your mercy and grace so long that I have forgotten how needy and unworthy I am apart from You. Holy Spirit, search my heart and reveal any sin in me. I repent of my sins and ask for forgiveness and total cleansing in the blood of the Lamb. Lord Jesus, I want to be ready so I can remain standing and pass the test when Your fire falls, but I can do it only by hiding in You.

COME OUT OF THE CLOSET AND DECLARE THE TRUTH

Today's Scripture Reading: Matthew 5:14–16 *Key Verse:* Matthew 5:16

Let your light so shine before men, that they may see your good works and glorify your Father in heaven.

It is time to come out of the closet.

I mean what I say. It is time for us to come out of the closet—and for all the right reasons. My passion is to step into public and religious arenas at God's direction and put everything on the line by challenging ungodly systems that hold people in bondage.

It is time for God's people to strip away the false cloak of secrecy our secular society has imposed on us and come out into the light. It is time to take a stand for the King and His kingdom! The prophets of the Old Testament often paid a dear price for their calling, because they were often the lone voice speaking the truth in a world of darkness.

We have the same mandate today, but we are many! We face the same devil, but he has already been defeated at the cross. We possess the same weaknesses and fears as the prophets of old, but we have the Holy Ghost dwelling within us and the name of Jesus on our lips.

Best of all, we have the promise of God's Word: "You are of God, little children, and have overcome them, because He who is in you is greater than he who is in the world" (1 John 4:4 NKJV).

What are we waiting for?

Heavenly Father, I want to do Your will and proclaim Your kingdom with boldness, but I know I cannot do it in my own strength or ability. Grant me a holy boldness to stand up in the face of men and demons to declare the kingdom. Anoint me to speak as a prince of the kingdom and as an oracle of God in Your name. I believe Your Word, and I trust that You will confirm the preached Word with signs following. In Jesus' name, amen.

NOVEMBER 10

CLEAN YOUR HOUSE BEFORE GOD CLEANS IT FOR YOU

Today's Scripture Reading: 1 Peter 4:17; Daniel 5:18–30 *Key Verse:* Daniel 5:27

You have been weighed in the balances, and found wanting.

God is about to judge this nation for its immorality. Our families are broken and our people are entangled in uncontrolled lust and widespread adultery. Our marriages are destroyed and our children scarred for life, and God is saying, "I will expose the immorality of this nation."

All of us have immoral friends and adulterous relatives, and some of us are caught up in affairs ourselves! Children born of our promiscuity are abandoned across the land, doomed to live fractured lives without wholeness, stability, or parents to meet their needs.

Our communities struggle to deal with an overwhelming flood of incest, rape, molestation, spousal abuse, pornography, and child abuse. Meanwhile, God asks you and me, "Are you going to sit there and put up with that? Why do you watch it on television?"

Everywhere I travel, I see Hollywood producing major movies based on the things we approve with our dollars at the box office. Our entertainment industry is literally teaching people how to be immoral. I say "our" industry because the dollars of blood-washed church people fund a lot of this garbage!

How can we demand that our leaders be moral when we live with such hypocrisy? We do not want people to tell us to follow a moral path in our entertainment tastes, yet we want to judge our leaders and everybody else by a moral standard.

The Bible is true, and it declares to you and me: "The time has come for judgment to begin at the house of God; and if it begins with us first, what will be the end of those who do not obey the gospel of God" (1 Peter 4:17 NKJV)? Judgment is not as painful if you voluntarily clean your house before the Judge arrives. I think we need to get busy.

Holy Father, I feel like I have been "weighed in the balances, and found wanting." I have fallen short on the righteousness scale again. I repent of my sins and wrong choices. Cleanse me so I can lift holy hands to You once again. I ask for mercy once more in Jesus' name, amen.

NOVEMBER 11

DROP THE PRIME-TIME HYPOCRISY OR BECOME ITS VICTIM

Today's Scripture Reading: Matthew 7:1–5 *Key Verse:* Matthew 7:2

With what judgment you judge, you will be judged;
and with the measure you use, it will be measured back to you.

This statement of Jesus is deadly serious. This is about an eternal judgment, and it applies directly to this nation. God is telling America, "I am going to do the same thing to you that you do to others."

America seems to thrive on the prime-time hypocrisy. There is no way in the world that I would want the private details of my life with my wife and family members broadcast on the Internet. I would not want my daily successes and mistakes discussed and analyzed on the evening news either, yet that is exactly what we do to government leaders and national celebrities.

Aren't you glad that God has not posted your mistakes and sins on the Internet or supplied color clips for the network news so the world could examine and judge you? I am thankful that God covers us in the blood.

With what measure we give, we will receive. With the judgment we judge, we will be judged. America's dirty laundry is about to go prime time unless we repent and change our ways as a nation. We can begin to make a difference by doing the right thing, saying the right thing, and reacting to the sins, mistakes, and failures of others God's way.

Pray this prayer with me:

Heavenly Father, I am determined to forgive others as You have freely forgiven me. Lord Jesus, I want to reach out to the unlovely and rejected in the same way You did during Your time on earth. I want to patiently work with others, even when they fail again and again—just as the Holy Spirit has worked with me in such grace and mercy. Freely I have received; now freely I will give.

NOVEMBER 12

WE MUST BRING HEALING AND UNITY TO OUR UNION

Today's Scripture Reading: 1 Timothy 2:1–3; 2 Chronicles 7:14

Key Verse: 2 Chronicles 7:14

If My people who are called by My name will humble themselves,
and pray and seek My face, and turn from their wicked ways,
then I will hear from heaven, and will forgive their sin and heal their land.

Can you imagine how much healing would blanket our nation if the House of Representatives and the Senate would say, "Let us call this nation to prayer regarding this issue"?

This nation is in moral decay and is divided on many issues. Repentant men on both sides of these issues must understand that there is only one side that matters—and that side is Jesus. Our nation needs to hook up with Jesus and call everyone to repentance. We must start working with families and bring God fully back into government. Who knows what changes would take place or what healing God would release?

God is calling the church to engage with the secular kingdom. It is time for us to bring healing and restoration to our nation!

Lord God, thank You for Your mercy. Thank You for Your kindness. Thank You for Your grace. Thank You for Your love. This nation has wandered far from You, but we thank You, for You are giving us another chance.

WILL YOU STAND WHEN FAITH AND FEAR COLLIDE?

Today's Scripture Reading: Matthew 5:14–15; Joel 3:13–14 *Key Verses:* Joel 3:13–14

"Put in the sickle, for the harvest is ripe.
Come, go down;
For the winepress is full,
The vats overflow—for their wickedness is great."
Multitudes, multitudes in the valley of decision!
For the day of the LORD is near in the valley of decision.

Some people think that God could not possibly judge our nation in the same way that He judged earlier cultures in the Bible. These people are deceiving themselves.

The slaughter of countless millions of babies alone makes us a prime candidate for judgment. The potential perils and opportunities of the future are very great, and it is inevitable that fear and faith will collide.

The very rich will suffer less and the very poor the most, and America may not be a pleasant place to live for a while. Our only guarantee, according to the history of God's dealings with nations, is that judgment is due.

Remember this: when the fire of judgment falls on a nation, the righteous will stand and the kingdom of God will thrive. God brings judgment not to destroy a nation but to restore it to godliness and truth.

If we love the people of our nation, we will pray for them, tell them the truth, and work tirelessly to establish the kingdom in their hearts. This is the only way to turn our nation around and avoid the consequences of judgment.

Are you prepared for judgment? Are you prepared to do what is necessary to establish the kingdom in our nation and save its people from condemnation? Pray with me:

Holy Father, You are both merciful and just, and gracious and holy. Help me to establish Your kingdom in my neighborhood, city, and state. Show me how to take Your light into the darkness that plagues our government and our key institutions. Help me join with other believers in the kingdom to plant righteousness in our nation and lead it to repentance. We, as a nation, have sinned against You. Please forgive us, Lord. We humble ourselves before You and ask for mercy. In Jesus' name I pray, amen.

BE BOLD AND SHINE

Today's Scripture Reading: Joshua 1:5–7; Matthew 5:14–16 *Key Verses:* Joshua 1:5–6

I will not leave you nor forsake you. Be strong and of good courage, for to this people you shall divide as an inheritance the land which I swore to their fathers to give them.

Judgment for America is inevitable. Things are occurring that could seriously affect the whole nation. More people could die than ever before because of deadly diseases and questionable actions buried under mountains of bureaucratic cover-up and political gamesmanship.

What is the church doing during all this? We are whimpering in the dark and worrying about the future when we should be at the head of the procession, leading the nation into the kingdom of light. We are supposed to be bringing kingdom principles to institutions, systems, and procedures that are indefensibly wrong. We are supposed to be the city of God, set on a hill, with a word from heaven in the midst of darkness.

We have no right to whine about how bad things are unless we are in the middle of the mess working around the clock to establish the kingdom. Jesus commanded (He did not *suggest*) that we go into all the world and preach the gospel of the kingdom. This does not mean that we should send a token number of missionaries into harm's way, and it definitely does not authorize us to build a fort in our backyard and hide out from the big, bad world. It is a summons for all who call themselves Christians to take Christ the King and His kingdom to the world.

It is time for the church to rise up and usher in the kingdom. We must take to heart God's word to Joshua just before he crossed the river of no return and possessed the land of promise: "No man shall be able to stand before you all the days of your life; as I was with Moses, so I will be with you. I will not leave you nor forsake you. Be strong and of good courage, for to this people you shall divide as an inheritance the land which I swore to their fathers to give them. Only be strong and very courageous" (Josh. 1:5–7 NKJV).

Pray this prayer with me:

Heavenly Father, the task is great, but You are more than enough for me. If You will stand with Me as You stood with Moses, then I cannot fail. Guide my steps and grant me the courage to take the kingdom to the very gates of hell in Jesus' name, amen.

OH, BY THE WAY—GOD STILL HATES SIN

Today's Scripture Reading: Micah 4; Proverbs 14:34; Acts 5; 1 Samuel 15:23 *Key Verse:* Proverbs 14:34

Righteousness exalts a nation,
But sin is a reproach to any people.

If you have read your Bible, then you know that God will not continue to reward disobedience with grace and mercy.

We live in one of the most blessed nations of the world, yet we may be the world's most irresponsible stewards of God's blessings! We do not respond to the gifts of God with gratitude, thanksgiving, or personal responsibility. We respond with rebellion and wholesale denial of God's goodness and importance in our lives. More and more Americans even deny His existence with their words or the way they live.

Given that scenario, how long can we go on before God sends judgment? The Bible reveals a cycle of judgment in God's dealings with nations and individuals. First the people obeyed and were blessed. Then they tended to become ungrateful, disgruntled, and increasingly disobedient; and God waited. When the cup of disobedience was full, God brought judgment to them like a parent who corrects a child to turn him from his wicked ways. Finally, God brought His people back to righteousness and blessings.

We think that we live in a season of grace because of the work of Jesus Christ on the cross. We do, but grace is not the same as "greasy grace," a term that describes our "no commitment, no transformation, no discipline, no boundaries" concept of Christianity. According to my Bible, God was still striking people dead in the season of grace if they dared to lie to the Holy Ghost! (See the story of Ananias and Sapphira in Acts 5.)

Do not think that God has developed a tolerance for deceit and disobedience just because you are a New Testament saint! He still hates sin, and rebellion is still as the sin of witchcraft. If you are waiting for "the right time" to take the kingdom to the streets, there is no better time than now! Pray with me:

Heavenly Father, You are holy, and You still expect Your people to walk in holiness as well. Cleanse me and purify my heart through the blood of Jesus. Make me a bold witness for Your kingdom in the midst of darkness in Jesus' name, amen.

WILL YOU? ARE YOU?

Today's Scripture Reading: John 14:23–24; 1 Samuel 15:22–23

Key Verses: 1 Samuel 15:22b–23

Behold, to obey is better than sacrifice,
And to heed than the fat of rams.
For rebellion is as the sin of witchcraft,
And stubbornness is as iniquity and idolatry.
Because you have rejected the word of the LORD,
He also has rejected you from being king.

We seem to acquire a taste for hypocrisy at an early age. It happens as we learn to say one thing and do another in childhood. Sometimes we learn it from our parents who promise to do something for or with us but do not keep their word. We quickly adapt that example to our own situation and glibly answer Mama or Daddy's order to do our chores, "I will," or "I am," when we really are not and have no intention of doing so.

We perfect the art of saying one thing and doing another in our personal relationships. We play the hypocrisy game at the altar during the wedding ceremony; we do it on the job with supervisors and coworkers; and we even do it in church when the preacher reads God's Word and presses us for an answer about our obedience to it. "I will." "I am." No, you will not. No, you are not.

Remember what happened to Ananias and Sapphira when they lied to the Holy Ghost? Remember what happened to King Saul? Now, he was God's anointed too. He was ordained to rule in the earth as a king and to establish a kingdom in God's name, just like you. He did not take long to ruin his life and his family's future by using the "say one thing and do another" method of serving God.

Jesus said it better than anyone: "If anyone loves Me, he will keep My word; and My Father will love him, and We will come to him and make Our home with him. He who does not love Me does not keep My words" (John 14:23b–24a NKJV). What does that make you? Think about it; then do something about it.

Heavenly Father, I really do love Your Son. Jesus is my Redeemer, my Savior, my Bright and Morning Star. He is my Hope, my Life, and my Salvation. Strengthen me in my weakness; empower me by Your Spirit to be a doer of Jesus' words and not a hearer only.

NOVEMBER 17

JUST PREPARE AND SHOW UP (GOD WILL DO THE FIGHTING)

Today's Scripture Reading: Ephesians 6:10–18 *Key Verses:* Ephesians 6:10–11

My brethren, be strong in the Lord and in the power of His might. Put on the whole armor of God, that you may be able to stand against the wiles of the devil.

It is time to fight, but we are nowhere near the boxing ring. We do not understand that all we have to do according to God's economy is make up our mind to be there and trust God. He does the rest.

The reason you are losing the battle day after day is because you refuse to discipline yourself with the Word and train. For that reason, you never show up at the fight. When the bell rings, God does not come in and fight for you because you are nowhere to be found in that arena. As a result, the enemy wins by default. Then he finds you where you are hiding and works you over just for the fun of it. Ignorance, fear, and poor discipline can wreck your life, even after you receive Jesus Christ into your heart and life!

We may get into scuffles and suffer bruises and falls from time to time, but the real battle on earth does not take place on earth at all. Paul—the man who was shipwrecked, beaten, and imprisoned for Christ in the physical realm—described the real battle in the spirit realm in Ephesians 6. God and His hosts will fight your enemy while you sit there and simply behold the salvation of God! But God will not fight for you until you show up at the battlefield.

You still have to have your battle equipment and maintain it. You still have to go through the training and the discipline because that is what empowers you to sit in the middle of a battle! You still have to fast. You still have to pray. You still have to read, study, and meditate upon God's Word. If you do these things, you will have the faith and discipline to take your seat at the side of the Most High God and watch Him destroy the works of the enemy once again.

Your help comes only when you are in action.

Heavenly Father, I think I have made this thing too hard by going about it the wrong way. I thought that I had to carry this thing on my back, but You never said that. You want me to show up in full battle gear in my home, on the job, at city hall, and on the streets. Then You will finish the fight for me. I bless You in Jesus' name, amen.

WHY WORRY? THE OUTCOME IS A SURE THING!

Today's Scripture Reading: Isaiah 54:17; Romans 8:31 *Key Verse:* Romans 8:31

If God is for us, who can be against us?

Most boxers go into the ring and fight to see if they have what it takes to be a champion. When they first duck under the ropes, though, they do not know if they will come back through those ropes as winners or losers.

The people of God go into the ring already knowing that they are champions. The battle was won even before it began. This is just a "cleanup operation," an occupation exercise for the winning army.

You should remember that the victory is yours even before you step into the ring. God says to you, "Whatever was lording it over you; whatever force, compulsion, or sin was controlling you, I have placed it in your hands along with the power to destroy it."

Jesus already hammered the devil in a humiliating defeat at Calvary. The Lord lets him up just enough for you to knock him down again from your place of rest in the corner of faith. You already know the outcome! You are a kingdom champion because God is on your side, and who can be against you?

Pray this prayer with me:

Heavenly Father, thank You for giving me the best seat in the house in this fight. Your Son already humiliated Satan, the would-be contender and offender, so all I have to do is take my seat beside You and believe. I must believe that Jesus is the risen Lord, the resurrected Savior, and the King of kings. I must believe that His name is above every name, and that there is healing, deliverance, and freedom in that name. Thank You, Father, for allowing me to take part in the defeat of darkness and the establishment of the kingdom of light! In Jesus' name I pray, amen.

STAND STILL AND STOP FRETTING

Today's Scripture Reading: 2 Timothy 1:7–8; Exodus 14:13 *Key Verse:* Exodus 14:13

Moses said to the people, "Do not be afraid. Stand still, and see the salvation of the LORD, which He will accomplish for you today. For the Egyptians whom you see today, you shall see again no more forever."

A lot may be going on in this nation and the world, and you may even see trouble brewing up and down your street. It does not matter—this is not the time for the people of God to be afraid. On the other hand, this is a great time for the unredeemed to be afraid.

As for you, remember Paul's counsel to young Timothy during the difficult times of the first-century church: "God has not given us a spirit of fear, but of power and of love and of a sound mind. Therefore do not be ashamed of the testimony of our Lord" (2 Tim. 1:7–8a NKJV).

God gave you—I said *you*—a Spirit of power. The Almighty also gave you a Spirit of love. Despite what you hear blaring on the evening news; no matter what you read in the newspapers about failing economies, corruption, and rising crime rates in your area, God also gave you the Spirit of a sound mind. No, you are not crazy; you are just different from the people who *should* be worrying.

Listen to Moses' advice. Put your trust in God and see His salvation pass right before your eyes. This is not a time to be afraid. Just stand still and watch God handle everything. Pray with me:

Heavenly Father, people everywhere are saying things look bad, and I suppose they do look bad from their point of view. As for me, I choose to believe Your Word. Things are well with my soul as long as I am found in You. You are my Rock and Shield, an ever-present help in time of need. You hold the destinies of kings and presidents in Your hand, and You raise up and put down nations and earthly powers when and how You choose. No, things look good from my point of view, seated in the heavens in Christ, right beside You.

NOVEMBER 20

DO NOT COMPLAIN—IT TELLS THE ENEMY HE HAS FOUND THE MARK

Today's Scripture Reading: 2 Timothy 2:1–10 *Key Verses:* 2 Timothy 2:3–4

You therefore must endure hardship as a good soldier of Jesus Christ. No one engaged in warfare entangles himself with the affairs of this life, that he may please him who enlisted him as a soldier.

Were you ever in the armed forces? Let me phrase that a little more specifically. Have you ever been in a war?

Our problem as saints is that we do not understand that we *are* in a war. If you fought in the rice paddies or jungles of Vietnam, then you know what it is like to sleep in the field. You had to contend with all kinds of exotic bugs and snakes crawling over your body at night, but you knew they came with the territory—you were in a war. You were not foolish enough to holler about those bugs and snakes, because you knew you might get shot—your complaint would give away your location to the unseen Vietcong lurking nearby.

Too many of us like to holler at the top of our lungs every time we get a little bug-bitten or feel something cold and slimy slither across our toes. I am telling you that you are going to get hit! Your complaints are music to Satan's pointed ears. They tell him that his weapons are hitting home. Naturally, he just starts pouring it on from that point!

God fights the battle, but do not think that you are going to come through this war without any scratches or scrapes. Do not howl, whine, or complain. Just get up, take your stand to continue the fight, and let Jesus Christ end the conflict! What a way to fight a war!

Holy Father, I am sorry for whining and complaining so much. I forgot for a moment who You are and what You have made me. In the heat of the conflict, I forgot that no weapon, no blow, no scheme, and no assault of the enemy can prosper against me. The enemy is not trying to defeat me; if he was, his job would be easy. He is trying to defeat You, and it will never happen. I will see this battle through to the end, Lord Jesus. Victory is mine because of You.

I GET THE FEELING YOU JUST WILL NOT QUIT!

Today's Scripture Reading: 2 Corinthians 6:4–10 *Key Verse:* 2 Corinthians 6:4

In all things we commend ourselves as ministers of God.

Something else you need to know about being in a battle is that you must know what to protect.

Inevitably your hide is going to get some nicks, scratches, and bruises in a battle. If God calls you to lay down your life, like the apostle Paul, to save the lives of a lot of people, then you might take a lot of hits in the course of the war.

Just accept that fact. You are going endure actual combat, but a wise person in battle knows what to protect. "I may have to lose such-and-such, but this other is the most important thing in the midst of this battle." "I am going to take some hits, but as long as I guard that which God has ordained for me to guard and take the land that God has ordained for me to take, I might limp in, but I am going in."

Paul, the seasoned battle veteran of the first century, put it this way: "In all things we commend ourselves as ministers of God: in much patience, in tribulations, in needs, in distresses, in stripes, in imprisonments, in tumults, in labors, in sleeplessness, in fastings" (2 Cor. 6:4–5 NKJV). Do you get the feeling that this man just would not quit? That is the attitude we need in this day and age. Advance the cause of the King and His kingdom, no matter what. It is your destiny.

Heavenly Father, I will not pretend that I can do this because I cannot do it in my own strength and ability. Be my strength, Lord. Rise up within me and accomplish that holy thing You revealed to me by Your Spirit. I will do my part—to believe, obey, and follow. In Jesus' name I pray, amen.

November 22

How Long Will You Straddle That Fence? (Isn't It Painful?)

Today's Scripture Reading: 1 Kings 18:20–24 *Key Verse:* 1 Kings 18:21

Elijah came to all the people, and said, "How long will you falter between two opinions? If the LORD is God, follow Him; but if Baal, follow him." But the people answered him not a word.

This is not the time to delay in what God has spoken to you. He is the only authority and direction you can trust, so you should listen to only His voice. Above all, do not let other people or circumstances dictate what you should do.

The only reason Elijah had to risk his life to face down 450 prophets of Baal was because the people of God could not make up their minds. They went with whoever was "on top" at the time. Long before that day on Mount Carmel, the Israelites had received the promised land with a command to possess the land and remove anybody and anything that would defile the kingdom. They delayed and compromised until those who followed God were in the minority. Does this sound familiar?

Do what God told you to do. The economy, changes in political structure, and the ever-changing whims of men do not affect Him. God has some secrets that He has held back from the devil, secrets that He wants to reveal to those who are faithful and who diligently seek Him.

Make God your first priority. Make Him your sole source for battle commands and orders. Pray this prayer with me:

Holy Father, I remember what You told me to do, and I will delay no longer. If You said it, I will do it. Forgive me for my hesitation, and anoint me as I step out by faith to do Your will Your way today. In Jesus' name I pray, amen.

JUST GIVE GOD YOUR MOUTH AND LET HIM TALK!

Today's Scripture Reading: Mark 16:20; Luke 12:11–12, 21:12–15 *Key Verses:* Luke 21:12–15

Before all these things, they will lay their hands on you and persecute you, delivering you up to the synagogues and prisons. You will be brought before kings and rulers for My name's sake. But it will turn out for you as an occasion for testimony. Therefore settle it in your hearts not to meditate beforehand on what you will answer; for I will give you a mouth and wisdom which all your adversaries will not be able to contradict or resist.

When you speak the things that Jesus said, when you walk in the things He told you to walk in, a glory comes to rest on and flow through you. This level of obedience prompts God to say, "Wherever you go, I am a witness for you. Do not even worry about what you are going to say when you are ordered to defend your obedience to Me—I will put divinely inspired words in your mouth."

Have you ever had those moments when you did not know what to say but God seemed to step in and take control of your mouth? You were amazed at yourself because you even threw in some big words that you had never heard before! You knew that it was not really "you" talking, but when the last word was said, you somehow ended up with the situation under control! You knew it was God all along, didn't you? He was "bearing witness" that you were representing Him and His kingdom.

Heavenly Father, sometimes I do not feel like much of a talker, but You have used the lips of a donkey, a rebellious prophet, a stuttering murderer, and unlearned fishermen to declare Your glory. It is obvious that You can use me, too, so I give myself—and my mouth—to You. I will faithfully preach the gospel of the kingdom if You will take over when you know I cannot go on. In Jesus' name, amen.

NOVEMBER 24

ARE YOU A TRANSFORMER OR A CONFORMER?

Today's Scripture Reading: Matthew 5:13–16 *Key Verse:* Matthew 5:15

Let your light so shine before men, that they may see your good works and glorify your Father in heaven.

Do you want to know whether or not you are walking in the authentic gospel? Just take this simple test: when you walk into a crowd, does the conversation change?

Some old-time saints just read and meditated on the Word and let God speak to them. They carried themselves in such a way that people knew not to cuss when they were around. Whether the people were churchgoers or sailors just off the boat did not matter. They did not know whether or not the saints were preachers, but they treated them with respect as if they were. It happened with Peter, the uneducated fisherman too. Jesus so changed his life that a holy boldness—and powerful words to match—came over him that could only have come from God (see Acts 4:13).

It happens to me today. I can walk into places for the first time and people who do not know me will say, "You are a preacher, are you not?" I do not have to tell them or announce my credentials over a loudspeaker. When the Spirit of the Lord is upon you, God bears witness to your calling and anointing with His tangible presence. It is as if He whispers, "This is My child. Do not mess with him."

People in my own congregation have shared about times when they were about to be robbed, but the assailants just could not rob them. One lady in my church actually turned around, took away her attacker's gun, and led him to Christ!

When people in the world see the genuine Spirit of God upon you, they cannot bother you. I am not talking about the imitation stuff. A superficial life with Jesus impresses or changes no one. I am talking about the real gospel on display through your life. Let me ask you again: When you walk into a crowd, does the conversation change?

Heavenly Father, I want the real thing in my life. I repent for not putting You above all things. Take first place in my heart and mind, and let my choice show up in the way I live each day. Transform me into a beacon of light with the power to affect the people to whom you lead me. In Jesus' name I pray, amen.

DOES HELL KNOW YOUR NAME?

Today's Scripture Reading: Acts 19:13–16 *Key Verse:* Acts 19:15

The evil spirit answered and said,
"Jesus I know, and Paul I know; but who are you?"

Does the devil know your name, or is he saying the same thing to you that the demons said to the seven sons of Sceva in the book of Acts: "I know Jesus and I know Paul, but who are you?"

You can go to church and do everything people like to do in your services—you can hear lofty sermons and take a bath in holy water, or you can jump, dance, holler, and speak in other tongues for hours. In the end, it all boils down to obedience or disobedience.

Are you living your life according to the Scriptures, or are you going your own way? What spirit rules your life? I guarantee you that all of the evil spirits in existence know and fear the Spirit of Jesus when they encounter Him. They knew Paul in the book of Acts because he was filled with the Spirit of Jesus. What are you full of?

The modern church is a joke in our society. The unsaved world views us as a bunch of overly pious hypocrites who say one thing and do another. When things get tough and the time comes to really cast out demons or heal the sick, we are powerless. The world is "going to hell in a handbasket" because we do not have the power to deal with anything. Evidently, we do not have enough of the Spirit of Jesus in us to get even a nod out of the devil and his bunch.

Is Jesus in you? Does hell know your name? Isn't it about time for us to change that situation? Pray this prayer with me:

Holy Father, I am tired of living a life of half-truths, religious pretense, and powerless phoniness. Lord Jesus, I have received You into my life as Lord and Savior, but somehow I went a different direction from Yours. I know it because there is not enough of You in my life to make an impact in my world. Holy Spirit, I yield to You and confess my hunger for the reality of Your presence and power every day. Father, possess me, transform me, and shoot me like an arrow into Your perfect will. In Jesus' name I pray, amen.

God Does Not Have Blackouts or Brownouts—That Is Our Problem

Today's Scripture Reading: Acts 1:8; 2 Timothy 3:12 *Key Verse:* Acts 1:8

You shall receive power when the Holy Spirit has come upon you; and you shall be witnesses to Me in Jerusalem, and in all Judea and Samaria, and to the end of the earth.

Never underestimate the ability of unsaved people to "read you" like a book. They can quickly recognize the presence of someone or something different from the world they live in. If you show up and say that you represent the kingdom, then you had better deliver the genuine goods. Otherwise they will say to you the same embarrassing thing the demons said to Sceva's boys in the first century: "I know Jesus and I know Paul, but who in the world are you? What kind of fake are you?" (See Acts 19:15.) They will not take long to discern whether or not you have power.

Too many churches today devote all their time and resources to preaching "another gospel." They go so far as to pervert the message to deliver it to the unsaved. They promise people that if they get saved, "Everything will be all right. You will get everything you are supposed to get here."

That is a lie. The Bible says that anyone who wants to live godly will face problems and persecution (2 Tim. 3:12). To say there will be no problems is the same as calling God a liar.

You will always have problems coming your way. The key is having the power to deal with the problems! This is how the church is supposed to stand out in the midst of a faithless and perverse generation. God is sending judgment to the church first so we will change our ways. We need to have the real thing, the power of the Spirit of Jesus, operating in and through our lives. That is the only way we can establish the kingdom of light in the middle of the kingdom of darkness. It may cost us more than we ever dreamed to acquire the power, but it is worth the cost.

Pray this prayer with me:

Holy Father, send Your fire to the church and cleanse us again. Purify our hearts and anoint our hands to do war in Your name. Fill us to overflowing with Your Holy Spirit so we can truly be witnesses for You at home, next door, across the city, and throughout the world. We ask it all by faith in Jesus' name, amen.

DO NOT LEAVE OUT THAT SIX-LETTER WORD: R-E-P-E-N-T

Today's Scripture Reading: Acts 3:12–20; Galatians 1:6–12 *Key Verse:* Acts 3:19

Repent therefore and be converted, that your sins may be blotted out, so that times of refreshing may come from the presence of the Lord.

What is our gospel? Peter said it all when he declared under the anointing of the Holy Ghost: "Repent therefore and be converted, that your sins may be blotted out, so that times of refreshing may come from the presence of the Lord." That is the gospel of the kingdom compressed into one sentence.

The problem with the body of Christ is that we preach another gospel. We are preaching something other than kingdom. We like to accidentally omit that difficult word *repent*. We imply that anybody can just "join up" in God's country club.

Our appeals to the lost resemble a low-dollar, used-car dealer's offer more than a biblical call to God: "No money down. It does not matter whether you keep your word or not. Just sign the dotted line—we will get you credit and hand you the keys. We turn no one away for any reason."

Repentance has never been a popular message with people. Repentance does not tickle people's ears. In fact, repentance may be the most unpopular message in the history of mankind. Still, any so-called preacher who does not preach repentance as part of the genuine gospel of the kingdom is *accursed,* according to the apostle Paul (see Gal. 1:8–9).

As a member of God's kingdom, you are officially called and anointed to share the gospel of the kingdom with other people. God does not require you to go to Bible college or seminary first. He does, however, demand that you tell people the truth. Share the pure and authentic gospel of the kingdom. Tell people that the only way into the kingdom is to repent and be converted in Jesus' name. If you do that, you are blessed. If you share another gospel . . .

Pray this prayer with me:

Heavenly Father, the gospel of Your kingdom is simple and straightforward. Help me to be the same way when I share Your gospel with those I meet today. Give me Holy Ghost boldness to tell the truth, no matter how afraid or intimidated I may feel. Once I obey and speak the truth in love, I know You will confirm the truth by Your Spirit. Thank You for hearing me and for answering my request in Jesus' name, amen.

NOVEMBER 28

"THE GOSPEL ACCORDING TO ME" IS SATAN'S FAVORITE

Today's Scripture Reading: 2 Timothy 4:2–5; Revelation 12:12; James 3:1

Key Verse: Revelation 12:12

The devil has come down to you, having great wrath, because he knows that he has a short time.

The devil is not stupid. He knows that he must prolong Jesus' return if he wants to delay his final defeat and destruction. He knows that he has already lost, but he still hopes to get back at God by messing with His children on earth. Unfortunately, we help Satan carry out his plans by playing games with the gospel. When we begin to preach "other gospels" and tamper with the truth, then the Lord Jesus cannot come back again.

Sad to say, one of the favorite false gospels preached in the church could be called "The Gospel According to Me." The church has always tended to focus too much on itself, but things took a turn for the worse when we allowed the secular doctrines of humanism and the New Age to infiltrate our thinking.

Most of our focus in the body of Christ today is directed to *us, me, you,* and *mine*. Some of America's most recognized church leaders have built massive congregations by preaching the always attractive "Gospel According to Me." This is alarmingly similar to the New Age doctrine that God is in everyone, that He can take any form and speak any way He chooses, and that "your god" is just as valid as "my god." It is also the essence of counterbiblical heresy.

God remembers every word we say, and He holds leaders especially accountable for the things they preach and teach (James 3:1). You and I have a holy mandate to preach the pure, unadulterated gospel of the kingdom to our lost world. This is the same gospel that Jesus Christ, James, Peter, John, and Paul the apostle preached. The true gospel brings new life in Jesus Christ, and it demands genuine repentance and true conversion. Anything less is heresy and worthy of a curse. Are you ready to buck the popular trends and reach out to the lost?

Pray this prayer with me:

Father, You put the choice in my hands, and I have made up my mind. You are going to have things Your way in my life. I will speak only Your Word; I will do only those things You tell me to do. I will follow only one Lord and Savior, Jesus Christ. I will give glory only to the one true God. I declare it in Jesus' name, amen.

ONLY GENUINE LIGHT CAN CUT THROUGH DARKNESS

Today's Scripture Reading: Galatians 1:8–11; John 10:1–2 Key Verse: Galatians 1:9

As we have said before, so now I say again, if anyone preaches any other gospel to you than what you have received, let him be accursed.

The problem of "other gospels" is not new to the kingdom of God. Many of the apostles' letters to the early churches warned Christians about the dangers of false teaching. The apostle Paul was concerned about the church in Galatia because its members had developed a taste for "pleasing preaching." He wrote, "For do I now persuade men, or God? Or do I seek to please men? For if I still pleased men, I would not be a bondservant of Christ. But I make known to you, brethren, that the gospel which was preached by me is not according to man" (Gal. 1:10–11 NKJV).

"Pleasing preaching" floods our world today. Countless numbers of people are preaching "another gospel" in the name of Christ, but their attractive words do not enlarge the kingdom. The true gospel *convicts of sin* before it frees people from sin. The false gospel encourages people to sneak into the kingdom by bypassing repentance and total surrender to the King of the kingdom. Jesus predicted it would happen. He said, "Most assuredly, I say to you, he who does not enter the sheepfold by the door, but climbs up some other way, the same is a thief and a robber. But he who enters by the door is the shepherd of the sheep" (John 10:1–2 NKJV).

Thousands of "other gospel" preachers and teachers are lining up to please you and fleece you. Avoid them the way you would avoid a plague because God has cursed them. Find a shepherd and pastor who preaches the truth of the genuine gospel, no matter how much it hurts. If you are called to preach, make sure you preach the truth and not a lie.

Pray this prayer with me:

Heavenly Father, even with all the noise I hear on religious television and radio, I can still hear Your voice. I can recognize the gentle voice of my Shepherd even on my worst days and in the most difficult of circumstances. I thank You for that, Lord. Help me do my part to shine Your light on the confusion and darkness being broadcast in the name of popularity. Make the light You placed in my life shine on all those I meet so they will know the genuine truth and be set free indeed. In Jesus' name I pray, amen.

November 30

Play Your Part or Be Replaced by Someone Who Will

Today's Scripture Reading: Matthew 25:14–30; Acts 20:24; 2 Timothy 4:7; Luke 9:62

Key Verse: Acts 20:24

None of these things move me; nor do I count my life dear to myself, so that I may finish my race with joy, and the ministry which I received from the Lord Jesus, to testify to the gospel of the grace of God.

Every actor playing a principal role in a stage play has an understudy. If he cannot show up for some reason, there is someone who can replace him.

I do not know about you, but when I go to a play to see a celebrated actor or actress perform, I expect to see that person step onto the stage and deliver the lines. It is disappointing to see someone else to play the part.

You need to understand that someone else is training for *your position* in the kingdom. No one but God knows this person's name. But if you fail to obey God's call and do not show up to play your part, God will announce that someone else will take your place!

If you get weary in the middle of the race and faint before you reap the reward, God will set someone else in your spot because the kingdom must go on. I am not making this up—this is the very heart of Jesus' teaching about the parable of the talents (see Matt. 25:14–30).

Pray this prayer with me:

Heavenly Father, it is a privilege to be chosen as part of Your kingdom cast. I have a part to play, and I will perform it with all my heart, soul, and strength. As You have been faithful to me, I must be faithful to you and those who depend upon me. I have put my hand to the plow, and I refuse to look back. Grant me the strength, the power, and the grace to stand, having done all. In Jesus' name I pray, amen.

Storing Up for the Next Generation

DECEMBER 1

CLEAN UP YOUR ACT NOW FOR YOUR CHILDREN'S TOMORROW

Today's Scripture Reading: Mark 8:1–21 *Key Verse:* Mark 8:18

Having eyes, do you not see? And having ears, do you not hear? And do you not remember?

Many of us in the church have some real sensory problems. We cannot see or hear properly, and we seem to forget easily as well. Jesus reprimanded His disciples because they could not perceive what should have been obvious to them. He was speaking of the seeing and hearing aspects of spiritual discernment and the ability to remember the things God said.

In general, a child's knowledge of God and his level of spiritual discernment are a reflection of his parents' knowledge and discernment levels. I have noticed two unsettling trends in generation-to-generation transfers. First, sin tends to grow progressively stronger with each succeeding generation, barring a genuine life-transforming encounter with God (for example, if Dad drinks moderately, Junior will drink excessively, and Grandson may be an alcoholic). Second, godliness tends to grow progressively weaker and less intimate with each succeeding generation where we simply pass down knowledge about God rather than lead our children into an intimate and vibrant relationship with God.

It is vital that you have twenty-twenty spiritual vision, highly developed listening skills, and an unfailing memory of God's counsel and kingdom principles. The future generations depend on it! We cannot afford to settle for a lazy spiritual lifestyle.

Clean up your spiritual act now so that on the great Day of Judgment, your child, grandchild, or great-grandchild will not come to you and say, "How could you be so unmotivated and unbelieving as to spend your life in church but let the devil beat you? We did not even have a chance because you never rose to your calling so we could walk into the callings God ordained for us."

God will not give you anything that you do not see first. He has no surprise deliverances. Pray this prayer with me:

Holy Father, open my eyes so that I can see You in Your beauty. Open my ears so I can hear Your Word and live the abundant life. Touch my mind so I can remember and apply the wealth of wisdom You have given to me in Your Word and by direct revelation. In Jesus' name I pray, Amen.

December 2

The Way You Treat Your Children Reflects the Real You

Today's Scripture Reading: Ephesians 4:1–6 *Key Verses:* Ephesians 4:1–2

Walk worthy of the calling with which you were called, with all lowliness and gentleness, with longsuffering, bearing with one another in love.

There is something that really makes me angry, and it gets me so hot that sometimes I wish I could just slap people for doing it! This happens when I see parents who are all dressed up in expensive "Sunday-go-to-meeting" clothes accompanied by their children—who are tagging along behind Mama and Daddy with their faces dirty, their hair a mess, and wearing clothes that look like third-generation hand-me-downs! What a shame! Those parents—presumably Christians if they are going to a church service—spent plenty of money on themselves while their children went ragged.

God owns everything, and unlike countless human parents, He wants to lavish His children with good gifts. We should take our cue from God. When people see you and your children, they should see what the kingdom looks like. Your Father sacrificed everything to clothe you in priceless robes of righteousness. What are your children wearing right now?

Have you sacrificed to meet your children's needs and clothe them to the best of your ability, or have your children suffered so you can look good at the mall? Are you modeling your parenting priorities after those of your heavenly Father?

The way you run your family and demonstrate your love in the home says more about the real you than all the posturing, posing, and pretending we see at church and on the street. God sees and knows all things, and the unsaved people next door to you can probably figure out the truth too. In the words of Paul, "Walk worthy of the calling with which you were called."

Pray this prayer with me:

Heavenly Father, You have been so good to me. You blessed and provided for me when I did not deserve anything but correction, You loved me when I was unlovable, and You stayed with me when I was sick. Help me to be that kind of parent to the children You have given me, as well as to other children in my extended family. Teach me how to cherish and nurture the children, Lord. In Jesus' name I pray, amen.

IF YOU NEGLECT THE CHILDREN, YOU ABORT YOUR FUTURE

Today's Scripture Reading: Psalm 127:3–5 *Key Verse:* Psalm 127:4

Like arrows in the hand of a warrior,
So are the children of one's youth.

Everything is generational in God's kingdom. He never thinks of one individual because He is not locked into time. He sees the end from the beginning. He knows that when Great-grandfather Joe got saved at the age of twelve, it had a ripple effect over time that literally opened the door for little Libby to be saved four generations and 120 years later!

When God spoke to Abram about blessings, He talked about his children and his children's children too! The same thing happened when God talked to David about blessing him—those gifts would continue from generation to generation.

Children are like God's arrows in our hands, and it is our responsibility and privilege to launch them into the future. But we need to examine how we are launching them. We need to prepare and equip them with all the accumulated knowledge, wisdom, wealth, and power that we have gained and that our forefathers left us.

I cannot stress this enough. If we neglect our children, we are aborting our own future.

Pray this prayer with me:

Holy Father, I am discovering just how much You treasure the children. Every child in my life actually belongs to You—I am just a steward of Your little ones. Give me the wisdom, grace, and gentleness I need to properly raise and train these children, Your heritage. Show me how to impart or pass down the things I have received from those before me and from You, Lord. In Jesus' name I pray, amen.

My Children Will *Not* Have to Go Through the Things I Did!

Today's Scripture Reading: Matthew 19:13–15; Deuteronomy 28:1–14 *Key Verses:* Matthew 19:13–14

Little children were brought to Him that He might put His hands on them and pray, but the disciples rebuked them. But Jesus said, "Let the little children come to Me, and do not forbid them; for of such is the kingdom of heaven."

You ought to be willing to bless anybody who will bless your children—even if your children have not been conceived or born yet! It is never too early to pray for the "kingdom team" that will help you raise and teach your children.

You need to bless the Sunday school teachers, children's ministers, and pastors who will labor over the Word for your children. Their hard work, in combination with the time you spend sharing God's Word and kingdom truths with your children, will allow your children and your children's children to stand up some day and be the head and not the tail!

There you go, thinking, *Bishop Long is making up things again*. But, my wildest imagination could not begin to compare with the reality of God's promises to His children! (Even this statement came from God's Word! See 1 Cor. 2:9.) It was God who said through Moses: "The LORD will open to you His good treasure, the heavens, to give the rain to your land in its season, and to bless all the work of your hand. You shall lend to many nations, but you shall not borrow. And the LORD will make you the head and not the tail; you shall be above only, and not be beneath, if you heed the commandments of the LORD your God" (Deut. 28:12–13 NKJV).

I do not know about you, but I made up my mind that my kids, grandkids, and great-grandkids were not going to go through the things I did. I decided to get right with Jesus. God is right in everything He says. Are you ready to do what it takes to make sure your children, your grandchildren, and your great-grandchildren are blessed and anointed in the Lord? Start right now with this prayer:

Heavenly Father, thank You for teaching me how to be a godly parent. Help me to provide more for my children than today's needs. Help me make provision for them twenty-five and fifty years from now. Teach me how to prepare the way for the blessing, training, and anointing of my great-grandchildren even after I return to You. I thank You for it all in Jesus' name, amen.

DECEMBER 5

THINK TRANSGENERATIONALLY: WHY START OVER WITH EACH GENERATION?

Today's Scripture Reading: Exodus 34:6–7; Proverbs 13:22; Luke 19:13; Ezekiel 44:30

Key Verse: Ezekiel 44:30, emphasis mine

The best of all firstfruits of any kind, and every sacrifice of any kind from all your sacrifices, shall be the priest's; also you shall give to the priest the first of your ground meal, to cause a blessing to rest on your house.

When this verse says "your house," it does not just mean your physical house or dwelling. Usually in the Old Testament, when the Bible speaks of a person's house, it is referring to his entire family at the time as well as all his descendants throughout time. It is a generational word similar to *seed.*

God wants us to think about more than ourselves when we do things, plan things, and pray. God is a generational God, the Bible is a generational book, and the Lord has called us to be a generational people—but we are not. We do not pass down generational wealth, and we do not pass along generational knowledge, insights, or skills either. In other words, we do not operate in the principles of God.

Many ethnic groups have operated on generational principles for hundreds or thousands of years. They combine a strong work ethic with generational principles to protect the future and wealth of the family.

Unlike many children of wealthy American business owners, children from generational cultures know they have an obligation and responsibility to work hard, study hard, and carefully guard and increase the things they receive from their fathers. The result is that the family's wealth, power, and influence grow significantly from generation to generation.

Why is the church not doing this? These are more biblical than ethnic or cultural principles. We essentially start over again with every new generation. Even the world would say we are not thinking smart. Are you ready to build the kingdom with the future in mind?

Heavenly Father, I am new at this but You are not. Guide me and teach me to plan and live with future generations on my mind. Regardless of when Jesus returns, I know You have commanded us to "occupy" until He comes. Show me how to plant eternity and righteousness in the hearts of my children for Your glory. In Jesus' name I pray, amen.

START A HOLY LANDSLIDE OF RIGHTEOUSNESS AND PROSPERITY

Today's Scripture Reading: Ezekiel 37:21–28 *Key Verse:* Ezekiel 37:25, emphasis mine

They shall dwell in the land that I have given to Jacob My servant, where your fathers dwelt; and they shall dwell there, they, their children, and their children's children, *forever; and My servant David shall be their prince forever.*

American Christians need a "mind transplant" to remove some wrong thinking. We must begin to filter everything we see and plan through a generational viewpoint. Instead of saying, How will this affect me? we need to ask, How will this affect my children, my children's children, and those who come after them? Truly lasting wealth is multigenerational, whether we are speaking of spiritual or economic wealth. This happens only when people live and plan for the long run, not the short span of their own lives.

Always remember that God called Himself "the God of Abraham, Isaac, and Jacob." He is a God with future generations on His mind. When He says that He is laying a blessing upon your house, He is talking about at least three generations!

In general, it takes at least three generations for a major character trait to be implemented or replaced in a family. That means when I start out and do exactly what God has ordained, I start a whole new kingdom thought in my home. That principle becomes embedded in the thinking, conversation, and teaching of my family from generation to generation to generation. If my great-great-grandchild decides not to walk in it, then it will take him three generations to reverse the godly training planted in my descendants.

This subject is incredibly serious! Parent, you are a failure if you do not leave a spiritual heritage of wealth for the next generation. You have failed God, no matter what you accomplish, accumulate, or possess. If you begin to be a good steward of what you have now—whether it is money, talent, time, or energy—God will start blessing and multiplying you. If you stick with it in obedience, it will endure for at least three generations! Pray with me:

Holy Father, I repent for being so nearsighted in my spirit. I want to start a holy landslide of righteousness and prosperity that will increase speed and power with each generation. I know it all begins with me, but I need Your help, Father. There is no one like You. I ask these things in Jesus' name, amen.

December 7

Plant a Seed to Meet Your Great-Great-Grandchild's Need

Today's Scripture Reading: Genesis 17:1–19 *Key Verse:* Genesis 17:7

I will establish My covenant between Me and you and your descendants after you in their generations, for an everlasting covenant, to be God to you and your descendants after you.

A spirit of poverty, which we inherited from those who went before us, weighs down the modern church. Our predecessors loved God and accomplished much, but most of them knew how to tackle poverty and other issues only within the time frame of a single generation. The reason God has not answered many of our prayers is because they mostly center around the word *me*. We also suffer from a serious case of "one-generation" vision.

God is reluctant to bless you if you do not understand that you represent a blessing line of three generations. Why? He knows you will just waste it. When He blesses you, He is already thinking about how that blessing will touch your grandchild. He wants to change the mind-set of an entire family line, not just yours. But God will hold up everything until you understand that you need to bless the next two generations after you by passing on everything God gives you.

I am serving notice to you right now that you should have a greater love for your unborn children and grandchildren than you have for yourself! Make up your mind to walk out this thing the way God told you to do it.

Stop murmuring, dishonoring, and robbing God. Sow your seed selflessly; declare to yourself: "I realize that I might not reap the full benefits, but I am sowing something for my son and grandson and granddaughter to walk in. I will spend eternity with them, and they will thank me for the good things I have put in store for them." Change the future! Sow something today that will change the generations. Pray with me:

Heavenly Father, You sowed divine promises, blessings, and Your only begotten Son to bless us long before we were ever born. Teach me how to sow seed today that will bless my great-great-grandchildren in the days when I am long gone from the earth. It blesses You when we bless our generations, and I will be obedient to do it. In Jesus' name I pray, amen.

SHORT-TERM THINKING PRODUCES LONG-TERM PROBLEMS

Today's Scripture Reading: Deuteronomy 7:7–9 *Key Verse:* Deuteronomy 7:9

Know that the LORD your God, He is God, the faithful God who keeps covenant and mercy for a thousand generations with those who love Him and keep His commandments.

I will say it again: everything is generational.

God has His hands full with us. He is trying to transform an entire church full of one-generation thinkers into transgenerational kingdom people. It takes the patience of God to handle the job!

Have you noticed that some families seem to have a built-in weakness for alcoholism, drug abuse, adultery, or poverty, while others seem impervious to these things? It is because transgenerational weaknesses call for transgenerational solutions. God has the power to instantly deliver any of us from these sins, but He wants to implant the spiritual antibody for these temptations in your family line. This will take several generations.

When God's Word and Spirit convince you to change something in your character (let us say you admit that you have a spiritual weakness leading to alcoholism), then your obedience will affect a minimum of three generations. If you pass down the spiritual wisdom that triggered the change, then each of the three generations will continue in that godly direction until it has fully embedded itself in your spiritual bloodline.

If the enemy comes against your great-grandchild with a spirit of alcoholism, that descendant will easily rebuke every curse related to that spirit and will then pass that "spiritual antibody" on to the next generation. This process should continue in your generations until it becomes automatic.

Our problem is that we still think short term. The solution is simple: think, plan, and live long term by the Spirit of God. Pray with me:

Holy Father, I confess that I have been a short-term thinker, and that has led to long-term problems. Transform me and change me, Lord. Help me make long-term changes according to Your Word and the leading of Your Spirit so the generations after me will not have to fall into the same pit I did. In Jesus' name I pray, amen.

DECLARE THE TRUTH TODAY AND SET GENERATIONS FREE TOMORROW

Today's Scripture Reading: Genesis 32–33 *Key Verse:* Genesis 32:28

He said, "Your name shall no longer be called Jacob, but Israel; for you have struggled with God and with men, and have prevailed."

When I step behind the pulpit of my church and ministry with boldness, I am not ministering as some kind of "shooting star" or spiritual upstart. I am walking in the spirit of my grandfathers, grandmothers, and of my mother and daddy. I stand and minister from the wealth of the spiritual heritage they passed down to me. I did not start from scratch; I am merely adding to what they already started.

If you are a first-generation Christian, you are not a spiritual pauper just because your parents and grandparents did not serve God. The Lord lends His grace and provision to you in abundance. Still, you do not have time to play around.

This is your chance to change your entire family line! Dig into God's Word and study it so you will know what it says and how to apply it in your life. Walk with it, and always remember that this thing is not just about *you*.

Jacob ("the deceiver") wrestled with God until his life was "put out of joint." God changed his name to Israel ("he will rule as God") and turned his life around. God is doing the same thing with you. Your obedience and careful seed planting today can save countless numbers of your relatives and descendants who have not even entered this world yet!

Put a new foundation of supernatural power and authority under your "house" today. Stand on God's uncompromising Word and declare these things with me in the authority of Jesus' name:

> *There are not going to be any more divorces in my bloodline. I kill that sickness in my bloodline. I take out depression. With these words of obedience and faith in God, I declare that I represent a whole new aspect of life in my house. I declare that from this generation forward to a thousand generations, we will serve the Lord and walk in His Kingdom. I declare it in Jesus' name, amen.*

DID YOU KNOW YOUR CHILDREN ARE FOLLOWING YOU?

Today's Scripture Reading: Deuteronomy 4:9, 11:18–21 *Key Verse:* Deuteronomy 4:9

Take heed to yourself, and diligently keep yourself, lest you forget the things your eyes have seen, and lest they depart from your heart all the days of your life. And teach them to your children and your grandchildren.

Our children follow in our footsteps, whether we like or not. If your children have already followed you into a mess, do not expect God to fix everything overnight. He does not work like that in most cases. Of course God can work miracles, but He might say, "I am not doing too many more miracles for you, because you are not learning principles. You are not passing on a spiritual heritage."

Do you own your own home, your car, your furniture? If not, then you are also teaching your children by your example not to own anything.

Whenever you have a problem, do you go see somebody in the church who is "spiritual"? You are teaching your children to depend on other people for their communication with God. If your children cannot find that "spiritual" person when they get in trouble, they may see the commercial on TV and dial somebody "spiritual" at a 900 number.

Whatever you are teaching your children by example, remember that everything is generational. Pray this prayer with me:

Heavenly Father, in Your mercy show me any hidden sins, evil ways, or dangerous habits in my life that could bring hurt to me, to my children, or to my children's children. I repent of my sins, for I want to walk holy before You and my family. Help me teach as much by godly example as by my spoken words of instruction. In Jesus' name I pray, amen.

DECEMBER 11

TEACH THEM FAITHFULNESS IN THE LEAST SO YOU WILL NOT WORRY MUCH

Today's Scripture Reading: Luke 16:10–13 *Key Verse:* Luke 16:10

He who is faithful in what is least is faithful also in much; and he who is unjust in what is least is unjust also in much.

Why wait until your son is fifteen before you teach him kingdom economics? It is almost too late by then.

Jesus said, "If you have not been faithful in the unrighteous mammon, who will commit to your trust the true riches?" (Luke 16:11 NKJV). This kingdom principle translates from the natural realm to the spiritual realm. If you cannot manage your own money wisely, why in the world would someone entrust his soul to you as a minister of God?

By the age of three, your child should be taught how to clean up his room and take care of the things entrusted to him. No one in my house leaves home with his bed unmade, and you will not find any underwear lying in the middle of the floor. I have room checks. After that, you move on to bigger things. Once you begin to give him an allowance, you have the opportunity to move into some spiritual things.

Kids want everything, basically because they do not understand what it costs. Give your child a dollar before he goes into the store. When he says, "I want that!" look at the price. If the item costs $1.50, ask, "How much do you have?"

"One dollar."

"Did you just get that dollar?"

"Yes, sir."

"Well, ten cents goes to the tithe because it belongs to the Lord who blessed you. So you really only have ninety cents. I know you want to sow in an offering, so why don't you double up? Now you have eighty cents. So no, you cannot have that $1.50 item."

When the boy finds something for eighty cents, say this: "If you spend this eighty cents, you will not have anything saved. You can spend forty cents now and save forty cents. Now remember that we are going to the store again next week, and you get only one dollar a week. If you really want that $1.50 item, you can save up."

In a wonderfully spiritual way, you begin to teach your child, and your grandchildren and great-grandchildren after him, how to manage money and be faithful in what they have. Pray with me:

Heavenly Father, show me practical ways to teach my children eternal truths about value, faithfulness, and stewardship in the kingdom. In Jesus' name I pray, amen.

RAISE YOUR CHILDREN TO BECOME GOD'S LIGHT TO FUTURE GENERATIONS

Today's Scripture Reading: Luke 11:36; Acts 13:47 *Key Verse:* Acts 13:47

The Lord has commanded us:
"I have set you as a light to the Gentiles,
That you should be for salvation to the ends of the earth."

You personally can lift a burden from pastors and churches in future generations by teaching your children at a young age how to manage their money the kingdom way. Your obedience now will help prepare the generation to come with kingdom understanding of godly principles for business, faithfulness, giving, blessing, budgeting, and much more.

Your young stewardship students may be just entering school this year, but keep up the godly work. When these kingdom rulers graduate, they will be able to stand on their own and do even more: they will carry the kingdom further than we ever dreamed! They are literally God's light sent to the unsaved world to bring salvation to the ends of the earth.

I guarantee you that many of the kids graduating from our nation's schools today choose to stay home and live with their parents because they are afraid to go out. They do not know what to do, and they know they cannot handle themselves in the real world.

The problem is that their school taught them only "book learning" and humanistic relativism. No one bothered to teach them the life-giving truth of kingdom principles, and many of them inherited nothing but wasted potential from previous generations. Frankly, their best hope may be in the children you are raising today, the future leaders with the fire of the kingdom and the hope of the King in their eyes.

Pray with me:

Holy Father, I know that destiny hinges on my willingness and ability to obey Your call today. You have called me to raise and train my children to be kingdom leaders and faithful stewards of Your gifts and resources. I feel inadequate for the task, but I put my trust in You. Show me how to train my children to touch the generations to come. In Jesus' name I pray, amen.

LORD, HELP ME LIVE RIGHT—THE FUTURE IS WATCHING

Today's Scripture Reading: Deuteronomy 11:19; Acts 2:38–39 *Key Verse:* Acts 2:39

The promise is to you and to your children, and to all who are afar off, as many as the Lord our God will call.

When you think kingdom, I hope that you think generations. If you do, then you may have to accept some difficult things. There also may be certain things that you want that you may not get. Anything worth having costs something.

For one thing, you have a special responsibility as a kingdom parent to steer your children straight for the goal. Make sure your children and your children's children become the rulers God called them to be. Do not let them struggle with the old clinging sins or mistakes that entrapped you because you were not taught.

Start studying and walking in God's will in those areas. Then turn around and teach your children how to avoid that device of the enemy altogether! You may have to sacrifice some things in your life to do it, but you have no greater kingdom assignment than this one!

Tithing is an example of something that can be difficult to teach from generation to generation. Very few Christians really walk in the truth of this kingdom principle. I know it is tough to tithe, but it is a direct indication of the nature of your relationship with God! In fact, that is all it is.

Perhaps the most difficult part of raising children generationally in the kingdom is this: God makes you examine yourself far more than you ever would on your own. It is crucial, because tomorrow's kingdom leaders are watching your every move (and mistake).

Pray this prayer with me:

Heavenly Father, it is easy to walk the Christian walk in front of strangers or with other Christians whom I see several times a week. It is nearly impossible to do it with my own children! Lord, they know me better than anyone else. They have seen me in my worst moments, at my lowest depths. They know the truth about me, Lord. Holy Spirit, let them see more than my failures and shortcomings. Let them see my total dependence upon You. Let them see how my heart burns for You and Your kingdom. Help me teach them what they need to know for the future. In Jesus' name I pray, amen.

December 14

Your Children Were Born to Rule

Today's Scripture Reading: 1 Chronicles 7:1–5, 26:4–6 *Key Verse:* 1 Chronicles 26:6

To Shemaiah [Obed-Edom's] son were sons born who governed their fathers' houses, because they were men of great ability.

God wants to bless your household, but He will do it through the generations. I have said it before, and I will say it again: All lasting wealth comes through family, and it is built generationally. Many of us have temporary wealth, and that is what is wrong with our people.

Even a casual reading of the Old Testament will tell you that the children of Israel valued their family relationships from generation to generation. Obed-Edom was faithful to house the ark of the covenant on his property, and he was faithful to respect God's holiness. God blessed him immediately, but He also blessed him *in his generations*.

What begins with one blessed man, such as Abraham, Joseph, or David, quickly expands in the course of one or two books of the Bible to include hundreds and thousands of descendants. For this reason, the Bible is a perfect textbook for the study of the accumulation of righteousness, wealth, and power, as well as of sin, from generation to generation. We need to catch on to God's way of doing things through the generations.

Every good gift, possession, blessing, or ability should grow stronger or more valuable, or increase in some way as it goes from generation to generation. If you do not come from a wealthy family, but you study your family history, I can almost guarantee that you will find someone in your family heritage who was building and growing with great success until something happened. At that point, everything collapsed and your family had to start over from scratch.

God ordained for you—and your children—to rule in this world. No one has a greater right to own property and manage resources than God and His people. He created it all, and then He bequeathed it to us. Now all we must do is possess it and establish His kingdom.

Heavenly Father, thank You for transforming me into a child of light. Anoint me, and my children after me, so we can follow and serve You all the days of our lives as we rule on the earth. In Jesus' name, amen.

IT IS TIME TO GO BACK TO BUSINESS SCHOOL

Today's Scripture Reading: Luke 2:42–50 *Key Verse:* Luke 2:49

He said to them, "Why did you seek Me? Did you not know that I must be about My Father's business?"

Jesus asked, "Did you not know that I must be about My Father's business?" If saints do not come to the understanding that God has set His kingdom up like a business, they will miss out. You must set up that same "family business" in your home and pass it down from generation to generation. (Some modern translators do not use the term *business* in this verse, but this does not bother me. The parable of the talents in Matthew 25:14–30 still proves my point: God set His kingdom up like a business.)

We have been mishandling the family business in recent generations because we have passed down some bad habits. Many of the families in the church have passed down a business ethic that sounds like this: "Get your paycheck Friday; be broke by Saturday. Buy, buy, buy!"

"That cannot be," you say. Just look at any of your children who work outside the home or do jobs for you. As soon as they get paid, they might buy those basketball shoes that cost ninety dollars or the latest fashion in casual slacks and outerwear at the mall. They will probably spend everything they earned because the culture and their peers (and maybe your example) have implanted it in them to be *consumers* and not *producers*. If this is not true of you and your home, then I applaud you. If you are guilty as charged, then I will go on just for you.

Consumer Christians support everybody else instead of having others buy from and work for them! They have nothing, and they continue to perpetuate their problem. They have mishandled the family business, which dooms them to be broke, busted, and disgusted. This needs to change. We need to learn how to conduct kingdom business God's way. Pray with me:

Heavenly Father, I think I need to some business advice. Whatever I am doing with my family is not working. It is time to find out what You do and duplicate it. Holy Spirit, help me to unlearn the things that need to go and to learn the Father's way of doing kingdom business. In Jesus' name I pray, amen.

December 16

Riches Come and Go, but Kingdom Wealth Is Forever

Today's Scripture Reading: Proverbs 3; Matthew 6:19–21 *Key Verses:* Matthew 6:19–21

Do not lay up for yourselves treasures on earth, where moth and rust destroy and where thieves break in and steal; but lay up for yourselves treasures in heaven, where neither moth nor rust destroys and where thieves do not break in and steal. For where your treasure is, there your heart will be also.

How do you bless your family and think generationally? Most of us think we do so with our wealth and riches. What is the difference between riches and wealth?

We all have wealth, but some of us have more riches than others. Riches are the perishable things, the temporary assets that Christ warned us about in the Word. Jesus warned us not to get hooked on money. We should use money as a tool, but when we let it get the upper hand it becomes a god to us.

Unfortunately, many parents train their children to go after stuff. Part of our ongoing spiritual anxiety is rooted in our resentment that God has not blessed us with all the money that we think we should have. God does not want us to focus on gathering material possessions because they usually end up possessing us!

People without ethics or morals can gain riches. I am afraid that many Christians would have to say yes if I asked, "Do you have any 'hot' or stolen items in your house?" You see, "good deals" become hard to pass up once your heart is hooked on accumulating more stuff. That addiction to acquisition can quickly lead you down the wrong path and into sin.

On the other hand, we can gain wealth only through skill, spiritual knowledge, and character development. In fact, true wealth comes only through our obeying God and doing what God has ordained for us to do as stewards. Wealth is what we pass on to our children, and it has far greater merit than riches. Worldly riches are fleeting, but kingdom wealth is eternal.

Pray with me:

Father, it is clear to me that I need to make some course corrections in my life. My heart is right, I do want to bless my family; but I admit to You that my methodology is all wrong. I have been going for stuff instead of true wealth. Holy Spirit, teach me how to gather wealth that will not fade with time or changing economies. Teach me how to acquire things that I can pass on to my children, things that really matter in the kingdom of God. In Jesus' name I pray, amen.

THE TRULY WEALTHY KEEP GOING DESPITE HARD TIMES AND HARD FALLS

Today's Scripture Reading: Psalm 37:23–26; Proverbs 24:16 *Key Verse:* Proverbs 24:16

A righteous man may fall seven times
And rise again,
But the wicked shall fall by calamity.

Why do so many multimillionaires acquire and lose so many businesses, yet still manage to come out on top? It is because they understand the difference between wealth and riches.

When you have been to hell and back and are still standing, *you are wealthy*. Do not let rich people intimidate you. You can look at them and say: "You have riches, but I have wealth. I can lose everything and gain it back, plus some. I have been in the fire, and I came out of the flames with character. It does not matter what happens; I know who I am and who my God is. I can get anything I want as long as God ordains it. Hell itself cannot stop me. I will not compromise because I am a man of truth. I pay my bills on time, and I stand as God has ordained me to stand."

True wealth is who you are, what you know about God, and how close you are to Him personally. Right in the middle of the worst economic crisis in history, God will honor your character. Everyone else will be going out of business, but they will wonder why you are thriving!

That is wealth.

Pray this prayer with me:

Father, I am beginning to understand the difference between riches and true wealth. Now I realize that You have made me wealthy indeed! I can see how true wealth from You can make it easy to acquire riches if I need them. Yet riches will have no grip on me as long as I value only true wealth in the kingdom.

YOU CAN TAKE MY STUFF BUT YOU CANNOT TOUCH MY WEALTH

Today's Scripture Reading: Matthew 6:20–21; Malachi 3:6–12

Key Verses: Matthew 6:20–21

Lay up for yourselves treasures in heaven, where neither moth nor rust destroys and where thieves do not break in and steal. For where your treasure is, there your heart will be also.

When you are wealthy, you do not need to worry about somebody breaking into your house and stealing things. You can replace things. So they can take your stuff, but they cannot take your wealth.

Riches are something that you have; wealth is something that you are. Let me say that again: riches are something that you have; wealth is something that you are. You can leave your earthly riches for the government, for foundations, or for other people after you die, but they have no life of their own. In fact, riches resemble a virus more than anything else. Most people who receive riches suddenly through a large inheritance or a lottery watch their personal lives fall apart in a feverish nightmare. They often end up broke several years later despite the millions of dollars they received. Riches have nothing to do with wealth.

You can pass on spiritual wealth, on the other hand, to live through your children even after you are dead. They will rise up in your generational blessing and understand kingdom principles. They will understand that they should not spend everything they have. They will understand the importance of blessing others, of walking holy before God, and of having a good character. They will have a thorough understanding about the tithe and how to give good offerings. Best of all, they will understand that God called them to be the head and not the tail, and they will understand that they are wealthy.

So no matter what the schoolkids say, no matter who tries to condemn them, your children will turn around and say, "If God be for me, then who can be against me? I can do all things through Christ that strengthens me." Now that is true wealth.

Holy Father, I want to leave more for my children than dollars, bank bonds, or deeds to property and cars. I know that things are not enough. In Jesus' name, I want to leave the wealth of the kingdom in their hearts.

This Is Your Wisdom and Understanding

Today's Scripture Reading: Deuteronomy 4:6–7; Daniel 4:3   *Key Verses:* Deuteronomy 4:6–7a

Be careful to observe [the statutes and judgments]; for this is your wisdom and your understanding in the sight of the peoples who will hear all these statutes, and say, "Surely this great nation is a wise and understanding people." For what great nation is there that has God so near to it, as the Lord our God is to us?

What is generational wealth? Here is a brief list.

- *Relational peace with God.* What good is a lot of stuff if you have no peace with God?
- *God-given relationships.* God will give you wonderful relationships with your spouse, children, friends, and family members. Do you have feuds in your family? Have you not spoken to a sibling in a long time? The devil is messing with you.
- *Revelational wealth.* This is your ability to hear things in the Spirit, including the deep revelations of the kingdom. Of course, the prerequisite is obedience to His commands.
- *Time.* Most of us talk about how we do not have enough time. The truth is that God gives you all the time you need to do what you have to do.
- *Material contentment.* This means that, like Paul the apostle, you have learned to be content in all situations.

Generational wealth, by definition, grows stronger with each generation. That assumes that each generation of folks will receive the true spiritual wealth that their parents acquired through obedience, and then add to it through greater and deeper obedience in their own lives. Have you caught the vision for transgenerational wealth and kingdom living?

Heavenly Father, Your vision for the generations is breathtaking in its scope. It is hard for me to think that way in the physical realm since my life is brief by heavenly standards, but by Your Spirit, I will change the way I live and raise my children. Help me to pass along to my children the true wealth and inheritance of the kingdom. In Jesus' name I pray, amen.

GOD'S "BLESSING LOVE LINE" IS CLOSER THAN YOU THINK

Today's Scripture Reading: Genesis 12:3; Acts 3:25 *Key Verse:* Acts 3:25b

In your seed all the families of the earth shall be blessed.

God wants you to pass your generational wealth on to your children. As a parent, He expects you to take the principles of the kingdom and learn them by practicing them. Then you can teach them to your children.

They must understand who they are in Christ. They should know that God wants to give them peace that passes all understanding so they can walk in contentment. The only way they will learn who they are is through their own obedience to God. It also will give them a deep understanding of the Word. Once that happens, holiness ceases to be "your thing" and becomes a family business that will go from generation to generation.

God told Abram, "I will bless those who bless you, / And I will curse him who curses you; / And in you all the families of the earth shall be blessed" (Gen. 12:3 NKJV). God never intended that the government rescue this nation, and that is why the nation has failed so miserably. God planned that the families of the kingdom would rescue America and the world! To put it another way, you are part of the rescue team for this planet!

In the book of Acts we read, "You are sons of the prophets, and of the covenant which God made with our fathers, saying to Abraham, 'And in your seed all the families of the earth shall be blessed'" (Acts 3:25 NKJV). God's blessing love line is closer than you think—it is the family!

Holy Father, no matter how much I would like to, I cannot avoid the responsibility you placed upon me to establish the kingdom in my family and in my children's hearts. Holy Spirit, teach me how to teach them by example as well as by word. Transform us into redeemers, saviors, healers, deliverers, and leaders in the name of the great Redeemer, Savior, Healer, Deliverer, and King of kings, Jesus Christ. Amen.

RESIST EVERY SPIRIT THAT WOULD TAKE YOUR CHILDREN'S GENERATIONAL WEALTH

Today's Scripture Reading: 1 John 4:1; 2 Corinthians 2:10–11

Key Verses: 2 Corinthians 2:10b–11, emphasis mine

I have forgiven that one for your sakes in the presence of Christ, lest Satan should take advantage of us; for we are not ignorant of his devices.

Do not be ignorant of the devil's schemes. He wants to close the ears of your children so that they will not receive your wealth. He wants to get you so frustrated as a parent that you stop teaching your child that he or she is wealthy.

Remember, riches automatically come once your children discover they are wealthy in the kingdom. If you start teaching them that they are wealthy, this teaching will go and grow from generation to generation. You do not have to worry about your child's welfare once you leave this earth if you put wealth into them. True wealth in the kingdom equips your children to get all the things that they need.

Stop fussing at the child. Instead, rebuke the spirit that has come between you to hinder the generational blessings God ordained for you to pass on to him.

If you allow this lifeline of wealth and blessing to be cut off, the next generation has to start over from scratch. This is the whole problem with inner-city families and communities. Families in inner-city regions are often messed up because there is no generational understanding of how wealth accumulates from family to family and from generation to generation. The result is that the next generation is cut off too, making it worse that the generation before. Pray with me:

Heavenly Father, thank You for reminding me about the really important things in life and the kingdom. Open my eyes so that I can discern the devices and schemes of the enemy, and give me wisdom on how to handle them by Your Spirit. I want nothing to separate me from my family or to block the transfer of kingdom wealth from Your heart to ours and from generation to generation. Keep us united in Christ Jesus I pray. Amen.

TEACH YOUR CHILDREN NOW

Today's Scripture Reading: Deuteronomy 4:6–10, 40 *Key Verse:* Deuteronomy 4:40

You shall therefore keep His statutes and His commandments which I command you today, that it may go well with you and with your children after you, and that you may prolong your days in the land which the LORD your God is giving you for all time.

The book of Deuteronomy is full of admonishments to fathers and parents to train their children while they are young.

Do you tell your children stories about your extended family? What do they know about your family's heritage? I hope you realize that the public school and the church can never teach your children what you should be teaching them.

Search the Scriptures and discover the truths God says are vital for them to learn at an early age. Teach them about Jesus Christ. Show them how He handled Himself when people challenged Him for doing the right thing. Show them how much He loved children, and point out that He rebuked the disciples when they tried to keep children away from Him. Tell them about the cross and make sure they know that Jesus died for them. Teach the kingdom truths about true wealth and the dangers of the love of money.

If you teach your children now, they will be a blessing to you all your days. Even better, they will be equipped to raise their children in the same way, but with even greater wisdom and kingdom wealth. Above all, do not wait until a more convenient time. It will never come. Just begin to obey God now, so you can reap His blessings.

Holy Father, I hear Your voice through the Word, and I will obey. It is time for me to begin teaching my children today. No matter how inconvenient or difficult it may be, I will press through and teach them anyway because our generations depend upon it. In Jesus' name, amen.

FATHERS MUST TEACH, TRAIN, AND INSTRUCT THEIR CHILDREN

Today's Scripture Reading: Ephesians 6:1–4 *Key Verse:* Ephesians 6:4

Fathers, do not provoke your children to wrath, but bring them up in the training and admonition of the Lord.

Fathers, God has charged you to keep open the blessing pipeline from generation to generation. A tremendous burden rests on you because you are responsible for training your children to walk in kingdom principles. It is your job to teach them that they are wealthy (and what that really means).

Your responsibility in the home is so awesome that I urge you to read Psalm 78. Then you will understand that you are to sit with your children and teach them what God has ordained. Tell them what has happened from generation to generation in your family. Teach them how you got out of your own "Egypt," and then tell them who they are in Christ. Describe their kingdom wealth, and outline their gifts and talents.

Brother, if you have a daughter who is old enough to walk and wear a dress, then you need to start taking her out on dates. Open and close the door for her and take her to dinner. Tell her that she is beautiful, and explain that you are showing her how a man is supposed to take care of her. Give her a standard she can understand, and then you will not have to worry when your daughter brings somebody home for you to meet. She will reach for the standard that you have set, so you can expect a carbon copy of yourself. If he is not like Daddy, she will automatically kick him out.

If you have a son, train him in the real meaning and role of manhood. Teach him how to treat girls and ladies with respect and honor. Teach him how to recognize and respond to authority so he will be qualified to wield authority as a ruler in the kingdom. Set the example and your children will follow. Do it all in Jesus' name, and He will bless your labor of obedience.

Heavenly Father, thank You for blessing me with my family. Help me to prepare, preserve, and bless them with true kingdom wealth and training. Give me strength, endurance, and insight to fulfill my responsibilities in my home and in the kingdom. In Jesus' name I pray, amen.

GOD HAS NOT FORGOTTEN YOU, MOTHER

Today's Scripture Reading: Judges 5:7–9; Hebrews 6:10 Key Verse: Hebrews 6:10

God is not unjust to forget your work and labor of love which you have shown toward His name, in that you have ministered to the saints, and do minister.

Mother, are you raising children on your own, with no one but God to help you?

If God is helping you, do not think you are inadequate. Do not allow anyone's idle chatter make you feel incapable. You are well equipped to teach kingdom principles to your children. Pray about those things you feel a man should deliver to your children, and God will send someone who will speak to your child and bring it to pass. Remember that God is faithful!

Do not use your lack of a husband as an excuse. Deborah was a mother in Israel, but when the chips were down she rose up and saved her nation (Judg. 5:7). You have a Man in your house, and Jesus Christ will speak into your children through you and tell them who they are. Stress to them how wealthy they are, and you will impart to them a spiritual heritage of wealth. (And tell them that the blessings and riches will come afterward.)

Remember that they are to build on what you have. If you teach them, they will go even further and deeper. Long after you are gone, you will see your great-grandchildren come into heaven and talk about how blessed they are and how they enjoyed great exploits in knowing the Lord. It will all take place because you took a stand and invested the time to speak into your children's lives. You were careful to correct them, and you made sure that they walked in the principles of the kingdom and knew who God called them to be.

You are blessed and you are a blessing, Mother. Keep up the good work, and remember this: God has not forgotten your labors in the night with your children. He knows the love you have invested in them. Pray with me:

Heavenly Father, thank You for walking with me through the hard and lonely times. Help me do what I never thought I would have to do—raise my children without the help of a husband and father. Supply all those things that I cannot, Lord. Send godly men into the lives of my children to model and teach them how a good man lives and blesses others. Give me the strength and wisdom to train them in Your Word and plant kingdom principles in their hearts. In Jesus' precious name I pray, amen.

FATHER, RESTORE THOSE THINGS THAT WERE CUT OFF THROUGH DISOBEDIENCE

Today's Scripture Reading: Psalm 37:21–22 *Key Verse:* Psalm 37:22

Those blessed by Him shall inherit the earth,
But those cursed by Him shall be cut off.

Do you feel that you have been cut off from the blessing lifeline of God because of disobedience from previous generations? Does evidence exist that your ancestors did not understand that spiritual obedience or lack of it can affect the generations to come?

If this is your situation, I have good news for you: God wants to establish a reconnection. He wants to see the things He ordained for you come to pass. He wants the favor He ordained to come back into your life and move from generation to generation because of *your* obedience.

Pray this prayer with me by faith:

Father, in the name of Jesus, I am forgiving the earlier generations in my bloodline who walked unrighteously out of ignorance or disobedience. In the name of Jesus, I ask You to reconnect me to Your blessing lifeline right now. First of all, help me understand that first I receive true wealth and then You will release my riches. Forgive me, Lord, for not walking in the faith I should have. I repent right now, Lord. Remove this curse and draw me close to You. Reestablish what has been cut off by the mistakes of the past. Lord, I receive the full blessing, the full wealth, and the full riches of the kingdom You have for me. I receive it all into my spirit right now. Thank You, Lord.

NOW IT IS YOUR TURN

Today's Scripture Reading: 2 Timothy 1:3–6 *Key Verses:* 2 Timothy 1:5–6

I call to remembrance the genuine faith that is in you, which dwelt first in your grandmother Lois and your mother Eunice, and I am persuaded is in you also. Therefore I remind you to stir up the gift of God which is in you through the laying on of my hands.

Perhaps you are like Timothy in the sense that your great-grandmother, your grandmother, and your parents were connected to a divine plan. Do not wander too far from that plan of kingdom understanding—it is your lifeline. When someone in a family decides to get back on track with God, He will pull down a lifeline and say, "Now you can start destroying Satan's curse on your family." Those who went before you already pulled on the lifeline and paved the way in prayer yesterday for your blessings today.

God has an eternal plan to make your family straight, no matter how many mistakes, sins, or failures have plagued its members over the years. He wants to bless them, lift them up, and make the family name great in the kingdom. But they must come under the umbrella of the kingdom first. They must understand God's mandate that we bring the kingdom of the living God all over this land.

This is that divine plan the old saints followed. Now it is your turn. Set your eyes on Jesus Christ and move forward. Pray with me:

Heavenly Father, keep me in line and focused on the goal in the days ahead. Help me keep the course by Your Spirit. Show me how to serve You and help build Your kingdom, Lord. You have given me the keys of the kingdom, with power to destroy the works of the enemy. Help me start the right way, the kingdom way. Then help me establish this kingdom in my children and my children's children. In Jesus' name I pray, amen.

Why Are People Not Talking About You?

Today's Scripture Reading: Hebrews 11 *Key Verses:* Hebrews 11:7–9, 11

By faith Noah, being divinely warned of things not yet seen, moved with godly fear, prepared an ark for the saving of his household . . . By faith Abraham obeyed when he was called to go out to the place which he would receive as an inheritance . . . By faith Sarah herself also received strength to conceive seed, and she bore a child when she was past the age.

Are you a comfortable saint who says, "I hear God and believe," but walk in unbelief? You are not alone, but answer this question: after going through everything you had to go through to get where you are, do you really want to watch your children to go through the messes, mistakes, and painful recovery you have endured?

The reason you have had to fight through so much hell in your life is because *you had to start all over*. In fact, you had to start out from a pit because you were forced to fight through some things in your bloodline that you had nothing to do with. You sweated and cried and crawled your way through a painful divorce, financial ruin, and crushing loneliness in the process, but God was faithful. How dare you stop short of the goal! *Why are people not talking about you?*

People talked about Abraham. That meant that they had to talk about Isaac and Jacob too, because of the impact Abraham had on his descendants. If you talk about Abraham, you literally have to talk about three generations! Will you have that kind of impact on the generations that follow you? Will people have to mention your children, your children's children, and their children after them if they start in on you?

Think about it. Do you have a grandfather or grandmother whom no one in the family can forget? Do family members say, "If it were not for Granddaddy So-and-so, we would not be where we are today! He was a man of such great faith that he moved mountains." When you open up your mouth, people can hear his kingdom wisdom and wealth in your words, covering three generations and working on a fourth.

Are you building an easy chair or a generational seat of authority? Are you impacting three generations, or will you take your seat in premature comfort and make the next generation start in a hole all over again? Pray with me:

Holy Father, I have come up short once again. I wanted to retire when You want me to refire. Lord, I will obey Your voice and put away my easy chair. Guide me as I work by faith to prepare the way for my future generations. In Jesus' name I pray, amen.

DO NOT FAIL TO PASS THE BATON

Today's Scripture Reading: Hebrews 12 *Key Verse:* Hebrews 12:1

Since we are surrounded by so great a cloud of witnesses,
let us lay aside every weight . . . and let us run with
endurance the race that is set before us.

I ran the second leg for a four-man relay team years ago. Several teams raced against each other in a single race, and everyone had to stay in his team's assigned lane. We could not hesitate in timed races, and we cannot hesitate in the kingdom race.

When I ran with the relay team, the first man started the race from the starting blocks. After he covered his allotted distance he handed the baton to me. I started running just before he arrived so we would have a smooth transfer and keep up our team momentum. In that moment of transfer, the person completing his course was nearly exhausted, yet he had to maintain his speed until he knew without doubt that I had a good grip on the baton.

Once I received the baton, I ran my allotted course and handed off the baton to the third man on the team. The vision of my coach was for the fourth man to cross the finish line before anyone else. He simply expected the first, second, and third runners on the team to do what they had to do to help the fourth man cross the line first. I did not get to feel the ribbon break across my chest like the fourth man did, but I shared in the victory.

Abraham knew that he had the first leg of the race. Isaac took the second leg, and Jacob knew he was number three. It was Joseph who broke the ribbon across his chest when he crossed the finish line and won the favor of Pharaoh in Egypt. No one knew it except through prophetic word, but it was in Egypt that Abraham's descendants began to increase so dramatically.

You may not realize it, but when you got here, someone handed you a baton. Now you must run your course. Perhaps you do not get to jump up and down for a couple of generations. All you can do when you pass the baton to another generation is watch.

The Bible says a great cloud of witnesses is watching you run this course (Heb. 12:1). You will join that crowd of witnesses after you pass on, but you must pass God's vision from generation to generation to generation. You are part of a team. Do not drop the baton.

Heavenly Father, guide my feet, strengthen my heart, and anoint me to fly. I have a race to win and a baton to pass on to my children and their children after them. This race will by won not by might, nor by power, but by Your Spirit. In Jesus' name I pray, amen.

DECEMBER 29

I WILL FINISH THIS RACE AND PASS ON THE BATON!

Today's Scripture Reading: 2 Timothy 4:1–8 *Key Verses:* 2 Timothy 4:6–8

The time of my departure is at hand. I have fought the good fight, I have finished the race, I have kept the faith. Finally, there is laid up for me the crown of righteousness.

Too many of us think life is just about "our season." It is not. This kind of thinking causes many of us to drop the baton on the exchange in the relay of life. We get selfish.

We have only a small window of time to pass on the baton, and timing is everything. If you come up to the next man too slowly, it forces him to decelerate. If you fail to prepare him and come too fast, you can lose all your momentum and team advantage. When I ran track and approached the next relay team member, I would say, "Go, go, go!" and he would start burning up the track. At that point it was my responsibility to give the baton to him.

The race goes not to the swift or the strong, but to the one who endures. You need a good burst of energy at the moment you pass on the baton to the next generation. The devil has destroyed many great men and women of God at the sunset of their lives. The enemy purposely tried to break up their generational handoff so he could make the work of their lives be in vain. If those men or women missed the exchange, the next generation had to start all over.

All of us need to repent for missing crucial exchanges in life. We need to endure so we will have the energy to hand off the kingdom baton to the next generation. Paul set a godly example for us all in his letter to young Timothy when he declared, "I have finished the race."

Pray this prayer with me:

Heavenly Father, the years are flashing by, and destiny is waiting. I want to make sure I pass on the baton of kingdom faith, hope, trust, power, and wisdom to my children and the generations that follow them. Keep my feet light and my heart strong. Give me a vision of the generations that will follow me so I can keep them before me in prayer and faithful love. I want to fulfill all Your will for my life. By Your grace and power, I will finish this race, pass on the baton, and keep the faith. In Jesus' name I pray, amen.

CHARGE YOUR CHILDREN TO BUILD A HOUSE . . .

Today's Scripture Reading: 1 Chronicles 22:5–19 *Key Verses:* 2 Chronicles 22:5–6

David made abundant preparations before his death.
Then he called for his son Solomon, and charged him
to build a house for the Lord God of Israel.

Whatever you do from this point on, do it unto the glory of God. I have to remind you that the kingdom business involves more than parents laying a foundation for their children. The children have responsibilities too. We do not want them to simply do what we did; we want them to stand on what we did as a platform, and then do better and go higher!

Challenge your children to go higher and further than you did. If they do only what you did, then they will have failed.

Teenagers have a natural boldness and incredible energy that they can easily lose or misdirect when they lack guidance. Tap that God-given well of creativity and courage for the kingdom. Dare them to think "outside the box" and to dream God's dreams and make them come to pass. Charge them to build the kingdom on earth for our God in heaven.

Get your teenagers together and task them with creating a business plan (make sure they know that it must make sense). Then help them to get started. Teach them how to do everything—banking, taxes, marketing, sales planning, and so on. Have them do it while they are still teenagers so that when they get into their twenties and thirties, they can tackle new ideas independently.

If you do these things and commit them to the Lord, your children will not be "looking for jobs" like everyone else their age. They will be creating jobs for others. It is all part of God's business plan for the kingdom, a kingdom destined and ordained to rule and reign in this life.

Pray this prayer with me:

Heavenly Father, I needed supernatural intervention to break out of my "box," and I am still dealing with the "small thinking" I picked up during my bondage. I want more and better things for my children and the generations to follow. Help me to challenge and train my children to dare to do great exploits in Your name under the leadership of the Holy Spirit. In Jesus' name I ask these things, amen.

DECEMBER 31

YOU CANNOT FAIL NOW! RISE UP HIGHER!

Today's Scripture Reading: Matthew 13:24–30; Proverbs 16:3

Key Verses: Matthew 13:24–25

The kingdom of heaven is like a man who sowed good seed in his field; but while men slept, his enemy came and sowed tares among the wheat and went his way.

The daughter of one my church members inspired me when she said, "We cannot fail now. We see what our parents are doing, and we have to rise up to an even greater level to carry on what has already been started."

Those words of wisdom came from a child! Frankly, many adults in the church do not even understand what that young girl was talking about. She was talking, of course, about the future of the people of God.

Many of us are suffering or playing catch-up today because at some point in our lives, we laid down and went to sleep in the Spirit. We chose not to move in what God ordained for us. We paused for a nap when we should have been about the Father's business. Then the enemy came in and sowed tares in God's wheat field. The enemy mixed bad with the good, and now there is extra work to be done at the end of our lives before the next generation can take off!

As you prepare to enter a new year, see it as an occasion to make a fresh start. This is a good time to pick up where you left off, to complete what you left undone. Seek God's face and ask Him to show you what to do. It is late, but it is not too late as long as you are willing to obey. In the terminology of a very wise young lady: "You cannot fail now. You see what others are doing, and you have to rise up to an even greater level to carry on what has already been started."

Pray this prayer with me:

Heavenly Father, forgive me for sleeping when I should have been leaping to do Your will. I am making a late start, but I commit my way to You, and I ask for mercy and grace to complete the race. I will do what You ask me to do so the generations after me can walk in a true kingdom inheritance of faith and power in Jesus. I cannot fail now. With Your help, I make a new start in the race. In Jesus' name I pray, amen.

Notes

March 11

1. Author's Note: Some diseases and sicknesses come upon us simply because we live in a fallen world where good people are born with degenerated DNA or are harmed by pollutants in the environment, poor nutrition, exposure to radiation, or childhood viruses that weaken the immune system.

We can attribute only a portion of the diseases that afflict us to sin or a lack of faith in the victim. We should be very slow to point the finger, but we should be quick to examine our own lives if these challenges come our way.

In any case, we should remember that God is not the author of evil in any form, and we should take our needs to Him who is able to heal and restore us.

June 19

1. I am not advocating or instructing you to divorce a spouse or "cut off" your family members. This is an appeal for you to put your relationships into biblical perspective. Put God first, but do not be surprised when some of the people closest to you disapprove. Do not allow them to sway or delay your obedience to God.